SURRENDER

AN ADDICT'S JOURNEY

SEX & SURRENDER follows the journey of A.D. Burks, a recovering sex addict. Raised predominantly in a single-parent religious-based home, A.D. was given every opportunity to succeed in life, and he did. He flourished in the education, entertainment and corporate arenas, and his life looked picture perfect from the outside. Yet deep down his personal life was tormenting him due to the conflict between his spiritual and sexual beliefs. Longing for the perfect/traditional family he never had with his female best-friend, he redirected his pain through countless forms of risky sexual behavior.

Sex & Surrender graphically recounts the addictive cycle which lasted nearly 12 years and almost ended his life— until he had a dream that helped him realize he had to find a way out. Therapy and spiritual counseling provided a temporary respite and helped him devise a four-step process to manage his addiction. Yet his true breakthrough didn't come until the root of his pain was uncovered.

Sex & SURRENDER

AN ADDICT'S JOURNEY

A.D. BURKS

BURLOC MEDIA GROUP

HOUSTON

SEX & SURRENDER

I have tried to recreate events, locales and conversations from my memories of them. In order to maintain their anonymity in some instances I have changed the names of individuals and places. I may have changed some identifying characteristics and details such as physical properties, occupations and places of residence.

ISBN 13: 978-0-983-8499-1-9

Published by: Burloc Media Group
Houston, TX

First Edition April 2013

Cover Design by: Albert Reef
Interior Layout by: A Reader's Perspective
Editing by: August Tarrier, Ph.D.

Printed in the United States of America

ADDICTION = PAIN

This book is dedicated to all the addicts and recovering addicts who were told their addiction wasn't real. Always remember, where you are today isn't where you have to be tomorrow.

Don't ever be afraid to tell your story because what you've been through might be the key to someone else's breakthrough.

Sex & SURRENDER

AN ADDICT'S JOURNEY

CONTENTS

Part Three: THE DELIVERED

Introduction

TIGER WOODS, Patrick Dempsey, Kobe Bryant, George Michael, Ted Haggard, Eric Benet, and Jesse James. What do they all allegedly have in common? An addiction that almost ruined their lives and the lives of the people around them.

It seems lately that every time we turn around a new sex addict is being busted by the media. Professional athletes, actors, entertainers, even religious leaders—no one seems to be able to escape the scrutiny. Luckily, I haven't had to truly endure the public humiliation these men have. Still, my story mirrors theirs. In fact, mine may be worse.

While the media has done a fine job of displaying the above-mentioned individuals' sexual indiscretions and transgressions for the whole world to see, they haven't thoroughly analyzed what was at the root of the addiction or examined what might need to happen for healing to take place. Nor have they documented the progress some of these men have made in picking up the pieces of their broken lives. Although it might be beneficial for others in similar circumstances to see the progress, it doesn't make for great headlines. So viewers and readers are left to make assumptions without all the relevant pieces to this most complex sex addiction puzzle.

Before labels are placed, judgments decided, and final conclusions drawn, it's imperative to take a closer look. Some crucial questions have to be answered: What caused or contributed to the addiction? What has the addict been through or is currently going through? And what can be done to alter the present state of the addiction? Without this insight, it becomes extremely easy to point a finger at others, since we really haven't had the opportunity to walk in their shoes.

While one's addiction may not be sex, it might be just as secretive and the addict is going to do his damnedest to keep it concealed. That's because if the secret were ever to be exposed, family, friends, coworkers and spouses would no doubt view that person in a very different light. They might abandon him or her entirely.

I endured a winding journey of both intense pleasure and pain on multiple levels, a journey that, in the end, brought me to the point where I am able to discuss the intimate details of my sex addiction. The facts and the language will definitely get graphic at times. My goal is not to entertain or titillate, but to offer readers a visceral and unflinching glimpse into the mind and world of one addict: me.

My goal is to offer insight and understanding in such a way that readers might recognize themselves in my story. My struggle—my triumphs, my setbacks, step by painstaking step—is instructive. Anyone can fail, as I did, anyone can rise, as I did. Anyone can reach out for help, as I did. And, most important, anyone will discover, as I did, that there is hope, if you just know where to look.

Part One

THE BACKSLIDER

Chapter One

TEMPTATION IN ITS MOST SEDUCTIVE FORM

My sexual appetite has got me feeling horny, right.
So I'm taking time to evaluate what's in sight.
If I play my cards right, I just might,
get the opportunity to blow your back out tonight.
— The Hunger, A.D.

EL INICIO

I FIRST MET Santiago on a Thursday night in late June 2011 while he was working at a strip club near downtown Houston. I had never been to that club and had stopped going to clubs altogether because I was focused on finding a woman who would be my wife and the mother of my children. I was an only child whose parents had divorced when I was four, so I could feel very alone at times. Having a family was the most important thing in my life.

When my uncle passed away unexpectedly the week before my mom's sixty-seventh birthday in 2010, I got the wakeup call I needed. My ex-boyfriend Mark loved me more than anything, but I knew that wouldn't be enough: after all, he couldn't bear children. We had been carrying on as a couple, without having sex, for over a year and a half during our almost five-year relationship. I had told him often that I only wanted to be friends, but he resisted that. It wasn't anything he did; I just wasn't in love with him. Our relationship/friendship forced me to maintain my sobriety from sex addiction because acting out would have made me feel guilty, even though we weren't technically together. For over a year I hadn't been having sex with anyone.

In June, Mark took a trip to Puerto Rico with his two best friends, and I was free to go out and see what I had been missing. I was a real estate representative at a major oil company with a 9/80 schedule, nine days on and the tenth day off, so on certain nights I could go out without worrying about what time I got home.

My first stop was the bars and clubs where I used to hang out in my sex addict heyday. Now, I knew this was a slippery slope. Yes, God had already called me out of my addiction, but as many addicts have discovered, you can be headed in the right direction of getting out of your addiction, and then suddenly you're forgoing all the progress you've made.

At the club that night, I wasn't seeing anyone who grabbed my attention. But I came across a local magazine which listed what clubs were open on a given night and I saw an ad which mentioned amateur strippers on Thursday nights. It featured a muscular Latin guy and I knew this new spot would be my next stop.

When I walked in I got that nervous shake which happens every time I go into a place that doesn't align with the Southern Christian values I was raised with. But I fought it off and focused on all the eye candy displayed before me. I made sure I took the time to scout out everything fine in the place, so I didn't miss the opportunity or person I really wanted to get to "know" in the Biblical sense.

Then I saw Santiago: it was attraction at first sight. But I knew if I was going to keep his attention, I'd have to resurrect my old sex addict persona. Everybody in the club wanted him. They were begging him to give them a moment of his time as they stuffed dollars in his bikini briefs. I knew the only way to get him would be to ignore him, but not totally. So I looked him in the eye every few moments but never approached him. Finally, we ended up crossing paths near the patio door and he approached me.

His smile was infectious. "How are you doing?"

In full sex addict mode, I retorted, "When am I going to get my private show?"

"Take my number down," he responded eagerly.

"No, you can follow me to my house when you get off." I wanted to maintain the control in this uncharted liaison.

"Okay," he said. His grin let me know he was up for playing my game.

When we got to my house, I pulled into the garage and he pulled into the driveway. Within seconds of the garage door slamming shut we started making out on the back of my convertible. In an effort to maintain some level of control, I stopped in the middle of our passionate tongue-fest and told him he had been working and needed to take a shower; I sent him to the guest bathroom and handed him a washcloth and towel. Knowing he had been sweating with everybody's dirty hands on him wasn't sitting well with me. (I have OCS—Only Child Syndrome, aka, selfishness—and it seems to rear its ugly head every time the addict comes out.)

I poured myself a glass of ice water and waited downstairs in the kitchen. Then it happened: he came down in nothing but a towel strategically wrapped around his waist, and he could have bought me for less than a penny. At that point, the ball was in his court and it has been ever since. His body was even more gorgeous wrapped in just the towel than it had been in barely anything at the club. His abs were lightly defined, his stomach completely flat, his chest and arms beautifully sculpted, and his culo (ass) absolutely perfect. I asked him what he wanted to drink and he looked in the pantry and grabbed an unopened bottle of Silver 1800 Tequila. Normally I didn't drink, but he was persuasive enough so I mixed some Hennessey and apple juice.

We went upstairs, where we had some of the most electrifying sex of my life. Once that towel came off, I got the full essence of his ass: well-manicured—hairless on the outside with just a little hair nicely trimmed as I spread his cheeks. We fucked in so many different positions that night you would have thought we were filming a user's guide to the Kama Sutra. I can still see his face and neck pressed up against the footboard of my bed as I rhythmically thrust myself inside of him. Then when we moved to the headboard to change positions he said, "You know I'm not gay, right?"

I thought: Sure, I'm just putting my dick in your ass but that doesn't make you gay. I told him, "I'm not either—I'm bi!"

"Yeah, I'm married with a child and when I'm with guys, I'm usually the one doing the fucking," he assured me.

While I had no reason to doubt him because he definitely had all the attributes of a "top"—the penetrating partner in a gay relationship—he was definitely taking my dick like a well-trained "bottom." Neither one of us wanted to be the first to come, a sign that we were both true sex addicts. Our uninterrupted session lasted four hours straight—a first for me.

As dawn was breaking, our pure exhilarating exhaustion (and my penis being rubbed raw) forced us to take a break. With my arms wrapped around his upper body and his ass flawlessly pressed against my pelvis, our bodies fit perfectly together; in thirty-four years, I had occasionally experienced this perfect fit with a woman, but rarely with a man. A sense of ecstasy overtook every fiber of my being and I never wanted it to leave.

After maybe two good hours of sleep, Santiago got up and said, "I need to head home."

So he got dressed and we headed downstairs. But as soon as we got to the bottom of the stairwell he started playing with my cock to get me aroused for another round. Seeing us downstairs standing together in front of my bathroom mirror was breathtaking, but I just couldn't have any more sex that morning.

"I'm sorry but I'm a little sore. We'll have to get together another time. What's your number?" I asked.

He gave me his number and I plugged it directly into my cell phone, but when I called I wasn't sure if it was the real number or not. I would have to wait to see when I'd be able to get another taste of the sweetest sex I had ever had.

I kept thinking about the fact that Santiago was married and had a child. It was so ironic—the exact thing I wanted in life was precisely what he was running from. Timing really is everything! At that moment I felt as if I would do almost anything to ensure that I could repeat the experience I had just shared with him.

JUST SPILL IT

As a recovering sex addict, you have to have one person who you can tell everything so you won't go too far off the deep end. This is the person you can trust with your life. So even if they berate you, you know deep down they are only telling you what you need to hear because of their unconditional love. For me, this person is Mitchell Morris.

Of all the people in the world, Mitch was the last person I would have picked for a best friend. We are polar opposites who just happen to have a lot in common. He's an introvert, I'm an extrovert. He's reserved, I'm unrestrained. He's genuinely caring, I'm selfish. But we both bring out the best in each other, as best friends always do.

While some people can claim they grew up in the same neighborhood as their best friend, Mitch and I can't. He was raised in what some might consider the rough part of the inner city, while I was brought up in the traditional ethnically diverse suburbs. The High School for Health Professions is where we first met: we really weren't in the same cliques, but we had the same mentor, Dr. Axelrod, a pediatrician who worked with the promising male students at our school. Now the fact we had attended the same college might have drawn us closer, but it actually pushed me further away.

Mitch would always tell people on campus, "Yeah, A.D. and I went to the same high school." Every time I would hear him say it or someone else would tell me they heard it, I would cringe. Mitch was a member of what my group called the "social untouchables." You didn't want to associate with them because they could potentially bring your stock value down. Besides having no fashion sense, Mitch was an un-ordained Christian preacher. For college students away from home, getting their first taste of freedom, the last thing they want to hear about is Jesus. Mitch loved the Lord and was vocal about it. Yet beneath all that professing of God's word, he was struggling with his sexuality.

In the best of all worlds, people grow—and, thankfully, Mitch and I had both matured. It wasn't until after we graduated that we finally became true friends. You might ask, what could bring a sex addict and a preacher together? That's easy: sexuality. Once each of us discovered that the other had experimented with men, the floodgates of our friendship opened like the parting of the Red Sea. I was flabbergasted to find out some of the guys he had been in relationships with during undergrad, while he was surprised to hear who I had had a crush on.

Our attempts to reconcile homosexuality and being a Christian are what really sealed our friendship. The Bible is constantly being used to condemn and alienate homosexuals from the church, and the "Body of Christ." Yet Christ's message was just the opposite: He that is without sin among you, let him first cast a stone (John 8:7). Judge not, that ye be not judged (Matthew 7:1). Mitch has both a thorough understanding of the Bible and an intimate relationship with God. Through my friendship with Mitch, I learned that when you know God for yourself, you don't have to be burdened with what Bible fundamentalists and interpreters say.

At this point in my life, Mitch and I have been best friends for twelve years. He knows the good, the bad and the dirty side of me. My relationship with Santiago was making me feel things that I hadn't felt in years, and I had to tell someone: Mitch was definitely one of the first on that list. He just happened to stop by my house on a night when Santiago was performing. I gave him a hug at my front door and commented on his dreadlocks as he headed into the living room. Mitch likes to dress for functionality and comfort, and he was wearing what I liked to call his "Jesus sandals," which are a fashion step down from Birkenstocks. Every time I see him, it appears as if he's added another pound of muscle to his well-built six-foot frame. He sat on the loveseat facing Allan Hill's "Hackensack Sessions," an artwork he had given me as a birthday present years earlier.

"Mitch, you're going to kill me."

"What did you do now?"

"Okay, you're not going to want to hear this."

"Just spill it."

"I had the best sex of my life. Four hours straight." I looked at him, elated.

"What? Uh, with whom? Cause I know it wasn't with your ex," he said.

I hesitated. "Mark? Nah, it was with a stripper."

"Have you lost your mind?" he said as his jaw dropped and his hazel eyes grew huge in disbelief.

"Yeah, he's Chilean and his body is out of this world." I couldn't help it; I knew Mitch was appalled, but even just thinking about Santiago made me feel exuberant.

"So where exactly did you meet?" he wanted to know.

I gave him all the details about how I had decided to go out and had stumbled upon the strip club. Mitch knew I had been doing well about resisting the seedy side of my past, so his shocked expression didn't surprise me. But I also sensed that he was at least cautiously happy for me—I hadn't been this excited about anyone in years.

"Oh and there's one more thing."

"What's that?" he asked, bracing himself.

"He's married with a son."

"Okay, so you really have lost your mind."

"I know. I know. But you've got to see him. We can go tonight."

"Uh, my boyfriend isn't going to be happy about me going to a strip club with you."

"He'll be alright. We aren't staying long," I promised.

"No sir. The last place I need to be is some strip club."

"Come on! We'll be in and out in no time. I just want you to see him," I pleaded.

After a bit more cajoling, Mitch agreed to go. There was just one minor problem—Mitch liked to be comfy when he wasn't planning on going out, and tonight was no exception. I knew he couldn't wear any of my clothes, since he's six feet tall and muscular with a shirt size of XXL. Luckily, one of my home-boys who I had hung out with months before had left his shirt in my car and it fit Mitch.

When we arrived at the club, we went through the back entrance, right where Santiago and I had spoken our first words. The show hadn't started so most of the dancers were mingling in the audience. It didn't take long for me to spot the reason I had selfishly dragged my best friend to a place he had adamantly resisted going.

"There he is," I said, looking in Santiago's direction.

"Where?"

"By the pool table."

Within a few minutes, Santiago saw me and headed in my direction.

"Hey, buddy," he said in that sexy accent.

"This is my friend Mitch."

"Nice to meet you," he said, smiling at us both.

"Likewise," Mitch responded.

Santiago and I exchanged a few words and then he had to go because it was almost show time. At this point, my mission was accomplished. My best friend had seen the person who was making me feel like I had reclaimed a part of my life I had lost, the part where I was with one singular person who made me want to conquer the world. With that being accomplished, we left without me subjecting Mitch to any more debauchery.

Technically, he could tell his boyfriend he just went to a club with me, since no one had actually stripped while we were there.

We went back to my car and I just sat there smiling from ear to ear thinking about Santiago. Yet Mitch wasn't saying anything.

"So what do you think?" I was so anxious to hear his opinion.

"You've had better," he said dismissively.

"Are you kidding me? That body and face are sick."

"Uh, he's cute but you've had better. And he looks like Mark," he added.

"No way! He's not as tall and his body is so much better. It fits into mine like a glove. It's true that Mark's face is flawless," I replied.

"Whatever. He looks like Mark. I do have to admit, though, that I haven't seen you this happy and excited about life in, I don't know when."

Mitch was absolutely right. Santiago made me feel like I wanted to conquer the world just so I could have him by my side.

THE LADY IN MY LIFE

NOW THAT MY best friend had weighed in on Santiago, it was time to get feedback from the most important woman in my life right behind my mom: Jeri Jones. Jeri grew up three houses down from me. The daughter of a biracial couple, she was beautiful, athletic and had a caring heart of pure gold. Whenever I thought about the woman I would marry, Jeri immediately came to mind: she was the epitome of perfection. Yet there were two quintessential problems: (1) Jeri was bisexual and was currently in a relationship with her new girlfriend and (2) Jeri saw me as her brother.

Jeri and I grew up together and we've spent a tremendous amount of time together, so it goes without saying that she is one of the most influential people in my life. My exposure to the GLTB (Gay Lesbian Transgender and Bisexual) alternative lifestyle scene came via Jeri. After I finished undergrad, I came home to Houston. My friends from high school went to schools out of state like I did, so when I got back, everyone was living in other cities. Naturally, I started hanging out with Jeri. She was intimately involved with the alternative scene, and I started tagging along.

Since I'm always looking for new experiences, I had to fight to get over my initial hesitation. Seeing men on men and women on women in bars, nightclubs, and house parties was totally different than what I had previously been exposed to. I was raised on church doctrine and I was well aware that the Bible said that homosexuality was a sin. I was in constant struggle and conflict around how I could be a Christian and be around what the church would consider debauchery. Yet at the same time there was such passion, intimacy, and sensuality taking place that I couldn't help but be intrigued. With so many guys complimenting me and wanting to get with me, I started to revel in all the attention.

Once I realized marrying Jeri wasn't going to happen anytime soon, because she was so deeply ensconced in the lifestyle, I became despondent and started turning to the adulation I was getting from men. Whether it was because I was trying to show her I could do the same thing or because I was devastated by her rejection of me, I'm not sure. I started having sex with men and that's how the addiction ultimately took root.

You might have heard it said that insanity is doing the same thing over and over, yet expecting different results. Well, addictions can drive sane people insane. You feel that you're psychologically and physically unable to do anything about the addiction, even though you know you have to do something. I harbored two versions of insanity: the first was the thought that Jeri and I would get married one day and have the family I had always dreamt about. This first version led to the second version, which was the idea that I wasn't a sex addict. I would see someone I wanted and wouldn't stop until I engaged in some form of sex with them—no matter who I ended up harming in the process. These moments of insanity would result in my sex addiction cycles.

The onset of the cycle might start with me seeing a guy around my age with a beautiful wife and a couple of kids. My cycle could also be initiated by a discussion with Jeri about our future children. We had said for years that if neither of us was married by twenty-eight, we'd get married. The insane part was that I actually believed it.

After our talks, I'd get my hopes up for having my ideal family, even though I knew that Jeri was bisexual, and that she was in a committed relationship with her girlfriend. But she was the only woman I wanted as the mother of my children, and so I didn't want to get attached to any other woman. Instead, I spent my time looking at various types of porn or I would check out men as potential sex partners. I'd engage in anonymous sex, or worse, I'd get in a "relationship" with a guy who genuinely loved me, only to leave him. It became a vicious cycle.

Every now and then, however, I'd run into a lady capable of placing a yield sign in my path. These women had beauty, intelligence, grace and class, and were definitely marriage material. They made me question whether Jeri was truly "The One." When I really sat back and analyzed what I valued (a more refined lifestyle) and what Jeri valued (a more laidback lifestyle), I would end up believing that our worlds had drifted apart like tectonic plates.

It was during those off periods when I was finally able to make headway in the direction I wanted my life to go. But subconsciously, something would tell me not to get too close because I was still waiting for Jeri. And like the laws of physics state, no two things can occupy the same space and time. I'd tell myself: just one more ride, you can get married and have a family when you turn thirty. It's okay to play now. And that's exactly what I did.

For me, the Holy Grail was to engage in sex as a spiritual act. I felt that if I could experience that I would be truly healed. What I wanted was a spiritual/sexual connection with an exceptional woman, one who would become the mother of my children, and I didn't think for a moment that I would find her in a club. And yet I was a man in his early thirties with a healthy libido who had been celibate for quite some time.

When it comes to sex, for me there has always been a neat dichotomy between men and women. Women are sexy, but ultimately I tend to see them as potential wives and moms-to-be. Men are who I turn to when I want great sex fast. I've had great loves with women and with men, but I have a very deeply ingrained rule: never have sex with a woman you don't love. This rule evolved because of the relationship I had with my mom. While I could have random sex with a guy and not give it a second thought, I never wanted to hurt a woman emotionally like my dad hurt my mom.

When anyone would ask why I hadn't settled down, I would often say, "I just haven't found the right one," and the person would invariably go on about how I was too attractive and nice not to be with anyone. But what they didn't realize was that there was one thought in the back of my mind—I want to get married and have children—and there was a radically different thought in the front of my mind: I want to fuck the finest thing I can lay my eyes on.

Over the years both Jeri and I had gone back and forth between men and women, but my idea that one day Jeri and I would be a family and have kids never wavered. Yet here we were at the age of 34, she in a committed relationship with a new woman and me falling for a new man.

Since Jeri's grandmother lives on my side of town, Jeri would typically swing by my place after her visits so we could catch up. It was always a pleasure to see those gleaming hazel eyes and warm bright beautiful smile. Before we sat down in my living room, she grabbed a piece of candy from the candy jar; Jeri makes sure to keep a stock of candy at my place, since she knows I try to avoid the stuff. If I'm going to eat something sweet, I'm going all out: cake, pie, cobbler, you name it.

"Jeri, you aren't going to believe who I've been doing," I began.

"Knowing you, I probably won't, but who?"

"He's Chilean and his name is Santiago. You have got to see him. His body is so right and you know I'm a face man. That smile of his is freaking contagious."

"That's what's up!"

"His smile has the ability to make me feel like I'm on top of the world. I don't know what it is! I feel so strong when I'm with him. The way he carries himself with so much confidence—it takes my own self-assurance to another level. There's no better feeling in the world than being with that one person who just makes you better."

"I definitely know what you mean. Just the way you're talking about him has you beaming. So when do I get to meet him?"

"Well, with all that joy he brings me, there are a few things which are a problem."

"Like what?"

"Well, he's a stripper, he's married, and he has a child. As a matter of fact, I'm quite pissed at him now because the only time we hook up is when I go to the club. I had made plans for us to go have sushi, since he said it was his favorite, and he stood me up."

"Hell, let's go to the club!"

"I can't keep going through this shit. I want to see him when I want to see him. But the sex is so good, Jeri. The first time we had sex, we went four hours straight. It took our third meeting before someone finally came. You know I made sure he was first and then I forced myself," I explained.

"Yeah, I see you 'won.' Well, if the sex is that good, he'll be back."

"True, but I want more. He's got me feeling the way Trevor made me feel." Trevor was the first man I had fallen in love with.

"What! I haven't heard that name in a long time. He must be special."

I smiled at her. "When I'm with him I think of all the things I want to accomplish so we can have a better life. Being with him makes me want to start a family—to create a better life for his son and maybe even a child you and I have one day. And the biggest thing of all is: I don't want to be with or have sex with anyone else."

Maybe a week or so later, Jeri unexpectedly showed up at my house on a night Santiago was going to be working. Looking very "butch," she was dressed in a plaid button-down shirt with some oversized khaki shorts and tennis shoes. I must have told her the club's strip show schedule. She had two female friends with her who I hadn't met before. They might have been heterosexual, but with Jeri one never knows. It wasn't like I cared either way because I was clearly infatuated with Santiago.

"Let's go see him," she demanded.

"I don't want to go," I replied, although I did want her to see him. If Jeri didn't think he was fine and didn't give her stamp of approval, it would be easy to let him go.

"Well, we want to see some strippers. So get in and drive," she demanded. It just so happened that both she and Santiago drove Mazda CX-7s. Hers was the Copper Red Mica and his was the Stormy Blue Mica.

As I was driving, I was so torn because I wanted Jeri to see him, and I wanted to see him, but I didn't want to be disappointed.

When we arrived, the club was packed and I made up my mind that I wasn't going to go in. I gave Jeri a detailed description of what he looked like. Besides, she knew my type to a tee.

"Man, come on and go in," she cajoled me.

"Nope! I'll wait for you all out here."

While they were inside, I was left to wonder if he was performing. What did he have on? What would Jeri think about him? It seemed like they had been in there forever and then I got a text from her saying the announcer said he was going on next. Within a couple of minutes, Jeri sent me a text with a picture of him standing on stage, shirtless and in sunglasses, with a red spotlight positioned directly on him. It was like I was looking at this irresistible temptation. All it took was one look and it was as if Satan's mighty power drew me right into the club.

Once inside, I maneuvered my way through the jam-packed crowd to the table where Jeri and her friends were seated. My heart sank when I saw that they were right in front of the stage—too much temptation.

"He's fine, but there's another one in here that's finer," she said.

"Yeah, but he can't dance worth shit," I replied.

"Your boy is definitely the sexiest in here."

When Santiago got off the stage I introduced him to Jeri, telling him that she was my sister.

"Your sister?"

"Yeah, my sister."

Once they had been introduced to him, the girls had had their fill of unavailable half-naked men and were ready to go. Of course, I wanted to stick around to make sure I would get to see Santiago that evening. He knew I was waiting and he intentionally kept talking to other patrons. At that point I was getting pissed, and everybody was waiting on me. So I made my way over to him.

"Are you going to swing by tonight?"

"No, I've got to get home."

It was just as I had known it would be. I should not have walked into that club; I should not have risked seeing him because once again I had ended up disappointed.

Chapter Two
AN ADDICT'S DREAM

If eyes are the window to the soul
And dreams are glimpses of the untold
Then there's no telling what results
An addict's dreams will unfold.
— Dreams, A.D.

WHAT WAS SO scary to me about my relationship with Santiago was that I had managed to step away from my old sex addict ways: God had called me out of my addiction years ago, back in 2006. But since I had met him it felt as if I was begging to be back in a twisted version of what I had been released from.

Back then my main priority was feeding my sex addiction. Not a day went by without me plotting when and whom I was going to fuck next. If I didn't have a regular "piece"— someone I was penetrating regularly—I'd pick up a new one at a club, gym or bar. And if I couldn't find a suitable piece at one of those locations I'd occasionally go to a bathhouse or bookstore/video store. This behavior was all-consuming for me.

Unlike drug and alcohol addictions, sex addiction is not seen by most people as a disease or a "true" addiction. The medical community continues to debate whether it's a legitimate disorder. So it can be a challenge to get help. We Americans have so many social hang-ups about sex, which forces the spouses of sex addicts to deal with feelings of inadequacy and may increase the likelihood that they'll be exposed to sexually transmitted diseases.

Sex addiction wreaks havoc on millions of families, and my own family was no exception. My father's infidelity ultimately changed the structure of my family and childhood. Once a person becomes addicted, they often spiral deeper and deeper until they hit rock bottom and are forced to make a decision to take control of their lives. The sad thing is that no matter how much help is given or who offers the help, an addict will not change until he or she makes the decision to change. In the meantime, everyone around them suffers.

I never let my addiction affect my work because I had become like most great sex addicts: I could function and even thrive in the throes of it all. It didn't matter if I stayed up until 1:00 or 2:00 a.m. The next morning, I was able to punch the clock without skipping a beat. As a matter of fact, I usually did my best work, because I had had a fix.

The most dangerous thing about sex addiction is this: the high doesn't have the after-affects that drugs or alcohol can have, so it's easier to conceal and, consequently, harder to get help. Great sex addicts are some of the brightest minds and best chameleons on the planet. We know exactly how to create the illusion that we have everything under control. I'd constantly tell myself, this is the last time, and then later I'd go right back to the addiction.

The reason I was able to make the kind of progress I had with getting out of my addiction was because of my relationship with God. I was blessed to have been raised by a family who knew the benefits which came when a person allowed God to lead his or her life. But all of that was irrelevant until I went down the road of seeking to know God for myself. By picking up the Bible, studying alone and allowing Him to speak to me directly, I was able to decipher how to get out of my sex addiction.

Church was a part of my life before I was even born. My grandfather was a Baptist minister in the Bible belt, Columbia, TN, and my parents attended church regularly when they moved to Texas. When I was a baby, the ladies in my mom's Sunday school class had to keep telling her to stop worrying about me and let me play on a blanket on the floor. They even named me "Miracle Child." My father was a deacon and my mother served on the count team, which would total the money taken up during the offering. They also made a significant financial contribution to the new church, which was being built when I was a pre-teen. Their names appear on the dedication wall in the sanctuary.

My gift for song manifested early, and by the age of four I was singing in the children's choir. To join the choir a member technically had to be at least five, but the director loved me and made an exception. From that point on, no matter where I am in the world, I have always made attending church a major priority.

So I wasn't particularly surprised when, in the early morning of December 2006, God spoke to me in a dream.

THE DREAM

THE NIGHT BEFORE, December 29, 2006, I almost had an encounter with a guy I had been sleeping with at the time. Although he and I had technically parted ways, we kept in constant contact. Most sex addicts have a person or persons they can call to always get a fix no matter what is going on. That person is like a sex extinguisher—in case of emergency, BREAK! During the call, he told me that his current lover was with his family and he was all alone. All it took was that simple phone call for me to start planning to head over to his house and have sex, which I kept promising myself I was giving up.

But we got our signals crossed: I called him, he didn't pick up, so I sent him a text message. When he didn't respond immediately to the text, I decided to drive home. Within two minutes of me arriving home, he called. He said he was in the shower when I called (that was God saying "enough"—if he had answered his phone, I would have been right back at the start of another cycle). When I told him I was already at home, he said, "Oh, well another time," and that was the end of our night.

The next morning my alarm went off at 5:15 a.m., the time I usually got up during the week, but it was Saturday so I decided to go back to sleep. When I dozed back off, I started dreaming my sex extinguisher and I were having sex in my mom's guest bedroom. During the illicit act, a few of my neighbors and church members came by and opened the door. My secret was out. Everybody now knew, but luckily, my mom never came by and saw me in the act. After being caught, I was forced to attend an outdoor town hall meeting, reminiscent of the Salem witch trials, to discuss the entire situation. Church clergy, neighbors, and family members were all there. It was literally the worst thing that could ever have happened to me. At the end of the meeting, a person who I didn't know was introduced to me and he said he was in the process of coming out of his addiction. He asked me the most important question: "What is your plan for coming out?"

When I awakened, all I could think about was how I never wanted to be put in such a predicament. I thought about all the time, effort, and money my mom had invested in me and there was no way on God's green earth I ever wanted her to have to endure such disgrace for raising a son addicted to sex. But most of all, I realized God was trying to tell me something.

It was 6:22 a.m. on December 30, 2006 and it was all I could do to stop myself from calling Emmett Keith, who was my pastor at the time, but I knew it was too early. So I decided the best thing to do was send him a text message asking to meet for breakfast.

I had a two-hour wait until it would be a decent hour for a phone call to Emmett, and during that time God gave me the outline for this book. So many thoughts were rushing through my head. In exactly one hour and thirty-eight minutes, I knew the content of each chapter, but more importantly, I knew I had to start making my way out of my addiction. Whoever said God doesn't speak through dreams doesn't really know God.

AN INTERPRETATION

LATER THAT MORNING, Emmett met me at my favorite Houston breakfast spot, LePeep. He and I had grown up together because our mothers were best friends. We walked in right about the same time and the waitress seated us at a table near the back wall, which was great because I didn't want strangers listening to our conversation.

Standing around six feet, with a genuine smile, Emmett meets most women's definition of tall, dark and handsome. Thankfully, he's married and not my type, which allows our relationship to stay purely spiritual. In addition to all the outward beauty he possesses, he is also a very warm, loving, and caring person, like his mother. He takes a predominantly literalist interpretation of the Bible, probably because his dad was a minister in the Church of God In Christ (COGIC) denomination, which has a very strict doctrine.

We greeted with a hug and sat down directly across from one another. He began with, "It's good to see you, and how are things? How's your mom?"

"She's fine. I have so much to tell you. I had a dream this morning and I think God is talking to me."

He gave me his discerning listening-ear look and said, "Okay, tell me about it."

I believe that Emmett has the gift of prophesy. One time we had an intense conversation regarding what the Bible said about homosexuality and sin; at the time, I was struggling with the issue, but I hadn't mentioned anything about my struggle to Emmett. He just knew somehow.

The waitress came over to take our order: I got my usual— one whole wheat pancake with blueberries, sugar-free syrup, a side order of turkey sausage, and water. Emmett ordered coffee and the Big Breakfast, which came with pancakes, sausage, hash browns and eggs.

Now that our orders were in, it was time to discuss both the dream and the proposed table of contents for the book.

"Once I had the dream, I knew I had to talk with you." I pulled out a sheet of paper with my notes. "Look, I even made an outline."

I relayed the dream in detail and started going through my notes, giving him my thoughts. He listened intently, giving me continuous eye contact so I knew he was taking in everything I said. Never once did he chastise me for my past behavior, although I knew he disapproved.

When I finished he smiled reassuringly. "This is definitely a message from God. I just started working on a book series that God gave to me. It doesn't touch on this topic, though, because I haven't experienced what you have. However, if your book is written well, it could help countless numbers of people."

I leaned toward him. "One of the biggest misconceptions addicts have about addiction is they think they don't have a problem. I kept thinking I was fine and had everything under control. The reality was, my addiction had taken over and consumed me. To keep the addictive cycle in motion, I created an environment where I could constantly feed the addiction. I strategically befriended fellow sex addicts, who frequented places where I could find more sex addicts. My addict friends created an atmosphere which was uncomfortable for my non-addict friends."

"Exactly!" he said, taking a gulp of coffee. "Frankly, that's why I stopped coming to your parties. My mission is to lead people to Christ, and how can I do that if I'm in the same places where they are being ungodly?"

"I see your point," I said, nodding. "So I ended up spending less time with my true friends, which kept me from realizing I needed help. It's a vicious cycle and I couldn't see it or comprehend it. When you can't understand how something operates, you can't do anything about it."

"You've got a strong network of people who will be there for you at times when you're struggling."

"Thankfully, I really do have true friends who know the real me—people like you, Jeri and Mitch who are able to tell if something is out of sorts. Every addict knows there are certain people who can tell them when they have gone too far."

The waitress brought our food and Emmett took a moment to say grace. As I closed my eyes I thanked God for friends like him.

"Emmett, this sex addiction had become such a way of life for me, I couldn't fathom how life would be without it." I took a sip of my water and a bite of my pancake.

Emmett put down his fork and gave me one of his sincere smiles. "What if you trust God to do what He does best, which is handle the situation?"

I had to laugh. There was something so sincere about Emmett: he knew where he stood with God, he knew what he wanted, and he knew who he would be spending his life with—his wife and stepdaughter. What he was saying to me was absolutely right.

"You know, I believe in this book—so much. I mean, like you said, it could really be a way for me to reach others, it could be my ministry."

He nodded vigorously and kept chewing.

"It's like I want to tell all the addicts out there—if you read what I wrote, I beg of you, when you can't see getting out of the cycle for yourself, do it for the people who love you unconditionally." I stopped and leaned toward him. "What I figured out is this: I am worth so much more to others if I stay alive than I would be out there chasing the temporary highs from the addiction. I have been endangering myself—I realize that now. It's a gift from God to have people in your life who love you more than you love yourself."

I glanced up at him; he was looking at me with great kindness and concern.

"Since I have a Type A personality, I never just sit and watch when I can be doing. All of these factors created a world of fantasy which was void of the main ingredient I was desperately searching for: love. The concept of love and fantasy gets blurry and convoluted in the addictive cycle."

Emmett folded his hands. "Just remember one thing. God is always pointing you in the same direction; He is always showing you the way out."

Hearing that confirmation from him was exactly what I needed. While I thought the dream was God's way of getting my attention, hearing it from a person I was certain God had spoken to before on countless occasions, was priceless.

A DIFFERENT PERSPECTIVE

WHILE I HAD no doubt God spoke directly to Emmett through his gift of prophesy, I also knew He spoke to others, including myself. The key is for each person to hear what God is telling them directly, because what He tells one person may be totally different than what He tells another. To get a clear understanding of God's message I have to settle myself and tune out all the distractions I sometimes allow the devil to surround me with. Once I do that, I'll seek out different perspectives at times. Although I love and treasure Emmett as a confidante, I couldn't confess to him then, in 2011, about my love for Santiago. I vividly remembered him telling me back in 2006 about his views on homosexual relationships between men: it was a sin against God.

Thankfully, I had another confidante, one who was both religious and more open-minded than Emmett. That was Ammon Davis, a minister who was the head of a congregation across town, and who had become a real sounding board for me.

We had initially met at my gym. Now usually I'm all business at the gym; if I know a person, I'll definitely speak but I'm not going to carry on an in-depth conversation unless I've finished my workout.

I noticed this one guy in his forties who always had a pleasant smile and was cordial every time I saw him. I would speak and keep it moving. One morning he caught me after I had finished my workout and introduced himself. Now I'm going to be completely honest! I have had countless numbers of people introduce themselves to me in a similar manner, but they only wanted to hook up, so I was slightly skeptical. But I try to refrain from judgment because everybody has something they can offer or you can offer them. I didn't know it at the time, but this man would be offering a blessing I never could have foreseen.

After he introduced himself, he asked about my Rice MBA shirt.

"Did you go to Rice?"

"Yeah. I graduated in '05."

"Yeah, I got my MBA," he explained. "So what are you doing now?"

"I work in real estate at an oil company," I said.

We talked for a bit, but I was headed to work so I had to cut it short. It turned out that we worked out at the same gym because he lived in a neighborhood up the street and my office building was around the corner.

After seeing each other a few more times, he suggested we do lunch one day to see if there were any areas we could collaborate on. I agreed and we met. Luckily, he didn't introduce himself initially as Pastor Davis. Like most people, I can have preconceived notions about men and women of the cloth. Yet here was a man of God who wasn't trying to be my pastor, but just my friend.

As our friendship grew, I became comfortable enough to begin telling him that I was writing a book. Telling most people you're writing a book on sex addiction immediately raises suspicion. Instead of using the Bible to lead our discussions around the topic, Ammon came from the basis of a true friend. I'm sure he didn't condone my past behavior, but he took on the characteristics of Christ by not judging but listening and encouraging me to foster healthy and beneficial relationships.

When I wanted to get an honest, non-judgmental, religious perspective on a situation I would call Ammon. He was someone who had become a beacon of sobriety and healing for me—a big brother, a guide.

Of course, I wanted to talk with him about my feelings for Santiago, but it was deeper than that. I had become angry with myself: the truth was that I had faced my sexual addiction and made a commitment to heal. I had started a four-step process to reach my goal. First, I made the decision I wanted to change and reestablish my relationship with God; second, I took a vow of abstinence; third, I changed my environment; and fourth, I established a supportive network.

Of course, a four-step process might make it sound like it was easy, but the reality is there really was and is nothing harder. I didn't just wake up one day and say, I'm going to do these four things and I'll be fixed. It took years to get to the point where I am now and I'm still moving forward.

Yes, I had setbacks. Yes, there were days I wanted to give up. And, yes, there were days I abandoned all four steps and did what I knew I shouldn't have done. But the good thing was that I had established a workable plan which enabled me to get back up and move forward.

I also got into treatment, which was based on Dr. Patrick Carnes books, *Facing the Shadow* and *Out of the Shadows*. Dr. Carnes is considered the expert in the field of sex addiction. When Tiger Woods went through his ordeal, he was admitted to Dr. Carnes' treatment program.

My main aim was to start a family, and to do that I had to find a woman who could be my wife, the mother of my children, and my soul mate. It was my top priority, but now I found myself falling in mad lust—and maybe it was love?—with Santiago. The more time I spent with Santiago, the more conflicted I became, so I really had to get Ammon's insight.

We met for lunch at La Griglia, a great Italian restaurant in River Oaks, which is the wealthiest neighborhood in Houston. When I arrived he was already seated working on his sermon notes for the week on his iPad. Dressed in a tailored long-sleeved shirt and suit pants, with his scholarly-looking glasses, he stood up to give me a handshake and said, "How are you doing, my brother?"

It was my Friday off, so I was dressed casually: V-neck Ralph Lauren t-shirt and khaki pants. The fact that we were eating at an upscale restaurant that served the corporate crowd made no difference to me: I had a heavy heart and I needed to talk to someone I trusted.

"I'm good," I responded, "but I might need someone to kick my ass."

He laughed. "So you better be looking elsewhere, bro. But if you want somebody to call in your better angels, I'm ready."

Ammon was slim, with a very energetic presence, and an easy laugh.

"I'm falling for this guy I met not too long ago. He's Chilean and a stripper," I explained.

"Wow! Okay!" He seemed a little shocked, but he recovered himself and asked, "So where did you guys meet?"

"Well, I went to this new bar near downtown. I was having a weak moment and he just happened to be working that night. Everybody wanted him, including me. I knew if I was going to get him I would have to revert back to my old sex addict persona. And then we came back to my house and had sex for four hours straight."

The waitress approached to take our orders and told us the specials for the day. He ordered a pasta dish and I requested the salmon and vegetable medley.

"Now let me get this straight. You went to a bar, saw him strip and took him back to your place the same night."

"Yep. And it was probably the best sex I've ever had."

"Exactly, but it was just sex!"

"But now I'm wanting more. The more time we spend together, the more I want to be in a real relationship. I haven't felt this alive since I don't know when. I really feel like I'm in love, but I also know that he's not available."

"Well, it sounds to me like you've got this figured out. Like you said, he's not available. Let's get real, he's a stripper."

"I know, I know, but he's who I really want. It's not like I'm trying to have sex with anyone else. Oh, and he has a wife and child, but they're separated."

"Yeah, I think you already know this isn't what God has in mind for you. Is this relationship going to provide the family you said you wanted? You deserve better than what you're telling me. But you know I'll be here supporting and praying for you. 'Cause obviously this situation needs much prayer."

"A truer statement has never been made," I said, laughing.

While I knew Santiago was definitely who I wanted, Ammon made me question whether he was what I really needed. I'm aware that often what we want isn't what we need, but it's still so hard to choose the "right" thing over what was, in this case, the immensely desirable thing. Although I had the blessing of people like Ammon praying for me, I felt like I was on the precipice and in danger of slipping back into my old sex addict ways.

Chapter Three
SWITCH HITTER

I should have the freedom to choose
Who I want to use as my muse
A woman today, a man tomorrow
It's my choice, why are you bothered?
— The Sexuality Spectrum, A.D.

IT'S COMPLICATED

THINGS GOT TO the point where I no longer needed or wanted to go inside the strip club where Santiago worked. Why should I waste time standing around in the club when I didn't drink and the only reason I had come was to see and hopefully hook up with Santiago? He wouldn't return my calls or texts, so I would just drive by after the club let out.

Santiago loved to smoke weed, which I definitely wasn't a fan of. Usually, after he finished working for the night, he would stand outside and smoke in the parking lot with a small group that included a few dancers and patrons. I'd drive up on the street alongside the parking lot, catch his eye and he'd walk over to my car with a mischievous grin on his face.

"Hey, baby, what's up?" he'd say.

"Nothing. You coming over tonight?"

"Of course!"

And just like that, he'd say goodbye, jump in his car and follow me home. I was so elated that he'd come over for another lovemaking session.

The first night we had sex Santiago had been adamant about letting me know he wasn't gay.

"You know I don't let anyone else do this," he said, referring to the fact that he had allowed me to penetrate him. He did have a very tight ass, and so I believed him.

And now, on one of our subsequent nights together, he had once again climaxed and I had been the one who had made him come. But then he got up to leave.

I couldn't believe that he was going. "You aren't staying?"

"I never stay," he said, and I couldn't help thinking that that was a standard line among strippers.

"You stayed the first night!"

"No, I didn't."

"Uh, yes you did. How could you forget? You woke up the next morning trying to get me to fuck you."

"Oh yeah, well, it's complicated," he told me.

As I watched him get dressed, I felt so empty. I had just been holding him in my arms after making love and already that was starting to feel like an unfulfilled fantasy. I had allowed myself to confuse great sex with true love. And that confusion led me to break a cardinal rule among experienced sex addicts: never let the other person know you really want them, much less need them.

The next time I drove by the club after it had let out, I noticed it was taking Santiago a long time to come out. I was obsessed with him and my desire for him was unbearable: I didn't care that our love was so unequal—I didn't want anyone else but him. So I pulled into the parking spot two cars away from his ride. When he came out, there were three or four women twenty-five yards in front of him. This was extremely unusual. And the way he greeted me was even stranger.

"Hey buddy, how's it going," he said in a very casual and detached manner. I immediately knew something was wrong.

"Hey, what's going on," I asked, as he headed straight for his car.

"Santiago, let's go," one of the women said as she got into her SUV. She was the heaviest of the three.

"My wife's over there. I've got to go!"

I couldn't imagine he was referring to the heavy set, unattractive one. The other two were significantly more attractive and in considerably better shape, although they were by no means beauty queens. They drove off and I was left disappointed, knowing I'd be spending the night alone— because no one else would do.

A few weeks went by and when I drove by I didn't see his car in the parking lot. By the end of August, he was nowhere to be found. Given the nature of the industry, I was extremely worried and wondered if someone might have harmed him. Finally, I decided to go into the club and do a little investigative work.

Trying to be somewhat discreet, I began by asking a couple of the other dancers what had happened to him. No one seemed to know. The other dancers were blatantly jealous of him because all the clientele loved him and he would almost always win first place in the strip contest.

I kept pressing for information, but I couldn't show how concerned I really was. It might have led the other dancers to suspect Santiago and I had been fooling around, and neither of us wanted them to know. I had become somewhat friendly with this one dancer and he told me that Santiago's wife had become interested in his whereabouts at night and so he had stopped dancing.

I thought immediately about the second time he had come to my house. When he got out of his car, I noticed an envelope was under his windshield wiper. It contained a check for $250, which he tore up right in front of me. I loved the fact that he couldn't be bought and that our relationship wasn't based on him getting anything from me except my undying love and affection.

But someone had written him a check for $250, someone had tried to buy him. And there was no telling what all he was doing to earn that money.

That night I pulled out of the parking lot, searching one last time for his car, and headed home. I was left to wonder what had happened and if I'd ever see him again. I was in a bad place, mired in worry and filled with uncertainty.

THE NEW MISSUS

ONCE I HAD my talk with Ammon, I began to feel stronger. I told myself that Santiago and I were taking a sabbatical from each other, and I refocused on my goal of finding a wife. Right about that time, Ralph Jonas, a friend and ex-coworker from my previous real estate development job, told me he wanted me to meet an ex-coworker of his, Megan Campbell.

"Man, you are going to love this girl," he insisted. "She's smart and good-looking."

"Okay, send me a picture."

Another buddy of mine had recently tried to hook me up with a coworker of his and it was an utter disaster, so I was being very cautious. My disaster date had been as sweet as could be, and a Christian, but her looks just didn't do it for me. So this time I was hesitant, but still trying my best to stay open.

Ralph himself had married a woman who was both intelligent and beautiful, so I figured that maybe I could trust his taste. When the picture arrived in my Hotmail account inbox, I saw a beautiful young lady who appeared to be sweet and unpretentious. Somehow, though, I wasn't wowed, so I told Ralph I wasn't interested.

A few months went by and Ralph mentioned that Megan wanted to meet me. I told him we could all get together for happy hour at Ra Sushi because some of my coworkers and friends would be gathering there next Friday. Happy Hour would be the perfect setting to meet her because I would have other people to attend to and I wouldn't look rude if I wasn't interested.

The following Friday my friends and coworkers all met up at Ra. The place was packed but we were able to get a corner section so all of us could sit down. At the time I really wasn't in the mindset to meet anyone because it had been a long week. Plus, I was finally able to catch up with my former coworkers I hadn't seen in months.

Megan and I were introduced, but we were seated at different ends of the table, so we really didn't get to talk. Besides, she seemed really shy. I'm an extreme extrovert, so if you don't grab my attention immediately, I'm usually on to something or someone else.

While I was chatting it up with the people around me, my boy Shawn Long was getting to know Megan and her cousin from San Antonio. The happy hour crowd was starting to fade and everybody started looking to me for the next spot.

"Let's hit the Flat. They have this great DJ over there on Friday night," I explained.

After the checks had been paid and people finally made their way to the exit, we caravanned over to the Flat. We were able to get one big table that all of us could sit around and actually hear each other. The seating arrangement at the Flat was similar to the one at Ra: Shawn was seated next to Megan. As we were talking, I mentioned something which prompted Shawn to say, "That's because he's in love with a stripper."

Shawn is one of my closest friends. We have known each other for over thirteen years and he is like a brother. Like me, he was conversant with both the straight and alternative scenes, so he knew about Santiago. There are certain lines you don't cross when you mix both scenes and he was usually good at following those unstated rules. But he had been drinking heavily and so he started airing my business. I tried to play his comment off and move the conversation along, but he said it again. Now I was livid. I gave him a look which let him know he had definitely crossed the line. Luckily, he got the message and shut up.

Eventually, we all decided to make it an early night and head home. As I was walking out with the ladies, Megan and her cousin were being escorted to her car by another ex-coworker of mine, who was known for trying to get into as much pussy as he could. So I said goodbye to the two ladies, and I went to find Shawn.

I let him know I was pissed about his little comment. While he hadn't mentioned that the stripper was a man, he had still said that I was in love with a stripper.

"Not cool," I said.

He quickly apologized and I told him it was okay because I knew it was the alcohol talking. He went on to say how intrigued he was by Megan.

"She's one of the few good ones left," he explained. "She's in her early thirties, well-educated and a genuine lady."

I couldn't deny what he said, but all I had seen was a nice young lady who didn't say much.

A few weeks passed and I was on the phone with my brother from another mother, Rem, short for Remington, who was working in Iraq for KBR. Before he left we had talked extensively about how I wanted to find a wife and settle down and have some kids. During this particular conversation, he reminded me that I was going to have to open myself up to dating women. While it wasn't what I wanted to hear, it was definitely what I needed to internalize.

Later that Saturday afternoon Ralph called and said he and some of his friends wanted to hang out again. It was a UFC (Ultimate Fighting Championship) night and I was supposed to meet up with my guys to watch the fight, so I told him where he could find us. When he said "some friends," I didn't realize that he was referring to his wife and Megan. As I reflected on my earlier conversation with Rem, I thought, okay, here is your chance to open yourself up because this girl is obviously interested in you. After the fight, I walked her to her car and got her number.

The following week was extremely hectic at work and I was headed out of town on Friday, but I hadn't had a chance to meet up with Megan yet. I have a seven day rule: if a person doesn't go out on a date within seven days of getting your number, they're not interested. The cutoff was approaching and I wanted to act fast. So I gave her a call and asked if she wanted to meet for dinner on Thursday. She agreed and we met at my favorite Vietnamese restaurant, Mai's.

It was raining that Thursday afternoon, which makes any commute in Houston a problem, plus Megan was coming from just outside the city limits. I called her to see if she would need a little more time. She thought she would make it, but we pushed back the time, just in case.

When I arrived she was already seated and answering a few work emails on her phone. Dressed in business attire, she looked gorgeous. I love to see a woman in a nice pair of heels and professional attire. It reminds me of Robin Givens in my favorite movie, Boomerang. I apologized for being slightly late and she said it was no problem as she greeted me with a warm smile.

Over dinner, we walked through all the traditional getting to know you questions and she seemed like a down-to-earth person. Intrigued and wanting to get more pieces to this puzzle, I suggested we go somewhere after dinner. When I go on a date I love giving the other person an experience they haven't had before. Since she was from Corpus Christi, she really hadn't been to all the spots in Houston yet.

After making a few calls to see what was going on that night, I decided to put her in my car and drive. Before I could get her in the passenger side and shut the door, my umbrella decided it wanted to act a fool and collapse in the wind. She said, "Don't worry, I've got one in my purse." Ah, a woman who's prepared, I like that.

I took her to Coco's, a quaint coffeehouse. As a lover of pastries, I thought she might enjoy some Nutella crepes (I fell in love with them when I was in Paris). Just as we got out of the car, it began to rain harder, so we had to share her umbrella. I put my arm around her waist and she put her arm around my shoulder and suddenly I was feeling a spark with a woman that I hadn't felt in years. It took me by surprise and lingered in my mind for several moments. Is this the one God has for me?

We ordered the Nutella crepes and started to get comfortable with each other. I could finally ask the questions which would allow me to know what made her tick. I was interested in what really got her excited because she was so even tempered, the exact opposite of me.

"I'm simple," she said. "I don't need to be in the spotlight."

Again, another way we were total opposites. Yet what we had in common was a love for family, God and travel. When she told me some of the financial sacrifices she had made for her family I knew I wasn't dealing with your everyday, run-of-the-mill woman. I knew I had a smart one on my hands: she had graduated as the first African-American valedictorian of her high school, finished Boston College, and then taken several key human resource positions in various companies across the nation. She went on to say she wanted children and a man who loved God.

At this point I'm thinking I've hit the lottery. Everything I wanted in a wife was sitting right before me. So we started hanging out and I started introducing her to my close friends. Everybody loved her, because she was such a personable woman. Still, there was one issue that annoyed the hell out of me. When we were together or on the phone she didn't really talk. I had grown up with two parents who would barely let me get a word in edgewise, so I wasn't used to silence.

Mitch enlightened me on what was going on.

"You have an introvert on your hands," he revealed.

"What?" I tried to wrap my brain around what he had just said.

"Yeah, buddy, she's got all the classic signs of an introvert," he explained. "She's not going to initiate the conversation because you're always talking. You have to learn to trust the silence. Then she'll open up."

"Trusting silence requires patience," I snapped, "a virtue I don't have."

"Well, if you want to be with her, you're going to have to find a way."

Mitch was an introvert so he was the perfect person to help me, a super extrovert, to evaluate things from a different perspective. And this was definitely a time when I needed his insight. Who better to explain how an introvert operates to an extrovert, than an introvert?

As soon as I got off the phone with him, I called her and told her I had just spoken with Mitch. Typical Megan, she asked how he was doing, even though she had never met him. I proceeded to tell her the gist of our conversation. While she didn't agree with everything he said, for the most part she thought his assessment was accurate. I was happy to have finally gained some insight into how her mind worked, but I wasn't thrilled to know she was an introvert. I'm all about letting things out at the moment and moving on, the exact opposite of most introverts and especially her.

THE TEST

WHEN I START to think I might be getting serious with some-one, the next step is to put them through my travel test. There is no better way to see who a person truly is than when you take them out of their normal setting and comfort zone.

I had to go to Brea, CA for work at the beginning of November, so I decided to fly Megan out for the weekend and see how things turned out. Honestly, I was really worried I was going to be bored out of my mind because she was so nonchalant about most things.

She arrived on the 9:00 p.m. flight from Houston that Thursday night. After I picked her up from the airport, we went straight to the hotel for her to drop off her bags and change clothes to go out. One of my best friends from undergrad, Javier Gonzalez, told me to check out the Standard on Thursday: it was a mix of two spots I like in Houston which have great club music and games. There was table tennis on the first level, with the ambient/house/drum & bass deejay. Megan and I had a blast. I'm a competitive person and a showoff and I ended up beating all the competition.

The next couple of days we did some sightseeing, the traditional L.A. stuff—Rodeo Drive, Hollywood Blvd.—along with a visit to the Getty Villa and a meal with Javier and his wife at Roscoe's Chicken and Waffle. Of course, they asked how we met, so we told them that it was through a mutual friend. We figured out that Ralph had been telling both of us that the other person was interested. We were both shocked.

While my friends seemed to like Megan, I needed to talk to Javier alone to see what he really thought. With so little time, I needed to find a place where Megan could entertain herself while Javier and I talked. To the Beverly Center! After we got a quick bite to eat, Megan went shopping and Javier and I got straight to the point. It takes someone who really knows me to set me straight. Javier, like me, was an only child, and he is also athletic, good-looking, and intelligent. The only difference between us was that he is Latin. Although his parents were still married, they had been living two separate lives and at times Javier was thrown in the middle. So he could relate to my situation on multiple levels.

"So what do you think?" I was anticipating an excited and joyful response from him concerning my new love interest.

"About what?" He looked at me, clearly confused.

"About Megan," I said.

He gave me a dubious look. "She's nice, but that's not you. What about Jeri?" Javier knew better than anyone how much I truly loved her. He reminded me that during and even after college, Jeri remained the second most important person in my life, right after my mom. And my love for her had never wavered.

"Why did you have to bring her up?" I asked, sulking.

I couldn't believe that I had brought Javier the perfect wife for me and he immediately made me realize I was missing the main ingredient: unconditional true love.

We headed back to Houston that Sunday and I knew, no matter how hard I tried, the reality was I wasn't in love with Megan. I kept hoping it would just happen one day, but so far it hadn't.

Before the plane took off, I sent Jeri a text telling her I wanted to talk with her as soon as I got back to Houston. When I was driving to my house from the airport Jeri called to say that she was near my house with Stephanie, her girlfriend, and Stephanie's kids, and was going to stop over.

When I got home, Megan headed back to her place and Jeri and Stephanie arrived with the kids. For the past 15 years, Jeri had been raising two high school kids and one preschool kid. She had unofficially adopted them, and then Stephanie and her two biological children had moved in.

We turned on a show for the kids to watch so the three of us could talk. They wanted to know about the trip and I told them I wasn't in love with Megan but I was forcing things because I wanted a baby.

Jeri jumped to her feet. "You won't believe it, but I woke up this morning wanting a baby. Didn't I, babe?" she asked, turning to Stephanie. Jeri had hazel eyes and when we were kids she would sometimes get so excited that her eyes would change color. I leaned in a little to see if maybe they were changing colors now.

"She did," Stephanie confirmed. Stephanie was in her late twenties, attractive and feminine, and very stable-minded. Jeri always had attractive girlfriends, yet Stephanie wasn't Jeri's typical petite type. But when she dressed up, she looked just as beautiful as all of Jeri's exes. Today was Sunday so both women were dressed casually in shorts, t-shirts and tennis shoes.

Jeri was standing next to me in the kitchen so I turned to her, shook my head and said, "You know, I sent you a text at 8:20 this morning while I was waiting on the runway. I realized, why am I forcing myself to try to fall in love with Megan just so I can have a baby?" I paused and smiled at Jeri. "When I can have a child with the person I've always wanted to be the mother of my children."

"Oh my God," she said. She laughed in a light-hearted way but I could tell she was a little shocked. "That was the same time I was telling Stephanie I wanted to have a baby of my own!" If Stephanie and Jeri stayed together, there would always be Stephanie's kids. But two of the children Jeri was raising were about to graduate from high school and the youngest one's mom had recently been released from jail. Once the mother got on her feet, she could take her child, leaving Jeri without any kids of her own.

Jeri turned to me. "And we both know you would be a great dad."

I couldn't believe that we'd both had baby thoughts running through our heads at the same time. I wondered if it was a sign from God that He was all right with my decision.

I leaned back against the counter and smiled at Jeri and Stephanie. "It must be a sign!"

Jeri nodded. "My information should still be on file at the fertility clinic. The last time I tried to do this, the guy backed out when it was time for him to pay to get his sperm analyzed. That was a blessing in disguise. He wasn't stable enough to be a father anyway."

I figured she was rationalizing about the other guy. After my initial excitement, I realized there was a two-hour time difference between Houston and Los Angeles, so we hadn't really had the thought at the exact same time. I was allowing myself an out just in case I got a sense that God wasn't in agreement with the decision. "Well, let me know," I said.

Although we were in accord about having a child together,

in the back of my mind I was holding out: to make it right, Jeri and I had to be married. That way our child would have both parents in the same house. I just couldn't bear the thought that my child might go through the same hell I had gone through: living in a divided family, with me shuttling back and forth between parents. But trying to force myself to fall in love just to have a child didn't sit well with me either. I knew that ultimately I would have to end things with Megan.

Later that Sunday evening, as I was leaving my mom's I noticed Jeri's car parked in the driveway at her parents' house so I stopped by. Her parents lived three doors down from my mom in a two-story brick house.

I found Jeri and her parents in the breakfast nook. "Hey, Mr. and Mrs. Jones," I said, as I gave them both a hug.

"How have you been doing, baby," Mrs. Jones asked.

"I'm doing. I just got back from L.A."

"Boy, you are always traveling. Was this for work or pleasure?" Mr. Jones asked.

"Both. My division just went through a restructuring and this was our first official meeting as the new group. But you know I'm not flying all the way to California without getting some vacation in."

"Yeah, yeah!" Jeri said, laughing. "He was also testing this new girl he's been dating. You know he always does the travel test to see if they'll last."

I shrugged. "What better way to see who a person really is than to get them out of their comfort zone and normal setting? You get to see how they operate under pressure." I sighed. "Too bad, I realized I didn't love her."

Jeri took that moment to break the news. "Well, we've decided we're going to have a baby."

"Finally," Mrs. Jones said.

Mr. Jones didn't say anything but I could tell he was listening keenly to the conversation. I was surprised he didn't say his classic line, "Jeri, that's nonsense."

Family was the most important thing in the Jones household and Jeri was the only daughter who didn't have biological children. Her parents had already accepted that she probably wouldn't be getting married, so I figured they were on board—this seemed like a viable option to them.

I nodded. "Yep, as soon as I get my book done."

"It's always going to be something. It's your book now; it'll be something else later," Jeri said, annoyed. "We just need to go ahead and do it before you change your mind. I don't have but another year and a half before I'm done with trying to have children."

Chapter Four
WHAT SHOULD I EXPECT?

No matter how meticulously I try
Something inevitably will go awry
Throwing all detailed plans out the door
Leaving me to wonder what's next in store
— The Unexpected, A.D.

BREAK UP THEN MAKE UP

THE NEXT DAY I started thinking about everything Jeri and I had said when we were standing in the Jones's breakfast nook. Jeri was right: I like everything to be perfect, which is why I was finding reasons to put off having a baby. There would always be some reason why it wasn't quite the right time. So I decided that we just needed to do it, and that meant we had to get around the one obstacle that was preventing me from moving forward: we needed to get married. That way we'd be living in the same house and my child would have an intact family.

I texted Jeri in the middle of the day, telling her to meet me at the Galleria the next day. She wanted to know what for, but I didn't want to let her in on my plan because I was afraid she'd shut me down. So I told her to just come and meet me. Because we're both so busy—she is a high school coach and I work in corporate real estate—it wasn't easy to find a time we could agree on, but we finally did.

We met at the mall the next day and I told her she was right. "We shouldn't wait," I said, "so let's go pick out a ring—right now."

Jeri looked at me in utter disbelief—she was so shocked, she couldn't say anything. We're both very vocal people, but at this point she was speechless. I had never seen her like that. I could see she was trying to process what I had just told her. I knew she was happy that I was proposing because that meant we would be having a baby, but she was also in conflict; she hadn't yet found the voice to explain the true source of her hesitation.

After she got over the initial shock, she was finally able to walk into Tiffany's. We looked around and she found a ring she liked. I got the contact information to call the following day to discuss pricing. As we walked back through the mall to return to our cars, Jeri found her voice. She turned to me and spoke slowly. "While I'm excited you proposed, you need to know that I'm in love with Stephanie. I really am in love with her."

The words were sincere, but Jeri had been in love before and it had never worked out: she had a knack for picking the wrong people. Besides, Stephanie and she hadn't been together a year, so I didn't put too much weight into her comment. The fact remained: Jeri wanted a child with me and she was willing to marry me in order to make that happen.

The next day I called the Tiffany rep and found out the ring she wanted was $50,000. Needless to say, she wasn't getting that one. So I called her and asked, "What's more important to you—the Tiffany brand or getting the exact style of ring you want?" Jeri's an eminently practical woman, so she said what mattered most was the style. Her oldest sister was a big proponent of our marriage, so I asked her for advice and she told me to go to Zales: The Diamond Store.

Luckily, I found a great ring, which I could return if things didn't work out, and I headed back to the Jones's house to ask if I could marry their daughter.

It was one of the oddest conversations I had had with her parents. Her dad said, "Hell no! I love my daughter and I love you—but Jeri's house, with all that riff-raff, is on a level 10. And that's way too chaotic for you. I know you wouldn't be able to take all of that." He was referring to the fact that we'd be adding a sixth child to the five Jeri and Stephanie already had together, and that would be a lot of chaos, maybe more than I could put up with.

"Yeah, but I'll be able to change things once we get together. I'll make her see there's only so much time and so many resources. If you want to have a baby, we'll need all of them focused on our baby versus other people's almost grown babies."

He looked at me like I had lost every sensible brain cell and exclaimed, "I can't wait to see that."

Her mom was even hesitant, which surprised me. Yet she said, "Jeri does have a lot going on. Well, I'll be praying for you. Now let me see the ring!"

As I laughed and pulled the ring out of the neatly wrapped Zales box, Mrs. Jones exclaimed, "Oh that's nice, A.D.! Well, good luck."

"Thanks, I'll take all I can get."

So I left the Jones's house with one "hell no" and one "I'll be praying for you." Either way, they knew if Jeri said yes, their daughter and future grandchild would be taken care of, which is all they really wanted.

The next stop was Megan's apartment. While telling Jeri's parents I wanted to marry their daughter wasn't the easiest thing in the world, finding the words to break up with Megan was even harder. We had just had a great trip to L.A., and it seemed pretty obvious that she was falling in love with me, so how was I going to tell her that I wanted to break up?

When I left the Jones's, it was getting close to 10:30 p.m. Normally, I wouldn't go to Megan's house that late because she had to get up early for work the next morning. Yet I didn't want her thinking I intended to be in a relationship with her when I was planning to ask Jeri to marry me the next day. So I called her as I left the Jones's to see if I could come over and talk.

When I got to Megan's apartment, she greeted me with her always beaming smile.

"Hey, babe," she said as she approached to kiss me.

I gave her a hug instead of a kiss and said, "Hey, you! We need to talk." This was so hard because she was such a wonderful woman inside and out, and yet I just wasn't in love with her. No matter how much I wanted to force myself to fall in love with her, I just couldn't.

We sat down on her sofa and she asked, "So what's up?"

I struggled to find the right words. I certainly didn't want to say that I wasn't in love with her because that would be too devastating. My main goal was to avoid hurting her, so I had to figure something else. I had to walk a very fine line. I feared that my backpedaling might leave the impression that I was falling in love, or was on the fence, and that would only cause her more pain.

After struggling through a few phrases about how wonderful she was and how I didn't have my shit together I said, "I need time to get me together."

Like a true introvert, Megan took the news well and didn't really show much emotion. She worked in human resources, so I figured that maybe she considered this situation similar to her having to lay someone off. Whatever the case, I was glad it wasn't as painful as I had thought it would be, at least for the selfish only child inside of me. I left knowing I could ask Jeri to marry me and I wouldn't feel guilty.

The next morning, Jeri drove her parents to the airport for one of their many vacations (oh, the joys of retirement) and that afternoon she rode with me to pick up my car from the mechanic. I had decided this was my time to actually present the ring. I had the little black box concealed neatly in the right pocket of my cargo shorts: in it was the sparkling 1.5 carat baguette-cut white-gold ring. After I picked her up, we chatted a bit, catching up. I was terribly nervous—it felt like I was waiting to get my test results back. Is this going to be it? Will the woman I trust more than anyone in the world accept my proposal of marriage?

When we got to the mechanic's, my car wasn't ready, and we had to wait. It's now or never, I told myself.

"So I went over to your parents' house last night," I began.

With a mischievous grin on her face she said, "Yeah, when I dropped my parents off this morning, they told me. Talking about, yeah, A.D. is going to pop the question. I've been so excited. I've been telling everyone at work."

Jeri mentioning her coworkers was a perfect segue.

"Speaking of coworkers, the Colombian lady who sits next to me attends Second Baptist. She asked me if I knew about the triangle/trinity. I said, of course I did: the Father, the Son and the Holy Ghost. She said, 'No, that's not it. It's God at the top, the husband on one side, and the wife on the other. As they both get closer to God they in turn get closer to each other. I was blown away and thought this is exactly how my marriage needs to be. If it's just me, my wife and God, everything else will fall in place."

"Are you done?" Jeri asked me.

"Yes."

"Good. Well, I know that's how you want it, but I want it to be, you, me and Stephanie. We can build a house on a plot of land I want that's near my house. Stephanie, the kids and I can live on one side of the house and you can live on the other side—because I know you like it quiet. Our child would be in the middle."

The minute the words traveled from her lips to my inner ear, passing through my cochlea to my acoustic nerve, my perfect fantasy came crashing down instantaneously. It was a cold, crystalline moment in which I realized that what I had so desperately longed for and carefully thought out would never be.

"I told Stephanie there would be times when you would have to be number one. I might have to fly out with you for book appearances and things, and she said as long as I wasn't sleeping with you she was fine."

I was filled with regret and all I could manage was, "Sorry, no deal, that's not going to work." The ring never saw the light of that disappointing day.

Having a marriage on paper was nothing like the marriage trinity I had envisioned. Although I knew we didn't share sexual intimacy, I was under the assumption that once we got married we'd make the intimacy thing work out later.

When we dropped off the car, Jeri said, "Well, let me know what you want to do."

"Okay," I muttered as I drove off.

The next day I was back at Zales. Maybe it was the business-man in me—when it came to purchase the ring, I made sure I had a safety net. I guess deep down inside I had somehow already known that a marriage between Jeri and me wouldn't work because we were missing an important piece of the union: sexual attraction and intimacy.

Although I still wasn't absolutely sure if Megan was the one God had sent as my future wife, it made sense to return to couple status with her. The following week, I invited her out to a restaurant with some friends. After a few quick introductions, I told her that I had made a mistake, that I had judged her too quickly, and we picked back up where we had left off.

I'LL TAKE YOU FOR A RIDE

ON DECEMBER 22, 2011, Megan and I were scheduled to take a helicopter ride from Ellington Field, near NASA. We had had a great Thanksgiving Day together. We went to three different house gatherings, which were all located in different counties of Texas. And I had to pick up my mom to attend two of the turkey day celebrations and drop her back off before we went to the third. Megan had been a trooper through it all, never complaining once.

Although there were plenty of opportunities for the intimacy we shared to turn sexual, we never had sex because

I didn't want to taint our relationship if this was who God intended as my wife. It was the rule I lived by: never have sex with a woman you don't love. At this point in our relationship, Megan had proven to be a woman worth investing time and money in. Since neither of us had been on a helicopter ride, I thought it would be a unique early Christmas present. After we took the helicopter ride, we went over my mom's house to put up Christmas decorations. Rem decided to come over and install the ceiling fan I had bought for my mom last Christmas, because Christmas was three days away and roughly forty people would be stopping by for our annual Christmas Dinner.

Normally, I always have my cell phone on me, but I had been moving back and forth between Megan and Rem, trying to help each of them with the decorations and the fan. When I went back into the family room where Rem was working, I heard a text message come through. After I read that initial one, I saw that Santiago had sent one earlier. His text read: Hey buddy, how's it going? :)

I thought, why now? Of all the times, it had to be today. I had just had a great time with Megan on a new adventure. Most of my friends were excited about us being together and now after four months he reaches out to me!

I was so frustrated: The one and only person I wanted, the one I had made up my mind I could no longer have, the one about whom I had decided it was best to move on, sends a text. I hadn't heard the text when it had come through three hours earlier, so I conveniently waited until Rem finished putting up the fan and Megan headed home before I responded.

In three days it would be Christmas morning and, like the Christmas mornings of my childhood, I was filled with uncontainable excitement and anticipation. He had texted me and I hoped this meant we would talk and perhaps get together. Rem and I were headed out to get dinner, but it was almost 10:00 P.M., around the time most restaurants are closing during the holidays. As we headed out in our separate cars, I exchanged a couple of texts and decided I had had enough, so I called Santiago.

"Hey, buddy! How are you?" he asked in a jovial tone.

"Where the hell have you been? I texted you and asked some of the guys at the club if they had seen you and nobody knew where you were. I was worried something had happened to you." I was so happy to be talking with him, but I was also frustrated and a little angry.

"There was no need to worry. I'm fine! I quit the club and started school. I miss you. I wanted to see if we could get together."

"Where are you now?" I tried to keep myself from sounding too eager.

"I'm at my sister's now, but we're about to eat dinner."

"Well, I'm headed to dinner myself. Give me a call when you get done and we can meet up at my house."

"It's too late tonight but soon."

I couldn't help myself and I blurted out, "I miss you so much."

"I miss you too. Soon! I'll see you soon."

I was so disappointed that I wouldn't get to see him that night, and yet I was walking on cloud nine: after four months he was still thinking about me. When Rem and I finally got to the restaurant, I couldn't restrain my elation.

"What are you are cheesing about?" he asked.

"The stripper dude I told you about, texted me tonight," I said with a huge smile on my face.

His brown eyes pierced mine. It was like he was my big brother and he was about to pummel me. "Don't mess up what you have with Megan. You've been talking about how this was what you wanted and now you're on the right path. Don't get off."

"Yeah, I know. But he . . . he just does it for me." And he did—I would have dropped everything and rushed to him if he had asked me to. I was filled with a mix of elation and regret, and even though Rem's words were wise, I couldn't listen.

I couldn't believe that I was turning my back on a woman I felt God had finally sent to me, one who wanted to give me what I so desperately sought: a family of my own. A woman with both beauty and brains, one who countless men would have died to call their own.

My past was stepping up to tap me on the shoulder. Very few people had any idea what I had lived through, and those who did believed I had left that crippling past behind. But had I?

Part Two
THE ADDICT

Chapter Five

LAYING THE FOUNDATION

What my eyes see, what my ears hear, what my spirit feels,
What you show me is what I'll grow up to become.
Not good or bad, not wrong or right,
Just what was destined to be.
— The Foundation, A.D

No ONE SAYS, "When I grow up I want to be a sex addict." Like everything in life, a foundation has to be established which either supports a person's success or failure. Even before my birth, my mom was laying the groundwork for me to become successful. Unfortunately, there were circumstances which were predominantly out of her control and ones she had no idea about which established the base for my sex addiction.

When I look at my father's family history, I realize that he witnessed his own father's unfaithfulness, and that in turn was passed on to my father and other members of his family. Eventually, the "curse," like a rattlesnake patiently waiting in the grass to attack its prey, injected its venom in me and the poison morphed into a different version of sexual addiction.

THE BIG "D"

MY PARENTS MET as undergraduates and got married at my maternal grandfather's church in Columbia, Tennessee, Labor Day weekend 1966. Now that they had both love and marriage, the only thing left would be me in a baby carriage, right? Not so fast! The ultimate planner, my mom politely informed my dad she would be taking the Pill until she started writing her dissertation and then she would focus on raising a family. Although my dad might have had a few objections, especially since he wanted "a baseball team" at that time, he loved her enough to go along with the plan.

As planned, when she began writing her dissertation, my mom quit taking the Pill. A year went by, the board approved her thesis and she received her doctorate in education at the age of twenty-one. Her undergraduate university hired her and everything seemed to be going according to schedule, except one minor detail— she couldn't get pregnant.

Both of my parents were overachievers, so they went back to focusing on their respective careers. A few years passed and my dad obtained his Masters and my mom was offered a job to head the psychology department at a small university in Texas. Two years later, my mom started having major cramps one day. At first she didn't think anything of it, but, yes, it turned out she was pregnant. Her pregnancy was high risk and she went through some pretty dire medical complications, but on April 5, 1977 at 8:51 p.m., God brought both of us successfully through a C-section surgery.

After all the love, time, effort and money it took to have a child, there is no way anyone would ever expect the two people who had me to get divorced. But before I turned five, my family became a part of a growing American statistic. Like most kids who experience a divorce at a young age, this one event would probably have the greatest effect on my entire life. Even today, some of the most important decisions I make are affected by my parents' divorce.

To put it bluntly, my father's infidelity/sex addiction was the reason my parents got divorced. Instead of delving deep into all the specifics of his indiscretions, which I wasn't truly able to comprehend at the time, I'll try to focus on the decisions which directly affected me and what might have led to his choices.

Based on the discussions I've had with my mother, after she found out about my dad's extramarital affairs and had proof, she went to him. Although I've made some attempts at it, my dad and I have never discussed what happened, so this story will be biased. My mother said that she was willing to work it out because she loved, and still does love, him. Like a typical addict, he said he would change but didn't. When my mom offered to pay for counseling, my dad turned her down.

Besides the stress of having to deal with a cheating spouse, my mom had to keep up the appearance that everything was fine. She did one hell of a job. As a child, I never knew anything was wrong because she held everything in, while drowning herself in Blue Bell Homemade Ice Cream. Her weight shot up and now that I'm older I realize that she must have been in a lot of pain as she downed bowls of ice cream with tears rolling down her face.

"Everybody plays the fool, sometimes. There's no exception to the rule," Aaron Neville sang. Whether it's true or not, one thing is certain: once reality hits, you'll wake up fast. My mom received the wake-up call when the foreclosure letter for our house came in the mail.

Here's the way foreclosures worked in Texas in those days: after a borrower was late three mortgage payments, the lender sent a letter informing them of a pending foreclosure. What made this communiqué so shocking was the fact that each month my parents would sit down together and write the bills. Much too late, my mom found out that instead of mailing the payments, my dad was spending the money on other women.

Manipulating the truth is one of the most often used tools in a sex addict's arsenal. It was a skill I started developing at an early age. There is only one way I can rationalize my father doing such a despicable thing: the need to feed his addiction was greater than taking care of the basic needs of his family. While it is beyond sad, I can actually empathize with him.

Eventually my mother initiated divorce proceedings against my father. Post-divorce, my mom never publicly slandered my father's name because she knew the importance of having him in my life. So instead of adhering to the court-appointed visitation, whenever I wanted to see my dad or whenever he wanted to see me, my mom would allow it. The situation created one of the biggest dichotomies in my life. On one hand, I knew who my dad was, but on the other hand, at times when I really needed a father, he wasn't there.

Children need stability in their lives, and my mom provided it the best way she knew how, by making sure all my needs were met. On the surface I didn't lack for anything and I got almost everything I wanted. My mom loved me to death and would do anything in her power to make me happy. I'll admit I was spoiled and I knew without a doubt that she loved me. Yet the single most important need she could not provide was a true and genuine relationship with my dad. That wasn't her job; that was his. The question that lingered in my mind was, "Does my father really love me?"

BUILDING BLOCKS OF SUCCESS

ALTHOUGH I WAS forced to deal with the unsettling reality of my parents' divorce in elementary school, an outsider looking in would never have known I was being raised primarily by a single parent. If there was something educational, spiritual or character building, my mom was going to move mountains to ensure I was involved. Plus, I found some solace singing in the church choir and being able to travel during the week of spring break.

I started singing in the church choir at four, one year before kids were eligible. There was something spiritual which took place when I sang and it became the time and space where I felt closest to God. It was like I was crying out to Him and He understood all my pain. The next thing my folks knew, I was singing a solo. I sang it perfectly, but when I finished I started weeping. My parents were so proud, but they asked, "Why did you cry at the end?" I told them it was because I was scared. They reassured me there was no need to be scared; I had done a great job. Once I received that assurance from both of my parents, I realized there was no need to be afraid of anything.

In addition to singing, nothing was more exciting than traveling with my mom during spring break. My mom was teaching in the Houston Independent School District and she started a Tours Club via American Student Travel (AST). AST's travel itinerary brought to life what the students were learning in the classroom. During the break, mom and Mrs. Keith, Emmett's mother who was a close friend and coworker of my mom, would take thirty or more kids to New York, Orlando, or the Washington, D.C. areas.

In New York, I bought my first bottle of expensive cologne, Tuscany, at Bloomingdales. We visited the Statue of Liberty and I got to see my first Broadway play, *Cats*. There was nothing but fun in the sun in Orlando, where we visited Epcot Center and Disney World. I was living the good life and didn't even know it. Traveling was an opportunity to see new things my little mind didn't even know to conceptualize. And I loved it. These trips laid the foundation for my sense of adventure and my need to experience something new.

In D.C., we toured national treasures and local sites. But what comes to mind when I think about our visit to D.C. was the time we spent in Union Station. Since the place had several shops and restaurants, the group had a couple of hours to look around. While strolling along, I came across a newsstand, which had a few dirty magazines. This was the first time I had seen such things up close and in person. While I knew I wasn't supposed to be looking at them, curiosity and temptation got the best of me. Besides, my mom wasn't around, so the likelihood of me getting caught was slim.

To be discreet, I took the pornographic magazine and sandwiched it between the pages of a regular magazine. As I turned the pages, the images caused me to become more and more aroused. After I got quite an eyeful, the next stop was the restroom, where I discreetly masturbated to the images I had just seen. It was at that moment I remember developing this fantasy of meeting a stranger and having sex in a bathroom stall. I was only eleven years old, so to this day I'm not clear where the fantasy originated from. But I have a good idea.

HOW THE SEED WAS PLANTED

PARENTS HAVE A tendency to want to protect their children from all the world's harms and dangers. Yet it's those experiences which enable all of us to become the people we were destined to become. I've been told that we all have a cross to bear and there will always be something we will have to deal or struggle with.

For me, I believe being sexually abused by a neighborhood boy when I was a child played a part. I never told anyone and it was as if it never occurred, but it affected me in lasting ways. In many ways, this secret served as the catalyst for my sex addiction but didn't cause me to have a desire for both men and women. Where I fell on the sexuality spectrum is where I fell. Thankfully, I've learned the reason God allowed me to carry this cross is because it forces me to rely on Him to help me carry it. I've also been enlightened to the fact I have been assigned a task and God never gives any of us more than we can handle.

The Evans, who lived on the street behind us, had a daughter several years older than me and a son who was one or two years my senior. Like most of the kids around the same age in my neighborhood, we all played together. Our families became close enough that my parents allowed their daughter to babysit me. It was a hot Houston summer afternoon and I was at the Evans' house. Anyone who has experienced June, July or August in Texas knows that during the peak hours of the day, most people are indoors soaking up the air conditioning.

Mr. and Mrs. Evans were either out or had to run an errand and they left their daughter in charge. Their son and I were playing, and he said, "Let's go in the other room. I want to show you something." Young, innocent and naïve, I didn't think twice about going.

We went into the closet and he shut the door. That's when the details become fuzzy. I remember the jackets and other clothes brushing against my face because I was small. The touching of private parts also comes to mind, but that's it. I have repressed the incident. With neither of us over the age of seven, I doubt intercourse actually occurred. However, I can't be absolutely certain.

All that I can accurately remember is him saying, "If you tell anyone what happened I'll tell your mom and dad and get you in trouble." At that moment, I automatically thought I had done something wrong and what was worse, I could potentially get a whipping for it. The last thing a child wants is to get in trouble, which is why I never said anything.

After that initial incident, the next few times I went over to their house, their son would consistently try to fondle me. It would take place as soon as his sister left the room or when we would go into his room to "play." I couldn't say anything because in the back of my mind was the thought he was going to tell my parents and I would be in big trouble. Luckily, my mom could sense a hesitation when she mentioned me visiting the Evans' household. So I told her I didn't want to stay over there anymore.

LIKE FATHER, LIKE SON

AFTER MY PARENTS were divorced in 1981, my mom taught me my first lesson in the consequences of lying. I did something at school I had no business doing and my mom got wind of it. She told me, "If you lie to me, it's going to be worse."

So I decided at that moment never to lie to my mom because the outcome could certainly be worse. (Notice I said I would never lie. I didn't say I wouldn't omit some of the pertinent details, a skill I learned from my father.)

Since I was mad at my mom for giving me a whipping, I told her I wanted to call my dad. She called him and politely handed me the phone. I cried as I told him, "Mom gave me a whipping." This would be one of my first lessons in manipulation. Since my dad wasn't living with us, I could use him as a chance to escape from my mother. He came over that night and took me to his apartment. Once I realized all of my good toys were back at my mom's house, I was ready to go.

Staying at my dad's also presented a totally different environment. While my mom never brought a man I didn't know into her house, at my dad's apartment I would often be introduced to new ladies. Instead of consistently spending quality time with me on our weekends together, our time would be shared or I'd have to just play alone until the door opened.

At night, his door was typically closed when he had a female visitor. Mostly, I didn't mind it because people were supposedly asleep at night, but I'll never forget this one Saturday. My dad was going to take me to Chuck E. Cheese to play, but instead he had a woman over. The next thing I knew, they went into his bedroom and he shut the door.

At first, I thought it would only be a minute, so I sat back down on the couch and watched TV. Well, it seemed like they were in there forever. I started banging on the door calling for my dad to come out.

"I'll be there in a minute," he responded.

So I went back and sat down. The fact that he had a one-bedroom apartment didn't help either. Staring at the door, I waited and then I went back to knocking, wondering what was taking so long.

"Sit back down. I'll be out in a minute," he said.

Once again I went back to waiting and kept waiting. Finally, the door opened. At the time, I didn't realize he was having sex. All I knew was we were supposed to go play and here I was sitting on the sofa by myself.

From that point on, it always seemed like one broken promise after another with my dad. A child's single-mindedness led me to believe that a certain outcome would occur, and so I would do whatever it took to try to make it happen. But with my father, it never did.

My dad knew I loved cars. During the week he'd call me and tell me we were going to look at cars on Saturday. Under the assumption we were going to get a new car, I'd be filled with anticipation. We'd go look at the newest models and he'd even test drive them. I'd come home telling my mom about the new car my dad was going to get. Saturday after Saturday we'd go on test drive after test drive and it never happened. It got to the point where I didn't even want to go anymore. Then he'd promise we'd go somewhere or do something and he wouldn't show up when he said he would. Broken promises lead to shattered dreams.

We started to drift further and further apart. To make matters worse, he gave me a whipping for doing the exact thing my mom told me I had to do: tell the truth. I had done something inappropriate in class (I no longer recall what it was). As soon as we got to the apartment, he gave me a whipping. When I returned to my mom, I was crying and she wanted to know why.

"He told on himself," was my dad's reply.

After that incident, I decided I'd have to live a double life, one of truth and honesty in front of my mom, and another of secrecy in front of my dad. He wouldn't ever have to worry about me "telling on myself" again. My calculation laid the groundwork for my eventual sex addiction in that I was already learning how to hide behind a façade of secrecy whenever the situation warranted it.

JERI JONES

WHEN I STARTED grade school, I was sort of an outcast. I just couldn't seem to find a place or space where I truly felt comfortable. Being overweight definitely didn't help. And since I wore "husky" sizes, I couldn't wear trendy clothes.

On top of being out of style, I didn't play sports. Strike two. The word "popular" wasn't in my vocabulary, which made getting a girlfriend next to impossible. I was in love with Alex. She was absolutely beautiful: thin, with hazel eyes, and beautiful honey brown skin. I remember fervently praying to God the night before I asked her to be my girlfriend, because I knew it was going to take a miracle for her to say yes. Unfortunately, that would turn out to be one of the prayers He didn't quite answer the way I wanted Him to.

Although I wouldn't get the girl of my dreams then, I got something better: Jeri Jones. Jeri was my best friend and she lived three houses down from me. Athletic, beautiful and biracial, Jeri was as popular as I was unpopular. Everybody knew Jeri. The girls wanted to be her and the guys wanted to date her. She was the baby girl with two older sisters and spoiled completely rotten. Her dad had always wanted a son, so I became the unofficial adopted child. Sad to say, my social life in elementary was lived vicariously through none other than Jeri.

We did everything together, especially during the summer. We'd wake up waiting for 10:00 a.m. to come so we could hang out. My mom wouldn't let me "disturb" the Jones' household until after 10:00. Once we could officially begin our day, it usually consisted of playing with her puppy, four-square, basketball and riding our bikes from neighborhood to neighborhood chasing the shade. We'd visit her friends, which in turn became my friends.

At one point, I saw this bike I wanted and my mom finally bought it for me. Jeri and I were so close that within a couple of days she had the matching girl's bike. If it was possible, we would have been together 24/7. But my mom would always call and tell one of Jeri's parents, "Tell that boy to get back over here. You all are going to have to add him to your income taxes."

Once I was in middle school, I began diligently working to make a name for myself both in the classroom and on the tennis court. Meanwhile, Jeri and I remained the closest of friends. In the morning, she would come over after my mom left for work and fix me up with the latest fashion trends and haircuts. This was when the rolled-up jeans and high-top fade were big because of the music and acting group Kid 'n Play. We'd play four-square with the other kids on our street as we waited for the bus. This was also around the time I was first exposed to pornographic videos.

Jeri had stumbled across her dad's porn collection and Brad Timbadeaux, my next door neighbor, had discovered his father's collection as well. There was nothing like watching my first porno. All the lust and nakedness being acted out on the screen kept me glued to the TV. I found myself taking any opportunity I could just to get a glimpse of that freaky action. Whenever Jeri's parents were going to be out of the house for an hour or so, we'd pop in a tape. We were very careful to make sure we remembered exactly where the tape was located in the drawer and to cue up the tape to the exact scene which had been in progress when the preceding viewer had ejected the video. Getting caught wasn't an option.

Brad's dad was a fireman, so we could usually count on him to be at the station for a good stretch of time. On a few rare occasions, I was able to borrow his dad's videos and return them the next day. Late at night, when my mom was asleep, I would sneak into the family room and watch them. I remember one film in particular. Unlike today's porn, with its minimal plot, this video featured a rich couple where the wife was cheating. The husband caught wind of the affair and then the story really got good. He brought the man his wife had been sleeping with to their mansion and made them have sex in front of him. After they finished, the husband said, "I hope you enjoyed it because it will be the last time you'll get any." He then kicked the man out of his house butt-naked and tied up his wife to a column outside near the swimming pool. In the pool were two beautiful women who fucked the hell out of him, as his wife watched, begging to join in. This man was large and in charge and it became my favorite video.

Now that the man in the video had become a new role model, I wasn't relying on Jeri anymore to be the sole source for my social life. I had to venture out and get my own girlfriend.

THE SEX IS IN THE MUSIC

As a lover of music, all I had to do was turn on the radio to get a nice dose of sexual enticement. I remember sexual lyrics as early as elementary school. Sittin' at home, watchin' Arsenio Hall, so I got my black book for a freak to call. . . Oh, me so horny . . . Oh, me so horny. Me love you long time. Those were the lyrics of 2 Live Crew's "Me So Horny." Of course, my mom quickly turned the channel once she realized what the rappers were saying. But the reality was that just about every genre (Country, Pop, R&B, Rock, Heavy Metal, Rap, Hip-Hop) had sexually explicit or suggestive lyrics.

After hearing Madonna's "Like a Virgin" for the first time, I remember singing the words and finally asking my mom what a virgin was. She probably said, someone who hasn't had sex, but we never really had the "sex talk." My mom was old school, so she probably thought my dad should and would handle it. But that never really happened.

The closest my dad and I came to talking about sex was when I had my first wet dream. I knew I hadn't peed, and yet my underwear was wet. My dad informed me I was becoming a man, but that was the extent of our conversation. Sex wasn't a topic which came up in our household, although being the precocious adolescent I was, I always had a natural curiosity about it. How ironic, a current sex addict wasn't able to communicate honestly about sex to a future addict.

Jeri use to love the rapper, Too Short. And he had some of

the nastiest lyrics, especially in his song entitled "Don't Fight the Feelin." Are you bleeding, can't think about sex? Irritated by your Kotex? We don't need to kiss, we don't have to fuck. I'll pull out my dick, bitch, you can suck . . . Since we hung out all the time, I'd recite the words right along with her.

HSHP

EVER SINCE I was a teenager, I wanted to be a doctor. The Houston Independent School District had a handful of magnet schools that specialized in a particular field of study. High School for Health Professions (HSHP) was a college-preparatory magnet school that gave its students the opportunity to work in the hospital setting during their junior and senior years. I was determined to get in, but it wasn't going to be easy. The school required potential students to take an aptitude test and to be a current resident within the school district. Taking the test wasn't difficult. But finding a way to legitimately live in the district was a major challenge.

They say God works in mysterious ways. Finally, my parents' divorce would work in my favor. My dad had an apartment in the city of Houston, which technically allowed me to meet the requirement of living in the school district. This meant my dad would have to pick me up and drop me off at school my freshman year and part of my sophomore year.

So I took the test and got accepted—I was thrilled. While most of my classmates in middle school would be going to the neighborhood high school, I would be the only one going to HSHP. By attending Health Professions, not only would I be headed in the direction of fulfilling my dream of becoming a doctor, I would also be in a new environment with some of the most astute minds in the city.

In addition to my academic pursuits, I was involved in several extracurricular activities. And I was now ready to actively pursue the activities that would allow me to make progress toward my goal of acting out what I had seen in my favorite video. My class had only 167 students, so we basically all knew each other. Sarah Carter, a cute, quiet, petite girl who played tennis, piqued my curiosity.

After getting to know each other, I finally convinced her to go on a date with me. The date didn't go as planned, but we became great friends and I started training with her tennis coach, lost the weight I had put on while in elementary and middle school, and played in several tournaments. But I would have to wait until my senior year to get my first taste of some horizontal action.

NEWCOMER

MY FIRST INTRODUCTION to the gym occurred during high school, at the Bally's Total Fitness near the middle school where my mom taught. I wanted to get a physique just like the men in the fitness magazines, so I persuaded my mom to get me a membership. She agreed, and I was on cloud nine because I was on my way to getting the "perfect" body.

My first day working out by myself was so exciting. Whether I was looking to my left or right, I saw someone attractive. The women were in great shape with their nice voluptuous breasts, round glutes and flat stomachs. And a sizable amount of the men were extremely muscular: from head to toe. Back then I wasn't aware of how prevalent the use of enhancement drugs, such as steroids, was among the fitness crowd.

For the most part, everyone at the gym had a very friendly and helpful attitude. Yet even as a teenager, I could see a certain percentage of guests were doing more socializing and flirting than training. There would always be a few ladies on the Stairmaster with workout shorts on right up to their kitty cat and others running on the treadmill in only a sports bra. The guys would hold conversations the entire time with big Kool-Aid smiles on their faces thinking, yeah baby, I can't wait to get some of that after this workout. And the ladies giggled as their breasts bounced up and down like miniature basketballs during a full-court press. I guess this was foreshadowing of what was to come for me.

DR. A

IN 1993, MY high school principal introduced me to Dr. William Axelrod. He was a pediatrician who worked at Texas Children's Hospital and mentored some of the promising male students at the school. Dr. Axelrod lived in a lavish condominium near the medical center. I had been to some nice places before, but this had to be one of the grandest I had seen at the time.

The first thing Dr. Axelrod wanted to know was a little bit about my background and what my goals were. He instantly saw I had the aptitude to become a doctor, but the passion and drive for something else. His type of intellect was one I had never been privy to: he was very wise but his presentation could be ponderous. As a listener, I wanted him to hurry up and get to the point. Yet he was slowly and strategically teaching me that I didn't know everything and that he was going to take his time proving to me that I didn't, and teach me some patience while he was at it. It was true genius, but torture for me.

Dr. Axelrod's mentoring was exactly what I needed because he was able to provide some of the critical insight I didn't receive from my father. Here was a man who looked like me, and who was financially, mentally, emotionally and spiritually successful. In essence, he served as a real role model I could look up to—the opposite of the porn star in the video collection of my friend's father.

GIRLS, GIRLS, GIRLS

EVEN THOUGH THINGS between Sarah and me didn't work out as originally planned, I was successful in finding other girls I was more romantically compatible with. During my junior year, there was this one girl who flirted with me and kept me wanting to know more: Rachel Johnson. She was wild and experienced, with beautiful shoulder length hair, a cute face and some of the biggest breasts in the school. She was somewhat overweight, but her other attributes and sex appeal more than made up for it, and I couldn't help but notice her. My attraction kept intensifying and I knew it was time for me to end my relationship with my girlfriend at the time.

Rachel knew just what to say and how to say it to get me turned on. In the middle of class she would blow on the back of my neck because she liked to see me squirm, trying to keep from being stimulated. On top of that, she had this crafty way of sneaking up behind me and putting her tongue in my ear and licking all around it. This girl was good and she knew it, and so did other people. I don't know if it was naiveté, raging hormones, or what, but I didn't care. I was ready to experience what she had to offer.

Fast forward to prom night. By this time, everybody knew me at school. I had become somewhat of a school-celebrity because I was in the National Honor Society, played tennis at another high school, and matriculated in almost every social scene on campus. When I look back at my school year book, it's hard for me to find an arena I wasn't engaged in. So I had plenty of options to choose from when it came to a prom date. But Rachel was a given in the equation because I knew if I went with her, I wouldn't be disappointed. The last thing a guy with raging hormones wants is to be disappointed on prom night.

A group of my friends made plans to rent the new 1995 Mustang convertibles and a suite and stay on Galveston beach prom weekend. In classic prom fashion, I drove to her house first and took pictures with her while her family commented on how nice we looked. Then I drove to my house and my mom, dad and the neighbors across the street came and took pictures and told us how great we looked. Normally, that would have been it, but I also had to go to Jeri's house, since we were still best friends, even though we had spent four years at separate schools.

After all of those house visits, we arrived at prom right on time—fashionably late. And soon as we got there, it was time to hit the dance floor. If there was one thing I inherited from my dad, it was dancing. For both of us, if there is a good song on, we are on the dance floor. After making my grand entrance on the dance floor, we took a break to socialize. The evening was a success and it was finally time for all of us, me and the crew, to head to Galveston, which was about an hour away.

To say I was physically exhausted would be an understatement. I had worn myself out the day before at field day and now it was prom night, or rather, it was the morning after, and I had to drive an hour before I could see a bed. While I'm pretty good at most things, being sleep deprived is not my strong suit. Regardless, this was the night I had been waiting for eighteen years. Rachel had an uncanny ability to get me aroused and I had no doubt I would rise to the occasion.

When we got to the hotel, someone decided we should watch Forrest Gump. The last thing on my mind was watching a movie, but this gave me time to rest up for the main event of the night. After I had my little nap, Rachel woke me up and we all headed to our respective rooms. Once the door closed, she put on some sexy lingerie and took out a basket of various sexual toys like handcuffs, feathers, massage oils and, of course, various types of condoms.

While I was trying not to let it show that I was truly a novice, as we progressed from foreplay it became quite apparent. This was the first girl I had ever had consensual sex with and while I was quite astute in sexual anatomy, the actual act became somewhat of a challenge. Once I was on top of her, she was trying to direct me into the right location, but I was having difficulty working my way around. Finally, I got to her secret garden and once inside, I thought I was the man. I was just going at it like a Formula One driver trying to reach the finish line, and then I climaxed. I'm quite sure I was the only one who did. While I enjoyed the climax, I remember thinking to myself, this wasn't as earth-shattering as I thought it would be. It must have been my inexperience.

While my first attempt wasn't a home run, if at first you don't succeed, try, try again. And that's exactly what I had planned to do once I got to college. When Jeri and I were in middle school, we watched the movie School Daze repeatedly. With all the sex that took place in that movie, I could only imagine what new experiences awaited me at college.

Chapter Six

WHERE THE HELL IS GRINNELL?

Though you never utter the words,
our emotional states are identical.
Lust for you solicits unfathomable thoughts,
fostering permanence in my heart.
— Insatiable Desire, A.D.

WHERE THE HELL Is Grinnell?" was the phrase on a t-shirt sold in the campus bookstore. This phrase was the response you got whenever someone asked you, "What school do you go to?" and you responded, "Grinnell." Grinnell, Iowa is definitely not the place I had envisioned living during undergrad, much less the place I thought I would find a group of guys I considered brothers, meet a girl I could have married, or kissed a guy for the first time.

While the college had the reputation of being the Harvard of the Midwest, when you arrive there you realize that you're very much in Iowa. There's nothing there but corn and open land. The winters are extremely harsh (the wind chill was 50 below during a blizzard my freshman year). If that wasn't enough, the summers were just as hot and muggy as Houston. But the one key reason why I stayed was really quite simple: I felt like I truly belonged.

Dr. Axelrod and his wife had accompanied me on a visit to Grinnell during Prospective Students Weekend, April 1995. Once I spent some time with the other prospective students, various members of the student body and a few campus organizations, my decision was made. I loved the fact that all the things I was interested in were at Grinnell: the Grinnell Singers, a traditional top-rate college choir; the tennis team, which played Division Three; and a host of various cultural organizations. I got to play tennis with Bobby Dent, a brother from Chicago who was on the tennis team and sang in the Young Gifted and Black Gospel Choir. At that moment, I realized there were other people at this school just like me: talented, concerned about their future, and set on having a good time.

When I paid my initial visit to the campus, I quickly realized that there were significant disparities between life on the north and south campus. Most of the athletic facilities were on the north side of campus. The south side contained the library, science labs, and music and art studios. Most of the jocks, girls next door, and All-Americans lived in dormitories on the north side, while south campus was populated with artsy types, druggies, Goths, gays and the socially "awkward."

When I checked in my freshman year, I realized I had been assigned to a quad on south campus. This was wrong on multiple levels. First and foremost, I couldn't stay in a room with three other guys. Worst of all, the room was on south campus. Although I had made plans to be in the Grinnell Singers, I also wanted to join the tennis team. Besides, I didn't want to be anywhere near gay people. I was raised as a Christian and homosexuality was what the Bible called an "abomination."

Grinnell is probably one of the most liberal colleges in the Midwest, so I knew for me to get reassigned I was going to have to come up with something major. I had just had minor surgery and I needed to be in a cool environment. There were two air-conditioned dorms on campus and they were both located on the north side. Thankfully, the dorm I was reassigned to was set up for only single and double occupancy.

THE BROTHERHOOD

ONE OF THE things I appreciated most about Grinnell was it allowed me to experience a platonic closeness with other men for the first time. Up until walking the hallowed grounds of Grinnell, I never really got to experience what might be called "male bonding." When I played on the football team in middle school, I got a taste of it. However, most of the guys on the team were already close friends with other teammates, which left me on the sidelines of well-established friendships. One good thing about going to a small liberal arts college is you have to forge new friendships because most of your close friends are at other schools.

Between the first and second semester of my freshman year, there was an interim session. This was not the norm for the school, but 1996 was Grinnell's sesquicentennial year. A hundred and fifty years for any institution is a milestone and the administration had events scheduled throughout the entire year. I ended up in the same class with three other guys—Javier Gonzalez, Hector Ramos, and Bobby Dent—all of whom were, like me, tennis players and "minorities."

The way our friendship formed was something I could never have imagined. The class we were in was led by two former alums who had become doctors. During the first session, one of the physicians said our next meeting would be early in the morning and we were to wear comfortable clothes and shoes. When we arrived the next morning at the designated spot, we found that our assignment was to run the campus. Since the four of us were athletes, especially Javier, who was a sprinter on the track team, we were all in the front of the pack. The competitive nature in us is what drove us together.

After we had finished the run and were waiting for everyone else to finish, we got to know each other. Hector was from Matamoros, Mexico, and Javier was from the other side of the border, Brownsville, TX, but they had attended the same high school.

From that point on, we were like a mini-fraternity. I named us "The Brotherhood" because they were truly like the brothers I never had (Grinnell didn't allow any fraternities or sororities on campus, so we weren't fraternity brothers). We supported each other in everything we did. While our schedules varied drastically at times, one constant was us getting together almost every night for dinner in Cowles, the north campus dining hall. (I remember one time I had just had sex with my girlfriend and she wanted to cuddle, but I politely informed her that I had to meet the guys for dinner.) It was such a ritual we had a designated table and most people knew it. The table was stationed right where we could see everyone coming out of the serving line into the dining hall. We strategically picked this location because we wanted to be able to ridicule our fellow students' fashion choices as they came through the line. While it was sad that we got pure enjoyment from laughing at our classmates' poor taste in clothing, it was honest clean fun and it didn't hurt anyone.

Besides talking about people during dinner, we also discussed issues which deeply concerned us. It could be family, romantic relationships, being homesick, coursework—you name it, we talked about it. Those times were sort of a therapy session, and the best part about it was I knew I was getting solid advice from people who really cared about me. This was the bond I had been looking for. That period was one of the best, if not the best, in my entire life. I had the perfect girlfriend, the perfect friends and the perfect environment where I could be 100 percent me.

We were so close that none of us was prepared for the day when a member of our Brotherhood might graduate. It happened, of course, and it was Hector who was the first to go. We all felt the loss, but we had added a few under-classmen to The Brotherhood. For Javier, who had been the closest to Hector, it was more than he let on. He didn't reveal it to me until several years after we all graduated. When Hector left, Javier plummeted into a tremendous loneliness, which caused him to do things he wasn't proud of. That same feeling of loneliness is probably what Bobby felt when he graduated.

The last time Javier saw Bobby, he was not entirely coherent, walking the streets in Iowa City high on some narcotic. And when I finally felt the same feeling of loneliness when Javier graduated, I turned to sexual media for comfort. It was so strange: we had become so dependent on each other that we found it hard to be alone.

A BURNING SENSATION

I STARTED GETTING involved in sexual relationships with a few women. In one particular relationship, we were totally committed to each other. We got to the point where we were having unprotected sex regularly and it seemed like it was not a problem. Then, out of nowhere, I woke up one morning, went to the bathroom, and I had a burning sensation.

In those days, most college students didn't have health insurance; fortunately, though, I was covered under my mom's insurance plan as long as I was in school and under twenty-five. So I made my way to the hospital emergency room. As I waited for the doctor to see me, I had no idea what was causing all this discomfort, but I knew I wasn't going to be thrilled to tell the doctor it felt like the tip of my dick had been dipped in sulfuric acid every time I urinated.

When the attending physician, who was slightly older than my parents, came in, he asked me, "What is the problem?"

Hesitantly, I told him I was having a problem urinating and it was burning. I had no idea that it was the result of having unprotected sex.

The doctor started asking a barrage of personal questions, which I wasn't too keen on answering. "How many times have you had sex in the last week? When was the last time you had unprotected sex?" The questions kept coming and coming. It felt like I was being interrogated. There was no good cop or bad cop here; it was just grandpa cop. Finally, after his intense round of questioning, I came to the conclusion: not using a condom had landed me where I was and if I lied, the doctor would find out from the lab results.

Based on his initial assessment the doctor thought I had a urinary tract infection (UTI). He also didn't hesitate to let me know I should be careful and more diligent about having safe sex.

I was hoping I could get away with making the copayment and I wouldn't have to tell my mom the reason I had been to the emergency room. But it wasn't that easy: since I was on her insurance, any time I made a visit to the emergency room, she received a letter from the insurance company. Everything had cleared up and I was back to normal. Then out of the blue, I got a call from my mom.

I told her I'd had a UTI but was fine now. She told me how worried she was and how much she loved me. "Next time something like this happens, you call me," Mom demanded.

Then she put my dad on the phone. While I might have been able to pass that story by my mom, my dad saw right through it. "Ah, next time you decide to put your thing in something, make sure you cover up," he instructed.

I was completely shocked. I managed to stammer out the words, "What are you talking about?"

Making sure I knew I wasn't fooling anybody, especially him, he sternly replied, "You know what I'm talking about!"

He was absolutely right and that was the end of the conversation. My dad had called me out, but when I look back I shouldn't have been surprised. It takes a sex addict to know a sex addict.

MY FIRST LOVE

DURING THE PROCESS of forming my great friendship with the fellas, I had already established some significant relationships with some of the ladies on campus. I was testing out the dating scene with a couple of girls. In addition, two fellow freshmen I had met during Prospective Weekend, Kim Provost and Dawn Northern, were becoming some of my best female sounding boards. I would visit them anytime I wanted to talk about Jeri, and they were great friends because they would amuse me by actually listening.

I was so in love with the idea of being with Jeri; I was convinced we would be the perfect couple. We had been friends forever and our families knew and loved each other. Emblazoned in my mind was the thought of how great our children would be. They would have her great athleticism and my intellect. On top of that, they would be the best-looking kids on the planet (look out Halle Berry and Shemar Moore). With the mixture of our genes, our offspring would have African, Native American, Greek and European blood. It would be a recipe for absolute beauty.

Kim and Dawn would encourage me to stop talking about Jeri and instead to pursue her—so that's exactly what I did. Jeri had spent her first semester at Texas A&M, so I decided I would drive from Houston to College Station to see her when I came home for fall break. When I got to the apartment, she was asleep and I was greeted at the door by a girl named Sherry. She told me Jeri had informed her I was coming and to make myself at home. I knew that one of our friends from Houston, Christy, was Jeri's roommate, but she had never mentioned Sherry. I didn't put too much thought into it because this was college. Nevertheless, I was in for a complete shock when I found out Jeri had been playing on both teams for quite awhile—and Sherry was the new starter.

Driving to College Station thinking I would profess my love for Jeri had been a debacle. I had been convinced that we would become a couple like Jeri's sister and her high school sweetheart. Then I came home for winter break. We went to Cinema 6 to watch a movie and when we were getting back into her car she told me. I'll never forget that day. I don't exactly remember how it came out, but maybe it had something to do with how close she was to Sherry and the fact that she didn't have a boyfriend.

Jeri had a natural inclination to do things which were considered rebellious. She had stolen her parents' car before she even had her driver's license, to go visit a friend. So being with another woman fit right in with Jeri's in-your-face nature. I had to admit she was good at covering it up, or maybe I had turned a blind eye because I still saw her as the sweet innocent girl who I had grown up with. In addition to dropping the bisexuality bomb on me, she informed me she wanted her future husband to have experienced playing on both sides of the fence as well.

LOVE OF MY OWN

I DON'T REMEMBER exactly when temporary reality set in, but I somehow decided to move on in regard to Jeri and me being together while I was in college. In the meantime, my friendship with Kim kept growing and I had begun to have feelings for her.

We had a talent show during my freshman year and Kim and Dawn were the hosts. Between the segments of the show, they would change clothes. And each time Kim changed, I noticed every outfit she was wearing. It was like each time Robin Givens made an appearance in Boomerang; I could recite exactly what she was wearing. Nothing turned me on more than a beautiful woman in stylish and sexy clothing. But Kim was more than just a beautiful woman in clothes; she had her own sense of style. At the time I didn't know if it was because she was from the Cleveland area and I wasn't used to seeing girls from Texas with that much style, or if it was just who she was as a person. Whatever it was, I knew I liked it. I happened to be dating a sophomore at that time, but there was something about Kim I couldn't let go of.

I came home for one of our breaks and showed Jeri and her family the tape of the talent show because they wanted to see how my performance went. In the process, it became clear I had developed a major crush on Kim. I kept going on and on about what Kim was wearing and what she had contributed to the show. "You really like this girl," Jeri said. I had it bad and I didn't realize it.

The summer between my freshman and sophomore year, I was going to be in Cleveland at Case Western Reserve University School of Medicine for the Health Careers Enhancement Program for Minorities in Medicine. This was going to be the opportunity I had been waiting for to see if Kim and I could be more than just friends.

One evening midway through the program Kim picked me up and took me to Shaker Heights. We got some frozen yogurt and walked around the area. I was having so much fun because she was the type of girl I could easily talk with about anything. During our conversation, I kept thinking, I've got to make her mine and she doesn't even know it.

A week or two after our unofficial first date, I called her to see if she would be interested in coming to one of our program outings. We went out and it was evident everybody liked her. Kim would call me the social butterfly and she said that if I was going to be with someone, she had to be gregarious like me.

The more time we spent together in Cleveland, the more I wanted to be with her. I wasn't going to let anything stop me—not even the fact that she didn't yet know I was attracted to her. The last day of the summer program I asked Kim to come meet me during her lunch break. I was beyond nervous because I knew it was either now or never. How was I going to let her know? The small talk was coming to an end and we were saying our goodbyes, but I still hadn't told her. And then, I did it—I kissed her! The ice had been broken and there was no turning back now. The look on her face was one of utter shock. Not in a bad way, but in the "I wasn't expecting that at all" way. We looked at each other and said, "Okay, I'll see you later." I walked away knowing she would be mine.

We returned to school the following semester and I had made up my mind we were going to be a couple. Unfortunately, she hadn't quite arrived at the same point yet. It might have been because she was currently dating an upperclassman. To ratchet up the stakes a bit more—he and I were casual friends. While I valued our friendship, if I had to lose it to get the woman I wanted, so be it. Someone worth having is worth fighting for and at this point I was literally willing to fight to be with Kim.

As classes began, we started seeing more and more of each other and I couldn't have been happier. At the same time, I did feel a little guilty knowing I was going to be the reason she ended her current relationship. So after a few more weeks of us sneaking around to be together, she finally ended the relationship with her boyfriend. I thought that since we were the new campus couple, I would finally get to have sex with her. While we both knew the sexual attraction between us had been growing ever since that first kiss in Cleveland, she wasn't just going to give it up that easily.

She made it known that she was just getting out of a relationship and she didn't want to jump right into a sexual relationship. Of course, this was the last thing I wanted to hear, but at the same time, I had to respect her decision. It also allowed our relationship to be more than just a friendship which had turned into a sex thing. I had to put in work and I did. I was the perfect gentleman. If she needed something, I was there. I stayed up many nights with her trying to convince her it was time. In the process of me anxiously awaiting the opportunity, it became more than just sex. I had truly fallen in love with her.

Then finally, one night it happened and it was magic. By nature men are visual and Kim had visually what almost every man at that school wanted: beautiful breasts, a nice round ass, and a gorgeous face. Her smile could light up any room and her skills definitely lit up the bedroom.

My sex drive was and is high, which is usually the case for most sex addicts, although my addiction hadn't taken root yet. I was more than thankful she was willing to accommodate the frequency. On a given day, we could have sex sometimes two or three times. Once in the morning, a quickie during lunch and the whole enchilada that night. The quickies were sometimes the most exhilarating because of their location. Kim was a house monitor during our sophomore year. This particular house was a two-story with a basement. The basement had a small library with computers and a bathroom, which students would use throughout the day, including at lunch. People would also come during lunch to watch "All My Children" in the family room, which was located on the first floor. The house monitors' bedrooms were on the second floor. Needless to say, any time we got the urge during lunch to play we could potentially have had a captive audience, and this only added to the exhilaration.

During the summer between our sophomore and junior years, Kim had an internship in Washington, D.C. Since my uncle had been the superintendent for the public school district there, he had plenty of contacts and still lived in the city. So I now had a ready excuse—I would visit my uncle—but in reality I was going to see Kim. In preparation for my trip I needed to make a stop at the local Victoria's Secret. I bought Kim a gift, but of course it was really a gift for me. She put the lingerie on under her business suit and all I could think about all day was coming back to her place and taking off that suit. The two pieces looked so good on her I didn't even want her to take them off. It had been a while and I was long overdue for some of what Anita Baker calls "Good Love."

We had grown so close while we were in D.C. that I told her what I had never told another soul—not even my mom. We were sitting on a couch in my uncle's basement and for some reason I got an urge to finally release my deepest secret. With an intense tightness engulfing my throat, I timidly started unveiling the fuzzy details of the abuse that occurred in my childhood. As I described the events to the best of my memory, the shame I felt was as vivid as if it had happened yesterday.

As tears streamed down my face, Kim looked me in the eye and reassured me everything would be alright. And I believed her. We never spoke about it afterward.

Our relationship flourished emotionally and spiritually. We attended services religiously and the female chaplain knew us both as a couple and individually. We must have looked like a married couple sitting in the pew next to each other.

Eventually, Kim and I went our separate ways: she had chosen to study abroad in London and I decided I wanted to pursue music, so I had planned to attend the Chicago Arts Program. We were apart for roughly a year. When Kim was in London, we communicated via email and phone. While I was still in love with her at this point, I still had needs and when those needs weren't getting met, my mind started to wander.

I managed to remain faithful, but it wasn't easy. Some of the girls on campus who were associates of hers (I call them associates because friends wouldn't do the things they did) tried to get me to do the horizontal mamba with them. It truly blew my mind when girls who knew Kim and I were in a committed relationship propositioned me to have sex.

Kim made it back from London and I could sense a change in our relationship. It wasn't anything major, but the closeness that had been there wasn't the same. Before she left, we could finish each other's sentences, but when she returned, that didn't happen. We had both grown over the semester, but unlike in the past, we were not growing together. As soon as a couple starts growing without each other, the relationship will quickly change, and usually not for the best.

In Spring 1998 it was time for me to move to Chicago for the Arts Program. Luckily, Chicago was only a four and a half hour drive from Grinnell and I had my truck. Having to be away from Kim another semester and being the only minority in the program didn't make my transition to Chicago the best. I took every opportunity I got to drive back to Grinnell. The only thing was, the more time we spent apart, the more I felt we were unconsciously growing apart. It had nothing to do with Kim because she did everything to make me feel loved during that time.

PORNIFICATION

WHEN I WAS attending the Chicago Arts Program, I began to change in other ways, too. By then the seed that had been planted when I was violated as a child was starting to sprout and see the light of day, or rather, the darkness of night. I had been tempted, but until that day I had resisted buying my first porno. I didn't know where the local porn shop was, so I searched local magazines and then called for directions.

When I arrived at the shop, I immediately got the sense I didn't belong. The cashier, who was probably in his late thirties to early forties, was wearing traditional gay leatherwear, with the leather cap, chaps, and metal-beaded shirt. He looked somewhat creepy, not in the Jason Friday the 13th way, but in a sexually dark way. It was as if I had entered another world, one I had never before been exposed to.

As I walked the aisles perusing the various titles, it seemed there was something for every sexual fetish imaginable—things I had never seen, much less thought about: fisting, threesomes, orgies, and Sadomasochism (S&M). I felt overwhelmed by the endless choices and found it difficult to decide what to buy. Before I knew it, fifteen minutes had already passed and I was still undecided. Finally, I selected a video which had several scenes with actors who looked like they had just come from a Men's Workout photo shoot.

The anticipation and excitement of finally purchasing my first porno and the prospect of watching it were quickly diminished when I arrived at my truck. While I was happy it hadn't been towed, the parking ticket on my windshield was definitely a letdown. In my haste to accomplish my errand, I had forgotten to read the parking sign up the street. I felt that the ticket was a clear indication and confirmation I had been doing something I wasn't supposed to do.

Now that the tape was in my possession, watching it was going to be another challenge. The arts program had paired each student with a roommate in a "studio" apartment. Because I was from Houston and had never lived in an apartment, I thought the term "studio" meant just a small apartment. No, studio was the Midwest real estate term for "efficiency." The two of us were in one room, so privacy was a luxury I didn't have. Luckily, I had learned my roommate's patterns, so I was able to predict when he would be gone for a few hours.

Popping in the porn was exhilarating. As I sat on the twin bed in a trance watching the graphic and arousing sex scenes, I couldn't help but yearn to be in the video myself. The more I watched, the better it got. There was this one scene in which a guy meets another guy outside in an alley and they start making out. Then two more guys come out the back door and join the party. And finally, another two join the fun. They were all in shape and attractive, some more than others, and they took turns fucking and sucking each other. By the end, cum was shooting everywhere, even from my own penis. And I had found my new fetish: group sex.

IS THIS THE END?

I HAD RECEIVED a grant from the college president for my band to record a demo tape. Kim rented a car and drove my band members to and from Chicago so that I could get the recording done. And that same semester she rode a Greyhound bus for six hours to meet me in Chicago to go to Eric Benet's concert before turning around the same night and riding with me back to Grinnell. She was amazing.

But it still wasn't enough for me. Or was it that I was afraid? Our relationship had gotten to the point where the next step would have been marriage and I wasn't ready. Kim wanted to go to law school and I had decided to forgo medical school and pursue a singing career. Those two paths didn't line up and I didn't want to sacrifice my dream. Also, I wouldn't have been able to live with myself if she had had to sacrifice her dream because she loved me. So that meant I had to end the relationship.

My initial attempt wasn't quite as successful as I'd planned. She loved me and was willing to do whatever it took to keep us together—but there was only so much she could take. During the summer between our junior and senior years, I was doing research at Grinnell to complete my chemistry degree. Kim wanted me to come visit her in Cleveland for the Fourth of July or one of those other summer holidays. I conveniently came up with some lame excuse as to why I couldn't come. She saw right though it and said, "Okay, I get it, it's over."

BI-CURIOUS

By THE END of my junior year, I had been exposed to Grinnell's free love environment. And Jeri had discussed her own bisexuality with me, explaining that whoever her future husband would be also had to be bisexual. The physical expression of lust and no-holds-barred attitude among the actors in the video I had purchased was like nothing I had ever seen before. Although I was still suppressing the memories of my own sexual abuse, Pandora's Box had officially been opened.

When I got back to campus, I decided I wanted to sing with the Grinnell Singers my last semester since I would be graduating a semester early. The choir was a big-time commitment but I enjoyed the music and the level of musicianship it required. During the first rehearsal, everyone was glad to see me and wanted to know how the Chicago Arts Program had gone. So

I gave them the update and I got back in the flow of practice.

At one of the evening rehearsals, I noticed an extremely attractive guy in the bass section. He was around six-feet tall, with an athletic muscular build and the prettiest cherry red lips I had ever seen on a man. Since I was just getting back from being off campus I hadn't seen him before. From that first glance, I immediately knew this was someone I had to get to know. My mind instantaneously started devising a way to get the 4-1-1 on him. I did my own initial due diligence during the next couple of rehearsals and then asked a couple of friends in the choir who he was. My initial observations suggested that he might be either bisexual or gay. He was extremely jovial and seemed like he enjoyed having a good time.

It was time to make my move and I wasn't about to waste any time. I introduced myself and we immediately hit it off. He said his name was Jack Perry and he was from North Dakota. At this point I'm thinking: what are the chances that I'd meet a white guy from North Dakota who I'd be attracted to?

Our friendship progressed quite rapidly. We went from not knowing each other's names one day, to having dinner two and three times a week within a couple of weeks. The more time we spent together, the more my attraction grew. At that time, Janet Jackson had released her album *Velvet Rope* and one song on it, entitled "Rope Burn," included the lyrics: Tie me up, tie me down. Make me moan real loud. Take off my clothes. No one has to know. Every time I was alone with Jack, in the back of my mind I would be thinking, I would love to tie you up and make you moan real loud. Yet he acted as if we were just great friends, or at least that's what he wanted to portray.

Since Jack had been at a military academy, I figured he would be a great workout partner (in more ways than one). But he hated working out, which I couldn't believe. How could someone who loathed the gym have such a gorgeous body? The people I had seen with his build stayed in the gym. Not Jack. He just had amazing genetics.

I finally convinced Jack to go work out with me one day. The great thing about working out with a partner is squats. In order to insure you don't injure yourself, your partner has to stand right behind you to spot. Depending on the amount of weight you are squatting, your spotter is almost doing the entire squat with you. It's definitely one of the most sexual exercises in the gym. Your hands are at your shoulder supporting the barbell while you bend your knees and squat, as if you're about to sit down in a chair. Needless to say, I totally enjoyed spotting that day. It was very apparent how strong Jack was—and that was a complete turn on.

By now people were beginning to guess that my friendship with Jack wasn't the typical friendship I had with most guys on campus. Two particular events clued me in to this fact: a concert I gave and a question Kim asked me.

The second semester of my sophomore year, my band Renaissance put on a standing-room-only-plus concert (I say "plus" because some people were outside listening because there was no room in the campus coffee shop, where the performance was held.) The concert was literally one of the best nights of my entire life: I have never felt so much love for doing something I loved. After that performance, any time I was scheduled to sing on campus the venue was packed. One night I decided to do a duet with Jack. We sang an obvious choice for a mixed-race duet: Michael Jackson and Paul McCartney's "The Girl Is Mine."

After the show, someone made the comment that they were surprised I would be singing a duet with Jack. The statement made me realize that people might be starting to suspect Jack and I had more going on than just a singing duet. What were people thinking and not saying? Jack was an accomplished bass in the Grinnell Singers. I had built a reputation of performing with the best musicians on campus, and this particular duet didn't fit the bill.

While I might have been able to dismiss the fact that a couple of people were reading between the lines of my new "friendship," what I couldn't brush off was the fact that Kim saw past my attempted smokescreen. Although Kim and I were no longer in a committed relationship at the time, we were still close and she knew me better than anyone on campus. One night we went to a campus party and she must have seen the interaction between Jack and me and picked up on it. As we left the party and were about to get in my truck she asked me, "Is it Jack?"

"What are you talking about?"

"Are you in love with Jack?"

I couldn't believe she knew. I thought I had been doing a great job of hiding my feelings and my ex was picking up on them like she had just found the real reason why we broke up.

I didn't know what to do. If I told the truth, she would question all the time we had spent together. She might begin to wonder what she had done wrong or start blaming herself. Our breakup wasn't her fault and I didn't want her to think it was. So I lied.

She said, "Look me in the eye and tell me."

So I did just that. I looked her in her eye and lied. Before that moment, I had never blatantly lied to her. The hurt penetrated my soul, not only because I had lied to her, but also because I knew she knew I was lying.

Right around this time, I told Jeri about Jack. Since she was bisexual, I didn't have to spare any details and she was more than willing to listen. In addition to her being the sounding board I needed, she also encouraged me to do what I had wanted to do since the first day I saw him— make a move. Jeri always had a way of making me feel like I could do anything. She reminded me I didn't have anything to lose because I was attractive, smart and a great catch.

So one evening I had finally had enough. I called Jack to see what he was doing. He said he was in his room relaxing, so I told him I was coming over. Once I got there, we sat on a two-person papa-san chair in his bedroom. Of course, I was nervous because I didn't know for sure if he had the same feelings. Nevertheless, the more I looked at his cherry red lips, the more convinced I became that I had to make a move. So I did. I kissed him.

Unlike the moment when I had kissed Kim, the look on Jack's face wasn't one of shock. He coolly explained that while he loved our friendship, he wasn't gay or bisexual. I was in total shock. I couldn't believe I had been wrong about him. All the signs were there. Usually, if I thought a person was bisexual or gay, nine times out of ten I was right. How could I have been so wrong?

Luckily, Jack was carefree and we had established such a great friendship that the moment passed and everything went back to normal. Besides, tons of guys and girls had come on to him before, so he was used to it.

I was graduating a semester early, so at the end of the 1998 fall semester I had to pack up all my belongings and head back to Texas. Before I left, Jack made me a tape that I still listen to today. It contained some of our favorite songs. The first side he labeled "The Hype Side." It included the remix of the theme song to a James Bond movie and other up-tempo rap and R&B artists such as R. Kelly, Mya and Tupac. The second side was labeled "The Chill Side." Of course, the "The Girl Is Mine" was on there, along with songs from Prince, Eric Benet and R. Kelly. There was also one song that I had never heard before—BT's "Remember." The lyrics sum up a significant part of our relationship: "I know how you feel. I'm feeling it to. I hold my heart, I dream of you. I see your face, I feel it too. Searching skies. I need you. I miss you." It's amazing how a song can say what we don't have the strength or courage to say.

I finally packed all my belongings, loaded up my truck, and was ready to embark on that sixteen-hour drive back to Houston. It was still early in the morning and the campus was quiet. Most of the students had already left school for winter break, but Jack was up hosting his radio show. So I went over to the studio to say goodbye. It was one of those goodbyes where you know a chapter of your life is ending but you don't want to turn the page.

I went into the disc jockey booth and told him I was leaving. He threw on a song and got up and gave me one of his classic big hugs. As the music played, we promised to stay in touch and looked forward to seeing each other at the end of spring semester for my official graduation. Trying to make this uncomfortable moment pass as quickly as possible, I told him I needed to get on the road. We exchanged a quick "I love you" and I was out. As I drove off, my radio tuned to the station, he sent me a huge shout-out and played one of my favorite songs. I thought, Goodbye Grinnell, for now.

PRIDE

ONCE I WAS back in Houston, I began to get my feet wet in the alternative lifestyle scene. In May 1999, I got my first taste of Splash, one of Houston's Gay Pride events. I didn't go to many of the events during the week because of my teaching schedule, and I wasn't able to go to the beach that Sunday because of church. However, there was a Farewell Party at Club Incognito that Monday night. Normally, I would never go out on a Monday night, but Bleu, Jeri's best friend, had piqued my interest. Bleu and Jeri were club running buddies. He would get the guys and she would get the girls. Standing just under six feet with a dark chocolate skin tone, he wasn't model fine but he had a sexual energy that was hard to resist. He convinced me that the gorgeous bodies at the beach were nothing compared to the strippers I would get to see. Several fine bodies in one place? Oh yeah, I'm there. And oh, how glad I was that I went.

One word sums up my first Splash: Shogun. There is "fine," and then there is "beyond fine," or "super fine," and Shogun was definitely the latter. Now when I say someone is "fine," I am generally thinking about their face; sure, the body counts, but 75 percent of the weight is given to the face. I'm a face man; always have been and always will be. Since I was a fat kid and later lost the weight, I believe anyone can change their body with a strict diet and a great exercise plan. The face, though—that you cannot change. Sure, you can have plastic surgery, but bone structure doesn't really change. Shogun's face was definitely fine and his body well-defined, which made him super fine/beyond fine.

I had been to a few strip clubs where women were the main attraction, and I had a great time. But I had never been in an environment where men were baring it all. There were two strip clubs in Houston that showcased men. One catered to a predominately Caucasian clientele and the other to African-Americans. But there was an unstated rule of women only at these establishments. Any male who wasn't dancing or working in the club would have immediately been considered gay (I later found out that most of the men stripping in the clubs were actually bisexual or gay).

It wasn't like I desperately wanted to see male strippers—that is, until Bleu took me to Incognito the Monday night after the Splash Sunday. We got to the club and it was packed. A few ladies were in the house, but there was an over-abundance of testosterone. I have to admit, at first I felt a little weird going to see other men take off their clothes, especially around so many other guys. But the sex addict in me was lusting to see something I had never seen before.

Once inside, Bleu strategically picked a table which allowed us to see everything taking place, but kept us out of the line of the cameras. The show was being taped and neither of us wanted to be filmed. As the show began, a few strippers came out and did their routine. Some had nice bodies, but only a few had great bodies. I wasn't really impressed with their dancing abilities.

With more than half of the show over, I thought: Is this what all the hype is about? A bunch of guys that either have great bodies with not-so-cute faces but who can dance or ones with cute faces and great bodies but who couldn't dance. Where's the sexiness in that? Bleu, on the other hand, was thoroughly enjoying the show. Then again, Bleu was a dick man. He loved them and had a PhD in "penisology." I have to admit, those strippers did have some big dicks— nine inches and up, by my estimation. Still, I wasn't impressed.

Then it happened. Out of nowhere emerged an artiste who had it all: Shogun. Unlike the other dancers before him, who were mostly from the Houston metropolitan area, this New Yorker came out with a presence that made everyone in the club stop what they were doing and pay attention. From the clothes he was wearing (a black cape that made him look like a sex superhero, adding mystery) to the music that was custom-mixed (a medley of songs and sounds perfectly timed to accentuate the methodical movements of his sexy body), he put on a show that resembled a master class for all the other dancers, teaching them how to truly perform.

To say Shogun was charismatic is an absolute understatement. I was truly mesmerized. It takes a lot to captivate and impress me and Shogun was doing it at a level I had never before experienced—it was total visual sexual stimulation. As the music started for his set, he hit each beat like a trained dancer. Incorporating the entire stage, he moved like he was floating on air— absolutely effortlessly. As the music became more and more erotic, he revealed more and more. First he removed his shirt, showing his perfectly chiseled arms and chest, which had a tattoo in the center resembling a crest with a sword transecting it. As his shoes and pants came off, I saw that he had perfectly manicured feet and sculpted calves and thighs. But what topped it off for me was what the G-string revealed— an ass that made you want to cum. To put the cherry on top for all the viewers like Bleu, he ended up in just a towel, flashing his manhood. And what a manhood it was: long and thick beyond measure. By the time his performance was over, everybody knew this was someone who you wanted to fuck and who could fuck the shit out of you, too.

I always wondered how men lost their entire paychecks going to strip clubs. After that performance, I finally understood. I was so sexually arousal that if he had whispered, "Let's go to the Hyatt and do whatever you and I want for a set price," I would have done it at the drop of a dime. (I found out later it could have been an option. Thank God I wasn't aware of the opportunity—there's no telling how much that would have messed me up mentally.)

After all the dancers had completed their sets, they worked their way through the crowd. Luckily, Shogun was one of the last performers, so my wait to see him up close and personal wasn't long. I had been up close with some fine people before, but no one who had the face, body, hair, skin tone and sex appeal like this one. Now that I think about it, it was like he had me in a trance. I intently gazed as he gave some of the other patrons lap dances, as they stuffed countless bills in his purple Crown Royal money bag to keep him momentarily engaged with them. As he worked his way through the crowd toward me, I was overcome with anticipation. Other dancers had come over to our table and Bleu might have tipped them. When they came in my direction, I gave them the "sorry, you aren't Shogun" look. Adding to the drama, Bleu kept psychologically building me up, saying, "Look, he's coming this way and he's looking right at you."

Bleu was absolutely right. When Shogun glided his sexy body in our direction, he bypassed several people who were literally grabbing for him and came straight over to me. The intensity of my heartbeat was staggering, but I had to play it cool. The last thing I wanted was for him to think I was nervous and not in control. I had to pretend like this was nothing for me and he should be honored just for me to want to look at him or touch him. Now let's be honest, it was just the opposite.

When we made eye contact, it was magic. He gave me that, "I know you want me and I want you too" look. It was a gaze

I'd seen tons of times, but this was the one time I couldn't act on it like I truly wanted. So I would have to settle with just touching him. My hand made its way immediately to the part of his chest where his tattoo was located, and it was like a spark of electricity shot through me. From there, I worked my way down to that beautiful six-pack, caressing each precious abdominal muscle one by one as he contracted them. With my other hand I grabbed his calf and worked my way up to his glutes. Needless to say, by this time I was hard as a rock and so was he. I could have stopped there, but I knew Bleu would have killed me if I didn't touch Shogun's cock. So I took one hand and pulled the front of his G-string and with the other wrapped a bill around the most coveted prize of the night. I remember leaning in and whispering in his ear, "Get away from me now before I have to take you home." A gorgeous smile came across his lovely face and then he seductively made his way to another table, giving me one last glimpse of that perfectly sculpted ass.

After that, I was ready to go. I didn't want to stay around to dance, mingle, talk, or hook up. My night had been made and I wanted to keep the memories of what had just happened untarnished. There was an official website set up for Splash which had pictures from all of the events. As expected, the pictures for this function were posted with great shots of Shogun. I can't tell you how many times I went to that website just to see those photos. I was in pure LUST.

UNADULTERATED JOY

GRADUATION WEEKEND WAS May 22-23, 1999 and it was definitely a weekend I'll never forget. I got back to the Grinnell campus a few days early so I could prepare for my family's arrival and catch up with all my friends. It was like I had never left. I went to some of the campus parties and had so much fun seeing teachers and friends, but I was also preparing for the graduates' talent show. My jazz instructor had agreed to play piano for me and some of my remaining band mates. I had decided that I wanted to do a mini-concert.

What better way to showcase my voice than by singing Jesse Powell's "You" and R. Kelly's "I Believe I Can Fly"? I was also going to need to sing the song that had made me a campus celebrity, my own "Renaissance Revolution." As I practiced with my professor, he could tell I had been working on my vocals since I had left campus. I told him I had been in Nashville working with a producer. He said I was sounding good and told me to start listening to some Donny Hathaway. I truly appreciated the compliment because I was in full pursuit of becoming a singing star.

Now that I had prepared for the show, it was time to go pick up my mom and grandparents from the airport. My small Mazda B2200 pickup truck wasn't going to be able to carry everyone, so Jack drove his car as well. On the way back from the airport, my mom said, "This is the Jack you've been talking about. It's so nice to finally meet you" (she had no idea that I wanted more than just a friendship with him—in her mind, he was just another great friend). We got back to campus and I was in for a total surprise. Some of my friends/fellow class-mates told me that some people from Texas were looking for me. I knew it wasn't my dad and his wife because I knew when they were coming in. It turned out to be Jeri, Satin, who was Jeri's girlfriend at the time, and Brad.

We finally caught up with each other, and I was in a whole new world. I couldn't believe they had driven all the way from Houston to see me. I knew Brad and Jeri were like my blood brother and sister, but for them to surprise me like that totally floored me. I had to show them the campus, introduce them to all my friends, and find somewhere for them to stay. Luckily, my friends at the house where Kim had been a house monitor allowed them to stay there. So when I introduced Jack to Jeri she said, "Oh yeah, he's fine. He looks like Superman." I died laughing. Of course they got along like they had known each other for years, and I was in heaven. My family, my old friends and my new friends were all in one setting.

Then it was time for the talent show. I killed it and got a standing ovation for my performance. After the show, everybody was coming up congratulating me on a magnificent concert. Several people asked, "When is the album coming out?" I was on cloud nine. But what made me feel even better was that even days after the show people I didn't even know were still raving about it. My mom told me that people were coming up to her and asking, "Are you A.D.'s mom?" before telling her how great my performance was.

After the graduation ceremony, the school had a campus-wide picnic. I couldn't have asked for anything more. My family and my friends all had a great time and would remember and talk about this experience for the rest of their lives.

Since I had just graduated and wasn't established, I had decided to move back in with my mom. But now it was time to say goodbye to Jack before I headed back. While we had done this before, this time would be different. Sometime during the weekend he told me that he had experimented with a guy well after our kiss. I of course rubbed it in his face, telling him that I had known all along that he was Bi. He laughed it off, but I thought: What would have happened if we had gone beyond that kiss?

Chapter Seven
SEX WITHOUT A CONDOM

While being enraptured by lust,
Never allow yourself to be naïve and trust
The thought "it's okay."
Today might very well be the day.
— Unprotected, A.D.

A S A SEX addict, the one thing which never changes is the craving to experience something new and more thrilling. You constantly look for the next fix and whenever the opportunity presents itself, you pounce on it automatically. It's what some call the "hunger." That hunger even persists when in a committed relationship, which is why finding oneself unconsciously engaging in unsafe sex comes as no surprise.

While I was painstakingly aware that having unprotected sex could lead to pregnancy and sexually transmitted diseases, it was the last thing I thought about when I was in a committed relationship. When my relationships reached the point where we engaged in sex, I initially would always use condoms. I had set lofty goals so I wasn't about to let an unplanned pregnancy or a baby put a stop sign in my path.

But the more sex I had with someone, the easier it was for me to forget to wrap up. Okay, let me be honest, I would skip wrapping up. And that's how it all starts. As soon as you have sex one time without anything happening, you get comfortable and start to believe that nothing is going to happen. This kind of logic is based on the man pulling out in time. After a couple of times, I was the king of the "withdrawal method."

I should have known better. Church folks always say that God gives a warning before destruction. What usually happens is that we ignore the warning signs. I had gotten lax to the point where I rarely used condoms whenever I made true love to a woman.

THE SLIP UP

LIKE MOST PEOPLE say, sex feels so much better without a condom. The sensation of the natural lubrication from a woman's vagina can't be replicated, especially when she is approaching the point of orgasm. It's like a tidal wave of wet moisture comes rushing toward you. And in my sex addict mind, it was like mission accomplished. Therefore, I got lax again and started having unprotected sex. And then it finally happened.

I had been in a committed relationship with a young lady. One night, I was going at it and it was feeling really good. Normally, I would pull out in plenty of time. But I was so in the moment that I was a couple of nanoseconds late and so ended up ejaculating during the process of pulling out. She had no idea anything was wrong because I had an average-size load. Yet in the back of my mind, I knew there was a strong possibility that I might have left some semen inside her.

The next morning I got up like nothing was bothering me. But as I've been told, my face tells everything I'm thinking on the inside. She knew me so well that if something was wrong she could pick up on it right away. So she asked what was on my mind. Initially I tried to downplay things, but as the day went on, I couldn't hold it in any longer. The risk of her getting pregnant had lifelong repercussions I didn't want either of us to have to endure, so finally, I broke down and told her.

Instead of yelling at me, which she was well within her rights to do, she took a considerable share of the responsibility like a grown woman and immediately called the local family planning clinic. I felt terrible that I had put her in such an awful predicament, but I was also relieved that I no longer had to keep it a secret. All my friends know I am horrible at keeping a secret, unless they specifically tell me not to say anything. Besides, when I make a mistake, I do everything in my power to correct it as soon as possible. Life has taught me that the longer you wait to tell the truth, the worse the outcome.

Thankfully, she was able to get an appointment the next day. Because there was a possibility, however slight, that she could have been pregnant, she went to the clinic to get the morning-after pill. The staff told her she might experience some side effects and she should go home, get some rest and take it easy the next couple of days.

When we got back from the clinic, I wanted to make sure she knew I was going to be there to provide whatever she needed. My dad had not always been there for my mom—and that was in the forefront of my mind. Abandonment and having an unsupportive mate were thoughts I didn't want her to contemplate. I had seen firsthand the emotional scars and damage those experiences left on a woman and I'd promised myself I would never be the reason a woman felt them. Later that afternoon, the side effects kicked in and she started getting nauseated. The one consolation in all of this mess was that she and I had gotten ourselves into this together and we were going to be there for each other as we got ourselves out.

After that, we reinstated the process of using condoms. But just like last time, we got comfortable a few months down the road and went back to the same thing. Yes, we were stupid as hell, but let's just say we were young, dumb, and in love.

TRANSMISSION

ADMITTING THAT I felt it was safe to have unprotected sex with women when I was in a committed relationship isn't something I'm necessary proud of because it was still risky. However, when I first started experimenting with men I always made sure I was strapped up during penetration. In the late nineties and early part of the two-thousands, information about the transmission of HIV/AIDS had been well documented. Yet the disease was still predominantly considered a disease of gay men.

The idea of my sex addiction being the cause of my death was scary. My biggest nightmare was my mom having to bury me because I had contracted the deadly disease; or worse, her having to visit me in the hospital as I slowly died. That would have been a slap in the face for the amount of time and money she had invested in me. Images of sick people living and dying with HIV/AIDS were ingrained in my head. Yes, there have been advancements in medical research and in drugs; yes, some HIV + people live relatively normal and productive lives, but HIV/AIDS is still a troubling disease that can kill you.

Accompanying those graphic images of patients lying in hospital beds with lesions and pain wracking their bodies were horror stories about individuals in the LGBT community maliciously spreading the disease. The tale went like this: An extremely attractive guy who had contracted HIV was so devastated, as anyone would be, that he decided he would not be the only one suffering. So he went around having unprotected sex, fully aware of the fact he was spreading the deadly illness. Why a person would want to inflict heartache and pain on innocent people is beyond my comprehension, but pain will make one do things that go well beyond logic and one's internal moral compass.

I had even heard stories about both women and men poking needle-sized holes in condoms, so that a person would assume they were having protected sex, but in reality they were unknowingly being fooled by their jaded sex partner. These stories became the catalyst that ensured I used condoms which I personally had purchased whenever I had anonymous sex. I never considered the double-wrapping method because I knew that the friction generated between two condoms could cause breakage.

When I look back, I realize that those stories were God's way of keeping me covered. It wasn't that I felt God was overlooking or sanctioning my lifestyle of anonymous sex. Deep inside, I knew He disapproved and was disappointed. But I'm thankful He was patient and forgiving. I figure that He must have a purpose for my life because, at the height of my addiction, it could easily have been my picture on the obituary page.

YOU NEVER KNOW

MR. POSITIVE WAS a kindhearted soul who appeared to fall in love with me from the first moment he laid eyes on me. He first saw me at Club Rascals and after a couple of long stares and glances he came over and approached me. With a beaming bright smile he said, "Hey, handsome, I'm Mr. Positive. What's your name?"

There was a certain level of sincerity along with boldness in his approach, which made me actually stop and pay attention. Normally, I would have blown off a guy like him because I wasn't attracted to him at all. Not because he wasn't cute, but he just wasn't physically my type. His conversation wasn't bad and he was nice, so I couldn't be rude. I ended up engaging him longer than I had originally intended, which gave him time to find out my relationship status.

"Why is such a handsome guy like you not with someone," he wanted to know. It was a question I often heard and never wanted to answer.

"Because I haven't found the right person and I'm working on myself," I said, giving him my standard answer.

"That's understandable. Well, why don't you let me take you out?"

While I appreciated the offer, at the time I wouldn't even consider dating someone who wasn't my "type," so I diplomatically declined the offer.

But he was not dissuaded and the next time we ran into each other, he came up to me and said, "Hey, handsome. How's A.D. doing this evening?"

We chatted again, but I kept declining his offers to go out. There was something about Mr. Positive I liked, but it wasn't physical. I couldn't put my finger on it and since it wasn't his body, I wasn't going to spend any time to find out.

In the midst of sex addiction, your mind doesn't allow you to see a person for who he truly is. All you're looking for is the next sex partner.

Well, as they say, timing is everything. Even though I wasn't interested in Mr. Positive, I was hurting emotionally. The first guy I ever fell in love with, Trevor, had recently ended our relationship. Nothing is more painful than realizing you've lost someone you truly love and that the blame rests solely on your shoulders. And that's exactly where I was: totally helpless and emotionally shutdown. I couldn't really talk to anyone about how I was feeling. If I expressed the true depth of my loss to Jeri, she would see how vulnerable I was, and she would realize that Trevor was the one I truly loved, not her. At that time, I was of the mind that a man never shows weakness in front of a woman he wants to marry. So I kept all the pain inside, and that gave Mr. Positive an opportunity to come in.

So I bumped into Mr. Positive at a club. It was so comforting to see a familiar face, someone who cared and who I could talk to. Instead of trying to pretend everything was cool and copacetic, I ended up opening up about my pain.

He listened to me with patience and true sincerity. "Well, obviously he doesn't realize what he lost," he said.

And there it was: the validation I wanted and so desperately needed to hear to remind me everything was going to be all right and I was still worthy of love, even if it was love from someone I didn't really know.

After that night, I decided I should get to know Mr. Positive. So we started hanging out and, just as I thought, he was a great person. Now there were two things that were huge strikes against Mr. Positive: he was a smoker and he had a cat. I detest smoke, and I'm allergic to cat dander. Normally, those would have been immediate deal breakers, but I was still getting over Trevor and it wasn't like we were spending every day together. Plus, the sex addict in me needed to get my fix.

After a couple weeks of hanging out at his place I was ready to get it on. Mr. Positive could tell I was getting to a point where my sexual appetite had to be fed, so while we were lying in his bed one night, he said he had something he needed to tell me. I was thinking that maybe he didn't like being penetrated or he had a favorite position or something. Nothing could have prepared me for the words that came out of his mouth.

"I have HIV/AIDS," he explained.

My heart felt like it dropped out of my chest and it took a couple of seconds for me to fully process what he had just said. So many thoughts were running through my mind at once, I didn't know what to say. At the same time, I was thanking God for allowing me to run into someone who cared about me enough to tell me. But all I could think about were the people I had had unprotected sex with who could have knowingly had the disease and never would have said a word. At that moment, I knew God was letting me know I could have been another statistic, but He chose to save my life. It's amazing how things quickly come into perspective when that realization hits.

I asked all the requisite questions. How did you get it? When did you find out? Are you going to be all right? I wanted to be considerate of his feelings since I was so grateful he was forthcoming with the information, but there were so many questions I wanted the answers to.

Mr. Positive had been through this interrogation before, so he was ready for the barrage of questions and he gave me the complete unabridged story. An ex, someone he had been in love with, had given it to him. Once Mr. Positive found out, he immediately went to the doctor and started on a "cocktail." He pulled out his labeled weekly medicine holder and showed me all the pills he had to take every day. If he didn't take the medication at the appointed time, he would start to feel extremely lethargic. He went on to say he had a few bad days every now and then, but for the most part, he was in good health.

What was so amazing to me was his positive attitude. Here was someone who was living with HIV/AIDS, taking his medication responsibly, and being honest with people. Instead of assuming he was going to die, he had decided this was something he had to live with and it wasn't going to kill him.

Because he had such a wealth of knowledge about the disease and knew how to care for himself and protect others, I felt confident I could have sex with him without contracting the virus. And to my surprise the sex session was quite nice. Still, in the back of my mind was the thought: you are playing Russian Roulette with your life.

Fear and ignorance result in bigotry and hatred toward people living with HIV/AIDS. While I prided myself on being educated about the disease, I couldn't keep putting myself at risk knowing that something as simple as a condom breaking could mean I'd end up just like Mr. Positive: living with AIDS. Although I appreciated his sincerity, I was definitely not in love. So like a typical sex addict, I took the immature little boy's way out and exited stage left.

This experience made me reevaluate my mode of operation when it came to using condoms. More importantly, I was forced to realize how God was protecting me in the midst of my mess. Looking back, I know it was wrong for me to allow Mr. Positive to get so emotionally attached to me. Here he was living with HIV/AIDS and all the physical and emotional pressure he had to battle and endure.

Sex addicts don't take into account another person's feelings or think about all the pain they're causing. It's all about getting your sexual needs met no matter what the cost.

Chapter Eight
MULTISEXMEDIA

With sights and sounds easily found
By all sources of media,
The addict is constantly tempted and teased;
Left searching for ways to be pleased.
— MultiSEXmedia, A.D.

MULTISEXMEDIA IS THE term I use to define how sex has proliferated throughout every form of modern day media. Sex can be found in obvious sources such as TV, the internet, and magazines, but it can also be found in some of the most unlikely places—such as your child's cell phone. We are bombarded with sex, which makes it easier for people to become addicted because they are constantly inundated by triggers. Both auditory and visual triggers keep sex at the top of one's mind, and keep sex addicts focused on finding their next fix. And I was no exception.

NOT-SO-DIRTY MAGAZINES

MAGAZINES LIKE PLAYBOY, Hustler and Inches weren't my only triggers. As I grew older I found my sexual triggers in the least expected places, like local city event newspapers and guides, such as the Houston Press and Creative Loafing in Atlanta and Chicago. In addition to all of the information on upcoming concerts and various events, there were seedy advertisements in the classified section located in the back. Ads for masseurs, dating and phone sex hotlines, and every other overt and covert sexual fantasy a person could have were only a phone call away. Some of the ads had visuals for extra stimulation.

Other entries to the print and publication world, right under hardcore porn, were magazines like King, FHM, Maxim and my favorite, Smooth. These magazines were very clever in their marketing. Give men a publication focused on entertainment, sports and other "male topics" while featuring a cover model centerfold spread. It was borderline genius, or maybe I should just say that it was the repackaging of porn. The reason Smooth was my favorite was because they featured the actress Stacey Dash in several of their issues. I don't remember if there was an article accompanying the spread. All I remember is the picture of her on the cover coming out of a swimming pool in a soaked white t-shirt. Can you say visual ecstasy?

Temptation from those magazines was just the beginning. What also did it for me were the workout magazines: Men's Health, Muscle & Fitness, Men's Fitness and Men's Workout. Men's Health catered to older, more professional men who were weekend warrior types. There were plenty of informative flowery articles about nutrition, relationships, fitness and health-related topics, including sex, and the female and male G-spots. While it ranked low on the visually stimulating scale, there were always advertisements by major designers such as Calvin Klein, Polo and Nike. Also in the back were condoms by mail and "The Better Sex Video Series" ads.

On the other end of the continuum was Muscle & Fitness (M&F), which focused on the hardcore, sometimes steroid-using, gym-rat audience. With page after page of often overly muscular men and women with veins popping out of their biceps and brains, the magazine offered great workout routines to go from scrawny to brawny. Attractive people definitely graced the cover of M&F, but they had nothing on the cover models of Men's Workout.

Muscular but not gigantic, the men gracing Men's Workout had everything needed to get me in the mood: gorgeous faces with six packs and nice round asses. Unlike the wordy articles in Men's Health, Men's Workout had almost cover-to-cover visuals of beautifully sculpted bodies and the workouts these breathtaking models used to train. It's no coincidence that each fitness model was usually shirtless and was wearing only swimming or workout shorts.

SEX-RATED

THEN, OF COURSE, there was television, VHS/DVDs, and the internet. As the number of senses required to process the information increased, so did the intensity of the sexual stimulation. When I was growing up, I didn't have cable television. My mom sat me down at a young age and said, "Either we can get cable or a VCR, but not both." She went on to highlight the advantages of getting the VCR versus cable, such as being able to rent movies.

I was a big movie fan, so I told her we should get the VCR so I could watch movies during the summer. Jeri and Brad had cable, so if I needed to watch something really important I could go to their houses. I didn't become a regular cable watcher until college.

In undergrad, I was finally able to fill my mind with all these new sexual images. But it wasn't just the television shows; it was also the illicit videos on MTV, VH1 and BET. As music lyrics became more provocative, so did the videos. BET After Dark was a great place to get to see all of the latest ones. Shooting a video in a strip club had become the new norm for the industry. With that new norm came a host of women waiting and willing to do whatever it took to be featured in a music video. Some of the moves these women were doing on stage and with a pole were worthy of an Academy Award. The nudity went beyond the strip club to the beach. Soaking wet breasts, asses, biceps and thighs were everywhere, making me instantly think about busting a nut even when I wasn't trying.

CYBERSEX

ONE OF THE most dangerous and addictive aspects of viewing porn was the way it provided me a portal to see new ways of having sex. Why have sex with only one person when I could have it with two? Why limit myself to two people when I could have sex with three or more? Why have sex with just a woman when I could have sex with both a woman and a man? The possibilities were endless and I wanted to try them all. And the more I watched, the more I tried out what I saw; porn turned out to be one of the biggest, if not the biggest, triggers in my sex addiction cycle.

The process of driving to a rental store and finding a new flick to watch had a built-in mechanism to deter the addictive cycle: (1) I might not be dressed to go out (2) if I didn't have enough cash on hand I would have to stop at the ATM and (3) once I got to the video store I might not find something I wanted to see. Those are just a few of the numerous deterrents which would sometimes prevent me from obtaining seedy cinema.

But the internet gave me instant access to porn. It didn't matter what time, day or night—as long as I could connect to the internet I could get a fix. I could see men on women, women on women, men on men, groups, singles, you name it, and I could watch over and over and over. I had full access to view anything I wanted if I was willing to pay, which I wasn't.

There were plenty of free websites, which had both photographs and videos of people engaging in every fetish under the sun. To get the entire video you would have to sign up and sometimes pay a membership fee. If the membership only required an email address, I would sign up. Of course, the majority of the sites I wanted to view required payment with a credit card number. Giving out my credit card number wasn't an option: I envisioned them overcharging my account and having to fight with the credit card company about charges from an online sex company.

So I would get creative and find links to other free sites. The web programs and marketers for the porn industry were very creative when it came to visiting their sites. As soon as I clicked on one site, a shitload of others would pop up. It's sad to think about the number of hours I wasted looking at porn.

Unlike true internet sex addicts, I wasn't about to watch porn at work and risk losing my job. That meant I had to watch it when I got home and I only had dial-up, which took forever to download graphics, pictures and videos. And I was too impatient to wait, so after about an hour I would have had enough.

The problem was this: spending an entire hour just watching people I really wanted to have sex with was freaking torture. I can only take so much teasing before I need to take action.

PERSONALS OR SEXONALS

BESIDES LOOKING AT photos and videos on the net, there were a few sites I would cruise, which allowed me to connect with other sex addicts. (I've chosen not to list those sites because I don't want to help promote them. In the days when I was regularly viewing porn, I found that the more I heard about a website, the more I was tempted to check it out. A person would mention a particular site and the next thing I knew, I'd be pulling it up and making it a part of my regular searches.) I would usually search profiles online. While most of the people posting their pictures didn't quite measure up to the "8" or higher that was my standard, there were a couple who made the cut. When I made the decision to visit those sites, I wasn't looking for a person's character, I was looking for anonymous sex, and physical attraction was the main criterion. Ironically, most of the people I was attracted to lived in other cities—that is, except for Mr. Six-Pack.

After viewing one particular site for a couple of months, I

ran across a profile and photo of a guy who seemed to be my type and who lived in Houston. To be completely honest, I can't remember what his profile said, and I probably didn't give it much thought when I read it. But I do still remember the photo like it was yesterday. He was lying on a chair wearing a jacket but no shirt; he had a cute face, curly hair, and was wearing sunglasses. All I could focus on in the picture was his six-pack.

Now that my eyes had been tempted, I immediately sent a note to his email account. After trading email messages for a couple of days, he asked me to send him a picture. Unlike most of the people who had profiles on the site, I would give as little information as possible, which meant no pictures. Some sites didn't even require a profile at all and those were the ones I usually visited. Once he got the picture, he wanted to meet.

We decided to meet at a gas station near his house. He drove up with his best friend in a new Lexus LS400 and I drove up alone in my '92 Mazda B2200 pickup. We both got out and introduced ourselves and then I followed him.

It could have been a potentially dangerous situation, but I felt pretty confident from our conversations on email that Mr. Six-Pack wasn't one of the millions of Looney Tunes scouring the internet.

I was a little shocked because what I had seen on the computer screen didn't exactly match what I assumed the rest of the package would look like in person. While he did have a cute face, curly hair and a six-pack, the rest of his body was extremely thin. The picture he posted for his profile led me to believe he had a muscular build, which couldn't have been farther from the truth.

I realized that I had been visually misled, and I thought, you can end this now and leave or you can tap that ass and then leave. I chose the latter and went back to focusing on his face and six-pack. It wasn't like I was looking to get into a real relationship. All I had planned to do was hit it and move on to the next one.

Well, that wasn't going to be as easy as I thought because he wanted to get to know me before we fucked. I was never one to run from a challenge or a new fuck, so I decided to play the game. Besides, posting that photo of himself was a very strategic move, which let me know he was obviously smarter than most of the people I had run into on the net.

Once a person gets to know the non-sex addict side of me, they are more susceptible to falling in love. It's the lovable side of me who is very caring and really wants to help people. Most sex addicts are great people who just have been extremely hurt prior to the addiction. We ended up hanging out for a few months and got to know each other. I have to admit that I was quite impressed with the fact that he owned and managed an income tax business while in his early twenties. But his materialistic mindset was a total turnoff. The Lexus and fur coats didn't impress me at all and he kept buying me expensive gifts. The gifts also became a turnoff and I wanted to teach him that money couldn't buy my love. Realistically, I was not that into him anyway.

We were at his office late one night and nobody else was there. It suddenly occurred to me: what better way to make a person remember you than by doing something sexual in the place where they work almost every day? So right then and there, I decided to give it to him on his desk. I'm not talking about just slightly tapping that ass. No, I'm talking about knocking papers, office supplies and files off the desk. His moans and screams let me know I was, as LL would say, "doin' it, doin' it and doin' it well."

Overall, he was a sweet and genuine person, but I was in the fucking business then, not the falling-in-love business. Besides, I had to teach him that money wasn't everything. And he taught me a very valuable lesson about the internet: don't always trust what you see. After the Mr. Six-Pack episode, I never again talked with or hooked up with anyone off the web. Once was enough.

Chapter Nine
24-HOUR MEAT MARKET

With running water down their backs,
They notice they're caught in the act.
With momentary intermissions from my gaze,
They wait to see if and when I'll engage.
— The Shower Stall, A.D.

N O MATTER WHAT major metropolitan city in America you go to, you can always find a sex addict in your local gym/ health club. They can literally be found everywhere: from the person at the receptionist desk, to the members who spend their entire workout in the locker room at the shower and/or sauna. The gym is the ideal place to nurture a sex addiction. Where else can one spend time with a bunch of people obsessed with their bodies who also just happen to be scantily clad? Add to that the effects of people sweating, with endorphins and hormones being released; it's the perfect setting for a prelude to a fuck. And I found a few of my best fucks at the gym.

RISE & SHINE OR BUMP & GRIND

THERE WERE BASICALLY two workout crowds at the gym— morning and after-work. These two crowds were like night and day. The morning crowd started around 5:00 a.m. and ended around 9:00 a.m. These members came in and focused on their workout. I'd say 95 percent of them were headed to work, so they didn't really have much time to socialize.

I loved working out at this time, partly because it was easy to get to the machines. I'd usually see the same people because they kept a set routine. But every now and then a newcomer would come in and it was like fresh meat. Everybody would have their eyes fixed on the person in between sets—but only if the person was attractive. Remember, being fit, beautiful, and fine was the name of the gym game. If you weren't a combination of those, you didn't get any play. You were like a benchwarmer watching from the sidelines.

Speaking of games, the after-work crowd was full of them. This was the herd which started after 3:00 p.m. and would go to about 9:00 p.m. After 5:00 p.m., the gym officially became Club 24-Hour Meat Market. Everyone was trying to make a connection. It didn't matter if you were old, young, black, white, gay or straight; everybody was looking for someone to get their groove on with that night or for the upcoming weekend. Club members would be perched on the treadmills pretending to workout. But as soon as someone they knew or wanted to know walked in, it was only their lips that were in motion.

While the after-work time slot wasn't the best for getting an optimal workout, it was definitely the best for finding fellow sex addicts. The typical scenario involved seeing someone you liked in the main workout area and working your way to the locker room. Some people would meet up in the sauna. Depending on the person or crowd on a given evening, you would see anything from men shirtless with shorts in the sauna, to men with absolutely nothing on. It could be one or two people in the sauna or a group, depending on the time of night. Although I never saw anyone actually having sex in the sauna at my gym, several of my friends had reported that it was a common occurrence at theirs. Now the shower was another story!

MEET ME IN THE SHOWER

As I SAID, my normal workout time was in the morning. Depending on how hectic the week had been, every once in a while I would have to train on a Friday night. One particular evening, I didn't get to the gym until after 7:00 p.m. The gym was pretty empty since the typical after-work crowd hits happy hour on Friday. So I got a good workout in and then headed for the shower. To my surprise there were two men, one Caucasian and the other African-American, engaging in oral sex. The white dude was on his knees going to town while the black guy was standing up enjoying the action.

When they realized I had caught them in the act, the guy giving oral got up and went to the adjacent stall. The setup of the shower area was basically open with two-to three-foot wide opaque plastic on each side of a stall. There were no doors, so anyone standing in the set of six stalls could see the others.

What made this situation truly awkward was the fact that these two were positioned in the middle of the showers, so no matter what stall I took, they were in my line of sight. I thought maybe once I had walked in on them that they would take their action to a more private place. I turned my back and proceeded to take a quick rinse so I could get out of there. By the time I turned around the black guy had started to jack off the other and had the audacity to look at me as if he were asking me to join in. The sex addict in me wanted to, but the fact that we were in the gym where anybody could come in wouldn't allow me to give it a second thought.

Although I didn't engage in any salacious acts in the showers while at the gym, I would flirt and pick up people. The odd thing was I rarely consciously initiated it. There would be some cute guy I'd seen while working out who expressed interest. I'd hit the shower and he'd come right in afterward and start flirting. After seeing me semi-erect from the attention, we'd get dressed and either a number would be exchanged or we would go somewhere and handle our business. While this technically qualifies as anonymous sex, the difference was I'd often see the person after I'd fucked them. They would end up wanting a relationship when for me it was just a fuck.

THE DANCER

ANOTHER TIME I once again had a hectic week, which forced me to push my workout to Friday night. After I finished training, I headed to the sauna thinking no one would be in there because the gym was pretty empty. Surprise! When I walked in, I noticed this cute little Latin guy who was about 5' 4." Wearing nothing but a pair of bikini shorts, he was drenched in sweat. We both said "hi" and struck up a conversation. The first thing that came to my mind was: why is he in here this time of night? So I asked him and he said he was getting ready to go dancing at the club later that night.

"Oh, so you're a dancer," I asked suggestively.

"Yes," he said, "at South Beach."

Now the "dancers" at South Beach weren't really dancers. Hell, if you ask me, I think the club let anyone who looked halfway decent and wasn't overweight "dance" on stage. These guys might as well have been underwear models—they didn't come anywhere close to professional male strippers. So I responded, "Cool."

During our conversation it became quite evident that he was sexually attracted to me, so I played right into it. The last thing a sex addict is going to do is turn down a nice tight ass, and he definitely had one. I told him, "good luck tonight," and "I'll see you later."

The next week, I came to the gym with the after-work crowd and he was there. Anytime I turned around during my workout, he was staring straight at me. At that point, I knew I had this one in the bag without even trying. We got to the locker room and he came over and asked how my workout was. The conversation went from casual to "when are we going to fuck?" in a matter of minutes. Because endorphins and hormone levels are high after a good workout, sex addicts take this as the ideal opportunity to fuck; our barometers are set to horny.

So I took one of the fastest showers ever and met him outside at his car.

He was ready to get it on and so was I, but we needed a place to go. I was staying at my mom's then and we couldn't go to his place, for some reason. I wasn't about to lose an opportunity to tap some new ass, so I told him to follow me. As I racked my brain trying to find a place to go, I thought of the "Cum Ball" on Allen Parkway. At Allen Parkway and Waugh, there is a giant piece of artwork, a ball on a stick with water shooting out of it.

We parked and walked to an area just behind the Cum Ball. As we walked further down, I noticed there was an isolated section secluded from the street level. Allen Parkway runs parallel to Buffalo Bayou, so the topography of the land varies tremendously in certain spots. This particular spot I stumbled upon made sort of a marshy/forested cave. I couldn't have imagined a better place. In addition to being secluded, there was a large log in the center, which served as a bench. With zero preliminaries, I took a seat, strapped on a condom, and he pulled down his pants so I could fuck him from behind.

To say this was an adrenaline rush is putting it mildly. I couldn't think of anywhere else we could have gone outdoors in broad daylight to have sex with only a 50/50 chance of being caught. With all the adrenaline, endorphins and hormones racing, I fucked that boy so good, he shot his load before I even realized it.

The next time I saw him at the gym, he had the same big Kool-Aid smile on his face, but, surprisingly, he kept his distance. Of course I didn't mind, because it was just a good fuck for me. Later I noticed he was working out with a guy. It turned out the guy was his boyfriend. Here I was about to mess up a "happy" home. He asked, "So when can we hook up again?"

I told him, "Sorry, you have a boyfriend."

While having great sex outside was undeniably one of my most memorable experiences, he wasn't worth another round. Like a true sex addict in the prime of an addiction, I don't even remember his name.

Chapter Ten

YOU CAN FIND ME IN THE CLUB

The club's syncopated rhythms,
Stimulate the catching of feelings.
For what most see as a pretty face,
True love rarely inhabits that place.
— Club Love, A.D.

For SOMEONE WHO loves to dance and has the potential to become a sex addict, nightclubs can become a second home. And that's exactly what happened when my sex addiction started to take root. Clubbing became the prerequisite. I would club from Wednesday through Sunday and repeat the same routine each week. From the thumping bass rhythms of the hip-hop beats to the fine women and men I met there, the club was perhaps the main culprit in the continual feeding of my sex addiction.

WEDNESDAYS

WHEN I RETURNED to Houston from undergrad in January 1999, I really didn't have a good group of friends to hang out with. My friends from high school went to colleges out of state, like I did, so when I got back, everyone was living in other cities. So I hung out with Jeri because she had been clubbing since high school, and by this time she was a pro.

Wednesday night at the Roxy was the spot. The Roxy was the place to be and be seen and it served as one the main venues for promotional hip-hop and rap concerts. The acoustics and sound system in the club were awful for putting on a high-quality show, but you would never know it by the amount of people in attendance. The club's capacity was probably around 2,000.

One of the best nights I ever had at the Roxy was when I went out with Jeri and a few of her college softball teammates, who were also members of her sorority. This particular sorority's members were known for their beauty, so these young ladies were turning heads as soon as they walked through the door. Of course, Jeri never wanted to be outdone, so she was dressed like a true lady. I don't think I've ever seen her looking sexier than that night. Her nicely fitted black pants hugged her athletic yet feminine calves and thighs, and her tight platinum blouse displayed her large breasts. Bring in to the mix the natural beauty of her face and her hazel eyes and you know she was Da Baddest Bitch, as Trina would rap.

Jeri and her friends came to party and put on a show. Since I was Jeri's brother from another mother, I had an all-access pass. Once the music really got going, I grabbed one of her team-mates, a girl with long gorgeous hair who was part Spanish. I had to let her know this boy who had just come back from Iowa knew how to move.

As the night quickly evolved, other guys in the club were coming up and buying drinks for the ladies. It didn't take long for the ladies to start getting inebriated. Since I didn't drink, I was able to make sure things didn't get too out of hand. To my surprise, Jeri and I started dancing and it wasn't our usual let's-act-a-fool dance. She had had a few drinks, so she grabbed my hand and held it up as she dropped to the floor, grinding her way back up my leg with a devilish smile. To say it was erotic would be putting it mildly.

While this was what I had been waiting for since my fresh-man year in college, I couldn't act on it like I wanted to because she was drunk. The alcohol was putting her in a less inhibited state, but this was the woman I wanted to marry, not some slut I wanted to fuck. So in my mind, trying to take things to the next level would have been easy, but it would have felt like I was taking advantage of her, the absolute last thing I would ever do. To keep myself in check, I started dancing with some other girls in the club, ones I didn't know, and was left with the memory of what could have been as I headed home that night alone.

THURSDAYS

THURSDAY NIGHTS I would sometimes go to a club called the Gatsby. It was one of the few traditional dance clubs with a truly ethnically diverse crowd. The club had some of the most attractive women in the city. Instead of R&B and Hip-Hop monopolizing the mix the way it did at the Roxy, the Gatsby's deejays played Pop and pure Dance tracks.

Now my regular Thursday night club spot was just as intense and interesting as the Roxy, but in a totally different way. The club was called Rascals and it was mixed gender. At the time, I wasn't aware there were clubs and bars that catered exclusively to one sex or the other in the alternative lifestyle scene. Also, there were less than a handful of establishments in Houston which had made the strategic business decision to cater to the African-American Lesbian Gay Bisexual and Transgendered (LGBT) community, which was probably the reason why both sexes were at Rascals. Whatever the rationale, it was quite comforting to know women were in the club. I felt awkward dancing with men at that time, so if I danced only with women I gave the impression I wasn't available. It came in extremely handy when I needed it.

I'll never forget the first time Jeri took me to Rascals. When we drove up there was a line extending out of the building along the street. The club was on Westheimer, one of the busiest streets in the city, and being seen at a gay club was not on my to-do list.

Once inside, I scanned the room to get my bearings. The club had a large dance floor, deejay booth and two bars on the first floor. The sexual tension in the air was so thick it was almost suffocating, and for the first time in a long time, I felt out of place.

I didn't know if Jeri could tell how nervous I was, but I definitely had the shakes going on, which is my body's way of telling me I was somewhere I shouldn't have been. After I got my bearings, I was ready to go back downstairs and "get my dance on."

Well, that task was going to be harder than I had initially thought. Jeri was dancing with Satin, and her other female friends were dancing with their respective lovers or other women. So I was left standing by myself, watching them have a good time.

After finally leaving the club, we made our way into the parking lot across the street, which was the site of the official/ unofficial after party. What usually happened was that some of the people who didn't have connections to get in or were too cheap to pay to get into the club would wait across the street. As soon as the club let out, they would blast their music and the people in the club would gather around their cars.

It was during this gathering phase when everyone who wasn't with someone already or who hadn't found their fuck for the night would get together. Unlike the club, which was dimly lit, the parking lot across the street, with a Wendy's right there, was well lit. For me, this became the best spot to window-shop and get plenty of attention. Most of the guys would circle around like vultures and finally work up the nerve to come up and ask if I had a girlfriend. When I said no, their next question would be whether I had a boyfriend. And when I would answer no to that, they would ask if I wanted one. I would laugh and tell them I was cool for right now.

By shooting everyone down that came my way, my stock value increased. Everyone was trying to see who would be the first person I'd get with. Even the manager of the club was trying to talk to me. Jeri's friend Bleu would give me updates, so I could determine who was not just a pretty face, or who had the "venom"—Jeri and Bleu's word for HIV/AIDS. A large part of sex addiction is about being in control and I made sure I was in control from day one.

Somewhere around 3:00 a.m., the cops came and cleared out the Wendy's parking lot and then some of the crowd either went to someone's house to have sex or stopped at an after-hours club. The fact that it was 3:00 a.m. on a weeknight meant it was well past my bedtime, even though it was summer and I didn't have to teach. (I taught science while I was pursing my music career in both Houston and Atlanta.) Also, I was informed that the after-hours spots were primarily a place for drugs and alcohol, which was not my cup of tea. After I placed Rascals in my club rotation, occasionally I'd head to someone's house for a quick roll in the hay or head home to get ready for the next night of clubbing.

FRIDAY'S CLUBBERS

FRIDAY NIGHT WAS one of the main club nights in Houston. This was in 1999 and 2000 when most of the clubs were located on the Richmond/Westheimer strip. It seemed like everything was open. Some of the well-known choices for the straight scene included Cabo, Polyester, Skybar, A-Bar, T-Town, Max's 2001 and Club Phoenix. For the gay scene there was Rascals, Incognito, Pacific Street, and South Beach.

Almost all of the venues had a decent crowd, but the key was timing. Because the club crowd was and still is fickle, T-Town and Max's 2001 might be near capacity around happy hour but almost empty at 10:00 p.m., while Phoenix and Cabo didn't get packed until 11:30 p.m. and stayed jumping until 2:30 a.m. Basically, there were three sets of clubbers on Friday night: happy hour, after happy hour, and both hours.

The happy hour clientele would arrive right after work, around 4:00 to 5:00 p.m., and by 6:00, the place was packed. They would stay until around 9:00 and that would be the last you saw of them. This was your more professional and married crowd, people who were ready to relieve some stress from the workweek. Once they got a couple of drinks, hit the dance floor and broke a little sweat, they headed home. Ladies would flirt, but the chance of taking them home was slim to none.

The after happy hour clubbers were the younger unmarried crowd. They were looking for a piece of ass for the night. So instead of heading to happy hour after work, they would head home and get ready for the evening. This might include a quick nap for some of the ladies and a quick workout for some of the men. But you could bet that by 10:00 p.m. both sexes were putting on their final touches: makeup for the ladies and cologne for the gents. The grand entrance for this group was just after 11:00 and they stayed until the club closed or until they found someone for the night.

Last, but definitely not least, were the both hours patrons (I ended up in this category on a few occasions). Since they knew they would be clubbing from sundown to possibly sunup, they prepared ahead of time. Depending on the Friday, they might carry their club attire with them to work and change there, or they would wear an outfit which could be easily altered and worn to the club. Some would go as far as leaving work slightly early. Whatever method they chose, you were sure to see them in the place. Not only would they be at all the happy hour spots, they were the first ones at the next spot for the night. The composition of this group varied: there were the people like me who were addicted to the excitement of the club, then there were the alcoholics posted at the bar like light fixtures, plowing through a night of drinks. Throw a few desperate and lonely clubbers into the mix and there was the cast and crew.

The music, dancing, and anticipation of something new were my primary drivers, which let me know my addiction to clubbing was the precursor to my sex addiction. I vividly remember one Friday night that I started off at Phoenix and then went to Rascals. Each club's deejay was jamming so hard that night that I went back and forth, which wasn't an easy feat. Just like living in both the straight and alternative worlds. My straight friends provided a certain level of camaraderie I wanted socially. And at the same time I wanted to hang out with my alternative lifestyle friends to feed my addiction.

SWITCH UP SATURDAYS

ONCE SATURDAY CAME, I was usually at Rascals because I would do the straight scene one night and gay the next. It was such a contrast in the club environments. You had to dance a certain way, dress a certain way, and act a certain way to fit in at the straight clubs, while you could be totally free at the alternative clubs. If I wanted to dance my ass off, nobody cared; in fact, it was celebrated.

Although I enjoyed the element of freedom which the gay clubs had, that freedom came at a price. It was called "the Shows." On Saturday night, and to a lesser extent on Thursday night, before the club really got jumping I would have to endure the Shows, which was hosted by comedian and drag queen extraordinaire, Ms. Carmen LaNook. It included everything from live individual and group singing performances, drag queen lip-synching, dance troop performances and semi-nude strip shows. While I hate to say it, because I truly detested the Shows, some of the acts and artists were very good. You could always tell how receptive the audience was to a particular performer by the amount of money scattered on the floor during and after their showcase. The fact still remained that the Shows was a temporary hindrance to me getting to enjoy myself and others on the dance floor.

Some weeks I would switch up my nights. I would go to Club Incognito for the gay scene on Friday night and the Skybar for the straight scene on Saturday night. Club Incognito had both men and women on Friday nights, which always made for an interesting evening. In addition to viewing some of the sexiest lesbian amateur burlesque shows, I saw my first no-holds-barred girl fight there.

From the endless mayhem at Incognito, I could escape to the Skybar on Saturday and get a totally different vibe. The Skybar was an upscale club for more mature and older clubbers. While the establishment catered to the late twenties and earlier thirties crowd, it wasn't unusual to see patrons in their late forties and fifties doing a "night out on the town." There was a strict dress code and the likelihood of seeing a fight was next to impossible. The women at this club were beautiful and looking for a sugar daddy. In addition to having a good deejay, the owner performed with a live band. He would showcase some of the best unsigned vocalists in Houston. Because I was both a singer and a dancer, Skybar became one of my favorite spots for a chill night.

THE SUNDAY CIRCUIT

AFTER GOING OUT Wednesday through Saturday, an average person would have been tired, not to mention a little tapped out on the spending front. Then again, I never have been a typical person and my out-of-pocket expense was extremely low. The biggest advantage I had on my side was that I didn't drink and I had learned to work the system. My friends in radio would get me in the straight clubs for free. Then I'd use my looks and charm to get into the gay clubs without paying a cover.

Until this point in the week, my primary focus wasn't on sex. It was all about having a good time and hanging out, things I really hadn't been able to do on this level when I was in Iowa. It was the Sunday circuit that facilitated the shift from my club addiction to a sex addiction. The circuit started at LaStrada for brunch and ended at JR's the next morning. As I slithered though the circuit, a major swing occurred. Sexual tension continually and consistently built all day and I would finally give in by midnight.

LaStrada was a very nice high-end restaurant and on Sundays it turned into Club LaStrada, the place to be seen. LaStrada's valet was the welcome center for some of Houston's most wealthy club-goers. (It was nothing to see Ferraris, Lamborghinis, and Bentleys strategically placed throughout the parking lot.) And once the nouveau riche got out of their posh luxury or sport cars, they were immediately ushered in, while the rest of the commoners had to occasionally wait in line.

Upstairs next to the VIP section was the deejay booth. This area became my official hangout. Besides having easy access to the deejay for requests, it was the starting point when the staff began removing tables and chairs. With those obstructions gone, the dancing was on. The deejay was another one of my favorites because even though the crowd was diverse both ethnically and sexually, he knew how to keep everybody gyrating.

In the section where I stood were a group of guys and girls who loved to dance and were innately good at it. Not only did the area get all of the attention because we got the party started, the sexual preferences of the section added another interesting and entertaining dynamic.

Houston's steamy weather, sexy people, dancing and alcohol—it was the perfect recipe for sexual titillation. As the grooves and booze kept flowing, so did the inhibitions of the crowd. The next thing you knew, guys would be kissing girls and girls would be kissing other girls. Every now and then, you would see a guy kiss another guy, but it was rare. What wasn't rare was the amount of flirting going on between everyone.

Because LaStrada closed at 6:00 p.m. on Sunday, which was way too early to call it a night for the hardcore Sunday club crowd, it served as the first stop on the Sunday Circuit and as what I called the "scout out." I would scout out potentials at LaStrada who I wanted and would get to know once I got to the second stop, Berryhill Baja Grill, about two or three blocks away.

There was a clear shift in the dynamics between LaStrada and Berryhill, and it probably had a lot to do with the layout. Berryhill had only one set of bathrooms because it was located on the end corner of a one-story strip mall. The police presence served as a deterrent to things getting too wild in the restrooms. There was only one large bar, and the majority of the square footage was devoted to dining. One benefit of this layout was that it allowed guests to sit down and talk instead of having to yell over the music.

Outside was a scaled down version of the patio at LaStrada. It seemed like the deejay changed each time I went. But one thing was constant: house music ruled the dance floor. While I am a fan of some styles of house, I would sit out the songs I didn't care for, spending my time instead getting to know the person or persons I had scoped out at the first stop.

Probably the biggest dynamic shift was the level of sobriety and the constituency at the second stop. Some people were just starting to drink at Berryhill, but a significant number of the circuit-goers who had been drinking Bellinis at LaStrada migrated over. As the alcohol flowed, inhibitions went out the window and the disinhibited flowed to the patio. The intensity of groping and flirting was easily turned up several notches. People were starting to make their moves and I loved it. Also, Berryhill was definitely a more alternative-friendly establishment. There was a rainbow flag hanging on the patio, but it didn't alienate any open-minded or sexually curious person from joining the party.

The crowd would slowly dwindle throughout the evening. Some people would hook up and head home, while others left around 8:00 to get ready to go to work the next day. JR's was the final stop on the Sunday circuit, and once I arrived there, it was time to finally decide who I would be fucking that night.

JR's was located right up the street. Nestled between LaStrada and Berryhill, the three spots formed a triangle of lust and enticement. I usually hit JR's around 9:00 p.m. and the only thing I and the majority of the alcohol-induced people were thinking about was sex.

Unlike the first two stops on the Sunday circuit, JR's didn't have an official dance floor because it was a more traditional bar. There were elevated platforms of varying sizes in the front and rear of the bar where guys I thought of as male underwear models (because they definitely weren't dancers) would get tips from horny patrons. The people who knew I could sing would always cajole me to go up and do a Karaoke performance at the platform/stage in the back. Normally I would have jumped at the chance to steal the spotlight, but something didn't feel right in my spirit about using one of my God-given talents in that place. My motives for being there were purely sexual, and it felt almost sacrilegious to express my singing voice while in a sinful state of mind.

There was only one purpose for me: to find some ass for the night. I chose a gay establishment because I wanted a no strings attached sexual encounter, at least on my end. And my goal was usually accomplished on the bar's outdoor patio. The patio had one of the five bars at JR's. Although I wasn't drinking, I'd bring the person I had scoped out on either the first or second stop of the circuit to the patio to talk. If I hadn't found someone at LaStrada or Berryhill, there was guaranteed to be at least one prospect in the inebriated, sexually over-stimulated multitudes.

The night would end with me following him to his place and having sex. Most of the encounters I enjoyed were based on the adrenaline rush of being in control and getting the person I wanted. Every blue moon, I'd find someone who really knew how to fuck and I'd think twice about coming back for more. But the reality was that I knew I wasn't going to be committed to anyone I was able to be sexual with on the first night. It was the equivalent of relationship suicide. Although I was quite skilled in manipulating the situation and getting what I wanted, if I could get a person in bed on the first night, I figured that someone else could probably do the same. What was mind-boggling was how quickly these people fell in love with me, even though I had absolutely no emotional attachment at all. I think it was a result of so many people looking for love in the wrong place and once they found a person who was halfway decent and treated them right, they fell in love. For me it was like being a sports fisherman. I'd catch them, "examine" them, and throw them right back and head home. I had no regard for their feelings and was focused only on my self-centered desires. This gave me a sense of control when in fact my world was spinning totally out of control. I didn't have the family I so desperately wanted because Jeri wasn't at a point where she was ready to settle down—at least not with me.

The cycle of going out Wednesday through Sunday continued week after week during the summer. Once school started and I had to teach, I'd skip Wednesday and Thursday and pick up where I left off on Friday. The Sunday circuit would usually end at Berryhill for me, so I had to be more efficient in finding my next sexual conquest. What made this cycle so hard to break was the fact that there were so many other sex addicts out there doing the same thing at different levels. Some were actually looking for love, but I always knew you couldn't find love in the club. Let me repeat that for anyone who is currently engaged in this sort of behavior: YOU CANNOT FIND LOVE IN THE CLUB. You can occasionally run up on a good fuck, sometimes even a great fuck, but not true love. Now I have to admit that I did experience love with a fellow clubber, but we didn't officially meet there.

Chapter Eleven
SPLASH

In a state of constant flux,
Life exists.
The beauty which exists today vanishes right before one's eyes.
Leaving only the memory of what used to be.
— Change, A.D

SPLASH!!! I'M NOT talking about the movie with Tom Hanks and the beautiful mermaid, but an annual Pride event. Each year, local and national members of the Lesbian Gay Bisexual and Transgendered (LGBT) community and other curious people gather from Wednesday to Monday in Houston and Galveston Island for various functions. The main event is held at Stewart beach on the Sunday following the first full week in May (which occasionally happens to fall on Mother's Day). In a nutshell, Splash is a sex addict's Fuck Fest.

Usually, Splash opens with a cultural awareness event—anything from a movie to an open forum discussion about a current issue within the community. It's held at one of the local gay or lesbian clubs, followed by a party. The next two days are filled with both male and female strippers, drag shows, and parties at various "family" friendly clubs. Saturday is officially "Galleria Day." You never know who you'll run into at Houston's premier mall on Splash Saturday. It could be anyone from brothers keeping a low profile or on the down low (DL) and "fish" (traditional feminine women), to full-blown drag queens and butch women, aka "Studs." Everybody is shopping or pretending to shop for the party that night and for beachwear for the next day. Although some of the retailers at the mall reportedly complained about the large number of African-American patrons in their exclusive shops, they didn't complain about how much merchandise they sold.

WE LIKE TO PARTY

AFTER MY SHOGUN experience, the next year when Splash came around, I didn't want to miss a thing. If the strip show was that entertaining and exciting, I could only imagine what I'd missed at the other events. While both men and women attended various functions together, there were some engagements which were either strictly men or exclusively women. So Jeri wasn't always able to be my wing woman. Plus, she had been to Splash before, so it was nothing new for her. Luckily, Bleu, Jeri's friend, agreed to serve as my personal tour guide. He knew what parties to go to and when to get there, which turned out to be more important than I had initially thought.

The events surrounding Splash were like nothing I had ever experienced before. I generally love the newest of things, and this was definitely something new. Thursday night Club Rascals was packed beyond capacity and the music was jammin' to an unheard of level. The deejay was one of the best deejays of all the clubs I'd ever been to, straight or gay. Everybody was dancing and having a good time, meeting and hooking up with new people. Usually newcomers do gain some level of attention, but during Splash you had to bring it or you wouldn't get any play. There was always someone waiting in the wings to take your place.

If a person was extremely attractive but had a reputation of sleeping around, their star didn't shine as bright. But if someone else was a bit less attractive and no one had had sex with them yet, they were like a piece of meat in a pack of ravenous wolves. Never one to be outdone, I had two weapons to keep heads turning: my shoulder length naturally curly hair and a lean muscular build. That one-two combo usually got me plenty of attention.

In addition, I had learned the key to keeping myself in the spotlight: flirt with almost everyone, but hook up with only one. The true beauty of the game was as soon as one key person started talking about you, it was like a domino effect—your name was on everyone's lips. I was getting invites to various gatherings and house parties, but there were certain parties you wanted to attend and others that you didn't want to be seen even driving past. To keep my reputation intact, I consulted Bleu because he knew almost everyone and their story. And if he didn't personally know, he could instantly find out.

After visiting a couple of these gatherings, it was clear they primarily served as a place to hook-up and be seen outside of the club in a somewhat exclusive crowd. Several of the house parties I visited and some I chose to avoid generated countless stories of people secretly or not-so-secretly making out in homeowners' bedrooms, bathrooms, pools, etc. While it's certainly true that if a homeowner is known for throwing sex parties, people assume that all decorum is left at the front door, I still believe that guests should display a certain level of dignity and respect when visiting someone's house. I admit that I engaged in various salacious acts, but attending a sex party just wasn't my cup of tea. As a sex addict, I coveted anonymity.

SO YOU'RE HAVING HIS BABY

Splash 2000 is one I will definitely never forget, particularly because of what I learned on the way to the beach.

I decided I wanted to go to church Sunday morning to make a preemptive strike, if you will, against whatever sinful acts I might need to repent for later that night. I went to the 7:30 a.m. service and then met up with Jeri, Satin and Bleu before noon so we could arrive at the beach on time. Jeri had prearranged the use of her sister's Mercedes Benz

ML to get us there. It was unquestionably the perfect mode of transportation at the time—one of the newest and most expensive SUVs with a sunroof.

We wanted to make sure our clothes were head-turning, so we stopped at Baybrook Mall, which was located right off I-45S on the way to Galveston Beach. I wanted a classy and sophisticated look, so I had worn white linen pants and sandals, but I needed something which would show off my physique. Jeri and the gang convinced me that an orange Nautica Competition muscle shirt was exactly what I needed. My calling card was my hair and my biceps, and this shirt was definitely doing them justice. Jeri got a blue version of the same shirt and Satin purchased a Nautica two-piece.

After our quick pit stop at the mall, we continued on our way to the beach. The wind was blowing, the sun was shining, the music was playing, and I was excited about all the sexiness and excitement I had been told would be at the beach. Then, out of nowhere, a bomb dropped on me. As Jeri was driving, she and Satin were talking, but I really couldn't hear what they were saying because 1) I wasn't really paying attention, and 2) the music was blasting, and 3) Bleu was in the back talking to me. But their discussion started to get heated, and I couldn't ignore them. The next thing I knew Satin was saying something about Drew and Jeri being pregnant.

My heart literally stopped for a moment—I was completely shocked and dumbfounded. The woman I thought I would one day marry and have kids with was pregnant by another man. In my mind, I was thinking, I can't believe you fucking did this to me, to us. Everything we could have had is OVER! To add insult to injury, everybody in the car already knew—I was the only one in the dark.

Jeri had just gotten out of a relationship with a woman (Sherry), was currently in a relationship with another woman (Satin), and was seeing a man on the side (Drew). How on God's green earth could I have come up with the idea I would

155

one day marry her? The answer is simple: I knew the "real" Jeri, or at least the one I had grown up with.

The Jeri I knew was surrounded by family and still is. She internally valued the concept of marriage and looked forward to having her own kids one day. She held on to the example of a good man, but—and this was counterintuitive to what she had been taught, to what her parents had instilled in her—she loved thrills and danger.

Most people with a brain would have said she was definitely not marriage material. But I was able to rationalize her behavior by telling myself that she was still young and was still trying to experience life. Besides, we would sit down once a year and say to each other, "If neither of us is married by 28, then we'll marry each other." So when I heard she was pregnant with Drew's baby, I was floored. She had broken our pact. There was no way in the world I was going to take care of another man's child, especially one that had Drew's genes.

Drew and I were polar opposites. He sold drugs, smoked weed, hadn't completed his education and had spent time in jail. Yet he had Jeri running behind him like a mouse on a string. That's not 100% accurate because she wasn't totally manipulated by him. She was using his money to pay for the apartment she and Sherry were living in at the time. The symbiotic/codependent destructive relationship Jeri had with Drew definitely had benefits for her.

Dealing with pain wasn't new to me, so I took the situation in and immediately compartmentalized it. I sat back and pretended everything was fine and we were headed to the beach to have the time of our lives. Yet deep inside, my world had come crashing down. I was sure that the future I had been so patiently waiting for would never materialize.

MISTAKEN IDENTITY

ARRIVING ON THE beach was definitely an event in itself. We arrived fashionably late to make sure we would be seen by everyone and scope out the scene. The beachgoers had strategically parked, allowing traffic to flow in and out of the beach and around the vehicles. Jeri made a loop around the beach to determine where we would set up shop. In the midst of making the loop, we kept seeing people we knew, so we had to stop, get out and take pictures, which held up traffic. It created a scene, which everybody was watching and wanted to be a part of. What was really comical was that people we had seen only once or twice but barely knew were stopping us.

At first it really blew my mind that people were just coming up to random strangers asking to take pictures. That was until I started seeing some fineness myself. One girl had a body that wouldn't quit with a two-piece showing every inch of it. To say she was wearing a two-piece might be a stretch. Her top covered her sand dollar nipples and a G-string went right up the center of her assets. The next thing I knew, I was telling Jeri to get this woman and her girlfriend to turn around so I could take a picture. All the fineness Bleu said would be there was.

Before we finally parked, we ran into Sherry, Jeri's ex-girlfriend. This was the ex Jeri had cheated on and left for Satin. Needless to say, Sherry wasn't too enthusiastic to see Satin sitting in the passenger's seat. I personally liked Sherry and her daughter. Sherry worshipped the ground Jeri walked on and was extremely nice to all of her family and friends.

As we were making our way toward the end of the loop, it became obvious that finding a spot was going to be harder than we had initially thought. Luckily, out of the corner of my eye, I saw a space that had a lounge chair in it. We had already passed it up but there were some girls next to it. I jumped out, worked my charm and asked if they would mind me moving the chair so my sister could park. Of course, these ladies weren't about to turn a handsome charismatic man with bulging biceps down, so they obliged. I gave Jeri the cue to drive back around as I held the place.

While I was waiting for them, several people were passing by on foot nodding, winking and saying hello. Naturally, I wasn't thinking anything was behind it. I'm a gregarious guy, so being cordial to people and them being cordial to me was nothing out of the norm. But something was a little different this time and I couldn't put my finger on it. Finally, two guys were walking by and said, "Great job last night!" with huge smiles on their faces.

I had no earthly idea what they were talking about, so I decided to ask them what they were referring to. One quickly responded by saying, "Aren't you that stripper from last night?"

The narcissist in me didn't want to believe I looked like anyone else. At the same time, it was like receiving the ultimate compliment from someone I didn't know. Somewhat aghast, I told them, "That wasn't me."

I could tell by the look on their faces and the slight head rolls that they didn't believe me. Strippers get a lot of adoration, but they also have to put up with the embarrassment and discomfort of being seen outside of work.

Not too long after the incident, Jeri pulled up and I immediately told everybody what had happened. Jeri had seen the actual dancer the two guys were talking about. With a naughty grin on her face she said, "He does look like you. He has long curly hair and drives a convertible BMW."

CATFIGHTS

NOW THAT WE had gotten settled, it was time to break away from the pack and see what was really out there. I didn't want anyone to think I was coupled up and end up missing a potential new "piece." As I walked along the beach, the groupings/cliques were so obvious. Various cute queens (feminine men) were grouped in certain areas of the beach, while the less attractive queens were grouped in the others. The gangster stud cliques were positioned next to the cute fish (feminine women) and so on and so forth. But the majority of the people were gathered at the lifeguard's guardhouse. People were busy playing volleyball—some games were competitive and others were just for fun.

As I looked around, there were gorgeous bodies all over the place, which brought a smile to my face. Relaxing at the guardhouse, I decided to use the restroom because I didn't know when I'd find another one. I went in thinking I was going to be able to take a piss and move on. In addition to the reek of urine, there was a whole lot going on in there. The stalls were serving as people's personal bedrooms. Yet that wasn't what amazed me. It was seeing guys climbing on top of the individual stalls to get a peek which did it. I knew I had to get out of there as fast as possible.

Stepping back onto the beach, I noticed a crowd slowly starting to form on my right. Suddenly, the people who were standing nearby started running toward the area. Not wanting to miss the action, I quickly made my way over so I could see what was going on. What I saw next was something I would never have imagined. Satin and Sherry were in a knockdown, drag-out catfight on the beach. By the time I got close enough to see what was happening, some onlookers had separated the two and Bleu was rushing to Satin's side. Jeri was nowhere to be found.

The crowd gradually dispersed and I walked up to Bleu and Satin to find out what had happened. Satin was totally enraged and wasn't about to let the incident go, even though she had won the fight. I found out this hadn't been the first incident and what I was seeing was the ending of the second fight. I was quite disturbed that these two women were fighting over Jeri.

I was so embarrassed. And that wasn't even the end of the drama for the day. Another friend of Jeri's kept egging Satin on, shouting, "I've got a knife. Let's find that bitch!"

Satin wasn't interested in the knife and told her, "I can beat the bitch with my bare hands."

Then they spotted Sherry and Round Three had begun. Satin approached Sherry, but Sherry insisted she didn't want to fight anymore. Satin wouldn't take no for an answer and began throwing punches. Sherry grabbed Satin's hair like an attacking pit bull and wouldn't let go. Finally, Bleu stepped in and began hitting Sherry, saying, "Let her go! Let her go!"

After Sherry loosened her tight-armed grip, she rushed over to get the policeman who was on horseback. Jeri screamed, "Everybody get in the car and let's go!"

We sped off like a classic scene out of The Dukes of Hazzard.

To say that the ride home was awkward would be putting mildly. Jeri was so upset that tears were streaming down her face. She and Satin were arguing over what happened, as Bleu chimed in. All the while I was thinking: What kind of shit have I gotten myself into? The realization that Jeri was pregnant with Drew's baby came crashing back into my consciousness. If she had that baby, everything would change. Our pact—that one day we might marry—would be null and void. After what had transpired that day, I knew I would never go back to the beach for Splash, if I ever went back to Splash at all.

EVERYTHING MUST CHANGE

WHEN I RETURNED from Atlanta a few years later, I realized something about Splash that I hadn't known earlier, and it was perfectly expressed in the lyrics to Bernard Ighner's "Everything Must Change." The event definitely wasn't the same. One of the best things about Splash was that the people who never went out to bars or clubs came out. It was a crowd that younger people looked up to because it was made up of people who were mature, successful and very attractive on multiple levels. Some constituents were in long-term relationships, and others were single because they were on the down low (DL). Whatever their status, they would come out once a year for Splash and it was a joy to see them.

But this crowd, the ones I was expecting to see, was nowhere to be found. It has been said that with age comes wisdom. That's debatable. But we gain experience as we age and those experiences change us. This current younger generation undoubtedly lacked the experiences, etiquette and cultural norms that were prevalent when I first went to Splash. A certain level of respect, class and dignity was also missing. In the past, newcomers looked to the older group to set the tone and decorum for events, but this younger generation wasn't looking to anyone but themselves.

While these new and extremely ostentatious attendees were definitely a downer in terms of attending the "New Splash," as I liked to call it, what truly disappointed me was the experience of witnessing the downfall of Shogun, the stripper I had been so enamored of back at Club Incognito. When Incognito closed, the strip show had been relocated to a club called Toyz. Originally, Toyz had catered to a lesbian clientele, but the venue was large enough to handle the anticipated crowd and the setup was conducive to hosting an all-male review.

Initially, I wasn't going to go that night, but a friend wanted me to go since he was meeting some of his friends there. When I arrived, I really wasn't in the mood, but hanging out with my friend was always fun because he was a show unto himself. When the actual show started, it began like the first one I had attended back in 1999; the performers were guys with not-so-cute faces but who had great bodies and could dance. Most of the dancers were new to me, but that might have been because most, if not all, of the dancers were not memorable. Since I didn't recognize any of the dancers, I wasn't expecting much from the rest of the show. I decided I'd just have a good time hanging out with some people I hadn't seen in awhile.

Then I heard, "Up next, live from New York: Shogun!" It was like someone had immediately taken me back to moment when I first laid eyes on him. I stopped mid-sentence and immediately made my way to a spot where I could view the performance area. Before that I definitely wasn't paying attention to what was going on or who was dancing.

The music started and it was reminiscent of Shogun's first performance: customized for him to put on another spectacular show. Sadly, the crowd wasn't the same and they didn't want a show. All this new audience wanted to see was the same dick and ass the rest of the strippers were displaying. The very thing that made Shogun stand out in 1999—he was a true dancer and an artist—resulted in him being booed. Not only had the type of patrons changed, but Shogun's body had also changed. Before he didn't even have to contract his muscles—you could see each and every muscle sculpted to perfection—but now he had gained a little weight and a miniscule layer of fat was covering parts of his body. Clothed or naked, he still looked better than 95 percent of the people in attendance.

What made his performance worse was the fact that he came out in a cheesy metallic Chippendale costume. The outfit matched the music and I understood the concept, but I was probably the only one who did. People kept jeering and it was getting louder; before he could finish his routine, the deejay was being prompted to bring up the next dancer. I could see the frustration and hurt on his face. Something inside, I don't know what it was, compelled me to make my way over to console him. When I finally reached him, I reminded him of the first time I saw him perform at Incognito and what an artist he was. He thanked me, but I knew the damage to his ego had already been done and no amount of encouragement was going to repair it that night.

Seeing Shogun being treated like a piece of trash reinforced what I already knew: everything must change. From that moment on, Splash would never be the same—it had become nothing more than a distant and bittersweet memory.

Chapter Twelve

EXPERIENCING LOVE IN WHAT STARTED AS LUST

If my mind could have conceptualized,
At the time what I've finally realized,
I would have turned back the hands of time
And tried to rewrite my lines.
— Regret, A.D.

I'T'S OFTEN SAID that you find in love when you aren't looking, and that does seem to be true in my case. But nothing is worse than realizing when it's too late that you had love.

THE LIAISONS

SINCE I WAS new to the game of dating guys, in 1999, Jeri decided that she wanted to hook me up with one of her classmates at her college. She told me that I would like him, that he was attractive, looked straight, had a job and was working on his undergraduate degree. Initially I was very hesitant because I've never been a fan of blind dates. So I told her I would pass, but she must have mentioned me to him and shown him a picture. A couple of months later, I offered one evening to take Bleu downtown for his traffic ticket hearing. As fate would have it, when we got to the courthouse the guy Jeri wanted me to meet was there, also for a minor traffic violation. Bleu said, "There's Mr. Blind Date!" He came over and told Bleu hello and immediately gave me that eye contact which says I want you. He introduced himself and the conversation quickly led to him asking for my number. Since he was handsome and looked straight, we exchanged numbers. As I drove Bleu home that night, he proceeded to give me the 4-1-1 on Mr. Blind Date.

Mr. Blind Date and I went on a couple of dates and hung out a bit, but after awhile it became evident we were not looking for the same thing. One time when we were hanging out at his apartment in student housing, Mr. Blind Date's bisexual classmate The Cousin came over. The Cousin and I exchanged greetings, talked about some random topic, and I didn't give it a second thought. While The Cousin seemed nice, I never envisioned our paths would cross in the future. How wrong I was!

Late one night, or rather early in the morning after going clubbing with some of my straight friends, I was hanging out at IHOP and I ran into The Cousin. At that stage in the game, when I was hanging out with my straight friends the last thing I wanted to do was run into someone who knew about the other side of my life. But The Cousin looked straight and there was nothing about him that would lead someone to question his sexual preference. So we started walking towards each other and began talking.

He asked me how I was doing and I told him things with Mr. Blind Date weren't really working out. The Cousin went on to tell me that he and his cousin were throwing a house party in a couple of weeks and I should stop by. I always loved a good house party, so I told him I was absolutely looking forward to it.

MEET & GREET

THE PARTY WAS set for a beautiful summer day in Houston, 1999. When I arrived The Cousin was barbecuing and he told me to come on in and meet everyone. As I walked from the garage into the kitchen, he introduced me to a couple of people and then quickly ran back to the pit to finish cooking. As I looked around I quickly noticed several people from the clubs and thought to myself, "These are the people from the cute clique."

In typical July fashion, the guys were in muscle shirts and the ladies in halter-tops, revealing plenty of bulging biceps and voluptuous breasts. And what could be better than a party full of eye candy? Since I was the "fresh meat" at the party, everybody was trying to find out who I was and I how I knew The Cousin. The body language in the room suggested I was in a scene from Melrose Place: any person there could easily have been with any other person at some point in the past. Determining who was currently partnered up was going to be an almost insurmountable task, but I was up to the challenge.

As I was meeting and getting to know people, I noticed a guy who was serving as host and deejay, and asked him to play a song I wanted next. He politely let me know he was about to play a song for his female best friend. And that's when Mary J. Blige's "All That I Can Say" video came on. Everyone in the room was jamming and I was forced to wait, but I didn't mind because this guy had an indescribably irresistible quality about him. Somehow he offered me a drink and then introduced himself as Trevor Huntington.

My normal mode of operation at parties then was not to drink. But there was something about Trevor I wanted to get to know, so I decided to change things up. I told him I normally didn't drink, so he said he'd give me something light and began to pour a glass of Beringer's White Zinfandel. (To this day, Beringer is still my favorite white zinfandel, and it's because of him.) We started chatting and I discovered that The Cousin, Trevor and his boyfriend, who was fine as hell, all lived together in the townhouse. I gave him a compliment on how well the place was decorated, but felt a tug of regret, given that he was already taken.

During the party I would occasionally flirt with Trevor, but not too much because I didn't want his boyfriend or anyone else to pick up on it. Besides, there were several attractive people to keep me occupied.

Ultimately, the party started winding down and I started to make my exit. On the way out, I thanked The Cousin for the invite and told him that I had had a good time. He gave me a hug that sort of surprised me. Given that we had met through Mr. Blind Date, I just considered him a cool person. I didn't have any idea he was attracted to me, but that hug definitely let me know otherwise.

Trevor was standing outside and saying goodbye to his guests. He told me that it was nice meeting me and made a point to make sure I knew he was interested. In our departing exchange the hint was subtle, yet blazingly obvious to both of us. He mentioned that he and his housemates would be having another get-together for his birthday in August and then added that he would get The Cousin to invite me. I told him I looked forward to coming, gave him "the eye" and finally left.

MIXED SIGNALS

RIGHT AROUND THAT same time, summer 1999, I met a woman. She was about 5'4" with a cute petite shape, gorgeous face and nice honey tone skin, and there was no way you could walk past Miss Petite and not say something to her. We were on the dance floor—my favorite place to be at the Roxy. Miss Petite was turning heads because of the way she was working her body, but she wasn't coming across as slutty, the way some girls did on the floor, which made me take note even more. So I made my move.

Walking up like a true alpha male, without fear or hesitation, I proceeded to show her that she wasn't the only one in the room who knew how to move. After I made my initial approach, she gave me a flirtatious glance, insinuating that she was interested. Now that I knew I had a chance, it was time to really turn it on, and I definitely didn't disappoint.

The deejay soon switched from booty-shaking to slow dance grooves, the perfect opportunity for me to display my vocal skills. I strategically slid around to her back side and slowly wrapped my arms around her waist as I crooned a couple of tenor notes. She turned her head to look back at me and said, "You can sing!"

"Yeah, I can do a little somethin', somethin'," was my nonchalant reply.

What surprised me as we slow-danced was how great our bodies felt next to each other. We danced some more and then exchanged numbers. I called her a couple of days later and found out that she was in school and working at a bank. Although she didn't have an undergraduate degree yet, I appreciated that she was working toward it while holding down a full-time job. Most important was the fact she didn't have any kids. It seemed so hard to find a woman of her caliber without a baby or two. I was in my early twenties and I didn't want to date a girl with a ready-made family. Avoiding "baby daddy drama" was a paramount concern of mine back then.

We officially started courting and being seen together. When we went to functions hosted by my close friends everybody seemed to like her. The Fourth of July weekend was coming up and Jeri's family was meeting at their vacation home in Baytown, TX. The Joneses' house backed up to the bay and they had built a small pier out into the water where family and friends could go fishing and crabbing. Whenever the Joneses got together it was always tons of fun, given the sheer volume of people and the blending of four generations. A setting where large non-argumentative families gathered seemed to always draw me because it was the exact opposite of what I had had with just my mom and me. Since I was "non-biological" family and Mr. Jones thought of me like a son, I thought it would be good to bring Miss Petite along and get his opinion.

I introduced Miss Petite to the family members and within minutes had the nod of approval from Mr. Jones. Jeri, however, was a different story. She was standoffish to Miss Petite, and super-attentive to me.

I quickly realized that Miss Petite had become a potential threat to Jeri. I admit that I enjoyed the attention but I ended up putting Miss Petite in an awkward situation. If I had known Jeri was going to get jealous, I wouldn't have brought Miss Petite. Nevertheless, it put a little water on the seed in the back of my mind that one day Jeri and I would get married and have the family I had always wanted. Even the suggestion that Jeri might want me for herself was enough that I began to rethink my decision to get close to Miss Petite, and I gradually ended the relationship.

MY FIRST HOUSE PARTY

I DON'T KNOW what it was about Trevor Huntington, but I knew this was someone I had to get to know ASAP. It was like when I had seen Jack at rehearsal for the first time. The birthday party Trevor was supposed to have had in August was cancelled. I later found out that Trevor's boyfriend had blown the money on drugs. So I immediately started plotting about how I was going to see Trevor again. The fact that he had a boyfriend and that both Trevor and his housemate, The Cousin, seemed to be attracted to me was going to make this more challenging than normal. I didn't have Trevor's phone number and my only means of contact was through The Cousin. Could there have been any more stumbling blocks?

Every summer my mom and I took a road trip when I was in grade school. We would typically leave Houston at the break of dawn and drive to Memphis, TN. My first babysitter, my mom's niece, lived there with her family. We'd stay the night and get up the next morning and drive to Nashville and stop by my grandparents on my father's side. After we spent a few hours catching up with them, we'd head to Columbia, my mom's hometown. Once there, I would spend time with my grandparents for a week or so before we'd head out to another city, usually in a neighboring state. We did this for ten summers straight. This year, though, my mom had decided to invite one of her friends so I didn't have to go. I had been living at her place since I moved back from Grinnell, and so now I was free to do whatever I wanted because I had the entire house to myself. I decided that the quickest way to see Trevor was to have a house party of my own.

The day of the party, I had the place spotless and I was so excited. This was going to be my first party I'd ever thrown without my parents being present or involved, at least to a certain extent. In my mind, I had everything ready to go, but since Jeri had given several of her own parties and she knew what was involved, I made sure she arrived a little early. Thank God she did.

As soon as she had finished looking around and I told her all the things I had set up, she asked about the drinks. I had purchased some bottled water and soft drinks, thinking that would be enough since I was supplying real food. Remember, I didn't drink, so I wasn't really concerned with alcoholic beverages. Jeri quickly enlightened me that I was having an adult party and adults expect liquor to be provided. She ran to the store and bought some cases of beer and wine coolers. Jeri saved the party—I had no earthly idea I was going to need all that alcohol.

The party was going as planned and everyone was having a good time. The music was jamming, people were playing cards and dominos, and everybody was getting their "eat" or "drink" on. As I said, I had invited people of all sexual preferences, which made for quite an interesting setting. The straight people were wondering if some of the guests were gay. The gays were wondering which guests were straight and the bisexual people were trying to determine who they would be sleeping with that night from the party. It was absolutely hilarious and complete entertainment to me.

People would come up to me with puzzled looks on their faces and then some would ask about a certain person. I was judicious with my responses: If the person was close to me and I knew that the person they were asking about didn't mind their business being told, I would let them know. Conversely, if I wasn't extremely close to the person asking or I didn't want to confirm their suspicion I would tell them to ask the person or give the "I don't know."

As more and more guests arrived, some who I didn't even know, I kept waiting for The Cousin to come because I knew he would bring Trevor. A couple of hours into the party, they finally arrived: The Cousin, his friend Mr. Jamaica, and Trevor. At that point I thought: mission accomplished! While I was ecstatic the party was going to be one everybody talked about for years, I was even happier to see that Trevor had come without his boyfriend.

When I get excited or mad my face reveals everything that's going on in my head. While I normally would have tried to hide my emotions, I was so ecstatic to finally get to see Trevor again I didn't care who knew. He was looking so good—his shaved head really made his eyes stand out. To say I was infatuated would have been an extreme understatement.

Once they were inside the house, I led them to the kitchen where Jeri and Satin were seated. The first thing on my agenda was to get Jeri's feedback on Trevor. Just as I had imagined, she quickly let him know he was sexy. Jeri and Satin also thought The Cousin's friend Mr. Jamaica was handsome, but they said that The Cousin just had a great body. I had to admit Mr. Jamaica's accent and gorgeous skin tone were turning me on as well. But my primary focus was definitely on getting to know Trevor better, now that he was literally on my home turf.

Of course, I thanked him for coming, let him know how good he was looking and how happy I was to see him. Then I immediately asked where his boyfriend was. He gave me that charming smile and said something about him being at home or at work, which was music to my ears. Just as I was getting deeper into our conversation, hosting duties called. I had to excuse myself and Trevor told me to go ahead and that he understood.

More people were coming and going and because I was the host I had to attend to my other guests. I kept trying to find a way to get back to Trevor, but then he came over and informed me that he had to go. Needless to say, I was pissed. The good thing was that I finally got his number. So I walked him to the door and anxiously awaited our next encounter.

Once Trevor was gone I got back to handling my hosting duties, talking with some of my friends I hadn't seen in a while, and playing a few games of cards and dominos. The night was winding down and at this point I was beyond ready for people to leave. I had spent the previous day getting things prepared and I was exhausted. But I wasn't too tired to give Jeri the 4-1-1 on what happened with Trevor.

Jeri is always very perceptive about what is going on. She tuned me in to the fact both Mr. Jamaica and The Cousin seemed interested in me. My ego had grown so big by this time, I usually thought that nearly everyone had some level of interest in me. Ego is the fuel which feeds the sex addict. Jeri and Satin left and the house was almost clear, except for Mr. Jamaica and The Cousin. I immediately thought Jeri must have been right. So the guys started talking about how the party went and discussing some of the guests. During the conversation I got to know Mr. Jamaica a bit more and thought, Um, this would be someone I'd be interested in getting to know. (Trevor had already left and he was tied up with his boyfriend, and besides, my ever-raging appetite for sex had to be fed.)

The night was turning into the morning and although I was starting to become interested in Mr. Jamaica, I really wanted both of them to leave but I didn't want to be rude. I mentioned I needed to get some rest so I could get up and go to the second church service. They finally took the hint and started making their way to the door. I wanted to get Mr. Jamaica's number but The Cousin kept lingering. Somehow I was able to get The Cousin into his car while Mr. Jamaica stayed around just long enough for me to get his number.

MENAGE A TROIS

ON SUNDAY I got up and headed to church, my mind full of the goings-on from the night before. Instead of truly focusing on the service, I was thinking about all the fun I had had and what I was going to wear to the Sunday Circuit. Since the second service didn't end until after brunch, I would have to catch the circuit at the tail end of LaStrada.

As the afternoon progressed, I ended up calling Mr. Jamaica that evening and meeting with him. I went over to his apartment and we commenced in some foreplay. Mr. Jamaica was sexy and his Jamaican accent made me want to see what he was working with. But I didn't know that I would be in for a surprise. Between the time I got to Mr. Jamaica's place and before we started to mess around, Mr. Jamaica had made a call to The Cousin, telling him to come over. I heard a knock at the door and there was The Cousin. The dynamics of the encounter were quickly heading to a place I had never been before and I was in a state of shock. It was exciting but also scary: I had never had a threesome before. So many conflicting feelings were swirling around in my heart and brain: this wasn't what I had planned and I felt railroaded, but at the same I relished the fact that both of them wanted to have sex with me. As I look back, this experience clearly demonstrates the level my addiction had reached. The fact that I would have sex with The Cousin, who I wasn't initially attracted to, speaks volumes. As I mentioned earlier, an addict's "hunger" always has him looking for the next sexual adventure. This ménage a trois was a perfect fit.

As we began to have sex, I was quite surprised that The Cousin was better at "fucking" than Mr. Jamaica. I used the word "fucking" because we definitely weren't making love.

Anytime you engage in a threesome, you aren't making love: it's just pure unadulterated sex. With more than one sexual partner there were multiple levels and layers of sexual stimulation. Hands, penises and tongues were going every which way. My body was feeling things it had never felt before and the sensations were happening so fast that it was overwhelming. I found out later that The Cousin and Mr. Jamaica were dating and that they often brought in a third party to spice up their sex life. These two fellow sex addicts were experienced and it definitely showed. In fact, The Cousin is probably one of the best sex partners I've had in my life, but I never told him because I wasn't initially attracted to him.

After everyone climaxed, The Cousin left and I stayed the night. It was so weird waking up that Monday morning to Mr. Jamaica ironing a shirt as he got ready for work. The thought that immediately popped into my mind: I can't believe I did what I did last night. While I had a deep sense of regret, because I hadn't initially planned for this to happen and I had lost control, I also had that feeling you get when you know you've experienced some of the best sex of your life. As Mr. Jamaica rushed to get out to work, I quickly threw on my clothes and headed home. When I walked out his door, I knew I would never come back. I had entered a new dimension of the cycle. Now that I had experimented sexually beyond just one person, there was no telling what I would allow myself to do next.

THE RENDEZVOUS

I COULD NOT stop obsessing about getting to know Trevor. There was just something about him that kept me wanting to know more: an insatiable lust. When I first met him at his house, he was dressed casually because he was at home. Yet he still had this sexiness about him even though he wasn't dressed to impress. Trevor's sense of style is what attracted me so strongly to him. When he graced me with his presence at my party, he was dressed quite differently and his shaved head made him look like a totally different man (one I wanted to fuck the shit out of).

In some ways he reminded me of Kim: they were both people who had a unique style but were also fashion-forward. Trevor also had an unspoken confidence about him that spoke volumes. It didn't matter what room he was standing in, people were going to notice him without him saying a thing—he looked that good.

The first time I called Trevor, he was in bed. I opened by asking how he was doing and saying how glad I was that he had come to my gathering. As the conversation continued, I quickly got the sense that something was going on because it seemed he was talking in code; either someone was listening to the conversation or he had company. I asked him where his boyfriend was, and it turned out that he was in bed with him during our conversation. I was floored. I couldn't believe Trevor was smooth enough to carry on a full conversation with me while his boyfriend was in the bed next to him. I decided to end the charade by suggesting he call me back or we meet later. And that's exactly what we did.

Once he called me back, we both knew we would have to meet in person to see if the infatuation that was brewing between us was just a crush or something more. I don't remember the details of what went on during that initial meeting, but we both knew the attraction between us was definitely more than a crush.

Our designated rendezvous was La Madeleine, a country French café, off Beltway 8 and Westheimer. It was an ideal location because it was close to his house but not close enough that anyone would know or come looking for him. It was also easy for me to get there from my mom's house. It took me no more than fifteen minutes, if there wasn't any traffic.

Each time we met there, I was like a kid on a new adventure. There was something always new with Trevor, which kept me always wanting more. From there we would go somewhere like a park and have sex. We even messed around in his van in the restaurant's parking lot. He must have remembered that I got bored easily, so he consistently kept me on my toes. At times I didn't know if I was coming or going and I absolutely loved it. His relationship with his boyfriend required us to be discreet, which only added to the excitement. The spiritual side of me felt guilty about having sex with someone who was in a relationship. But the cocky and arrogant addict side of me relished the fact that I was getting what I wanted, no matter who got hurt.

LOVING ME FOR ME

TREVOR WAS COMPLETELY attuned to who I was as a person and what made me tick quite early in our relationship. One day we were riding in my truck and stopped at the ATM. While waiting in line, out of nowhere he turned to me and said, "You have it and you don't even know it!" I asked, "What did you say?" and he repeated what he had said. "You have it and you don't even know it!" Totally perplexed, I looked at him and asked, "What are you talking about?"

"The total package. You have the looks, the talent and the education."

This was the first time I had ever heard someone I was totally enthralled with convey such a thing to me. He clearly thought that I was a gifted, rare and truly blessed person. It was as if he was able to look deep into my soul.

That one conversation changed my life. I always had the feeling God had put a special gifting on my life, but for Trevor to realize it put things in a different context. I knew I was smart and talented but not gorgeous. In elementary and middle school, I was made fun of because I was fat. In high school, I lost the weight but several people were jealous of me because I was smart. And while I was at Grinnell, at times I felt like an average Joe. Once I heard a person like Trevor say I had the total package but didn't realize it, my eyes were opened to what had been there all along; I began to feel like a beautiful person from the inside out.

Not only could he see the authentic me, he also did little things I didn't even know I would like. It freakin' blew my mind. He always knew how to keep my mind focused on him. Although he and his boyfriend still lived together, I knew I was number one in his heart. While we were dating, I was teaching chemistry at my high school and doing concert promotions on the side for Catch 22 Promotions. The owner of Catch 22 had given me a pager just in case he needed to reach me to pick up or distribute some promotional flyers. I would be in the middle of teaching a lesson and all of a sudden my pager would go off with the numbers 143—that was Trevor's code to let me know he missed me (this was well before Musiq Soulchild's song "143" was released). A huge smile would come across my face and my students would say, "Who is that, Mr. Burks?" It definitely made my day. It didn't matter if I was having the worst day of my life, when I got that page, everything was fine.

THE ESSENCE OF THE FASHION CONNOISSEUR

WHEN IT CAME to fashion, Trevor was one of the most creative persons I've ever known. To see things styled in a magazine is one thing, but to see someone come up with a look right on the spot is another. One day I was visiting him at Buyakah, one of the trendiest clothing stores in Houston back then, and he decided he wanted to style me. My typical dress was usually conservative or preppy chic. Trevor wanted to show me that I had the body to go well beyond those styles. So he picked out a couple of different outfits. The one I remember clearly was a Playboy shirt with a black background and a pattern of

SEX & SURRENDER

Playboy Playmates. It was something I would never have worn, much less picked for myself, but I had to admit that the shirt actually looked good on me. I hated being wrong and he knew it and he wasn't afraid to let me know. He would say, "You might know those books, but I know fashion." And he was absolutely right.

All this made sense once I found out that he used to be a model and had served as a model scout for Page Parkes, which is, according to their website, "the largest model and talent group in the Southwest." He was so good at what he did that under his tutelage he was able to get his boyfriend a job setting up and styling mannequins. It's no wonder Trevor moved on to work at Bebe and ultimately got picked up by one of Houston's most renowned singing groups. He works as a celebrity stylist today.

Although Trevor was into fashion and always looked like a million bucks, what made him so amazing was his ability to make people happy. He could put a smile on anyone's face. Whether it was saying something nice to lift their spirits or physically giving them something he had, his giving spirit was inspiring and it made me want to be a better man. As an only child I was used to everyone taking care of me, but for the first time in my life, I wanted to take care of someone. I set my sights on making enough money for the both of us so he could choose if he wanted to work or not. Artists are known to have their muse and it was clear Trevor was mine.

IF I COULD TURN

I WAS SO devoted to Trevor that it might seem as though nothing could have gone wrong between us. But my lack of experience with intimate relationships between men created a few problems. One day during the week, both of us were off, which was extremely rare, and we decided to hang out at Rice Village. The Village was a great place to shop because it was an outdoor mall in a ritzy part of Houston. We went in and out of various shops while he showed me what he liked and I was captivated just being with him. We ended the evening with dinner at Café Express. We were talking about how much fun we had and then suddenly he said something, which to this day I can't remember, and I said, "Stop being so fake!"

I didn't realize I had just made one of the biggest mistakes of our relationship. He diplomatically let me know he wasn't being fake, and said that if I really knew who he was as a person those words would never have come out of my mouth. He was livid. Our wonderful afternoon turned instantly into an awful evening. The situation was spinning out of control so fast I didn't know what to do. Needless to say, dinner was over at that point. We got up and I drove him home.

When I got back to my mom's house to assess what had happened, I kept thinking about the fact that I had called him fake. Whatever he said had something to do with me thinking that wasn't what "a man would do" in that particular situation. At the time, my pea-brain couldn't imagine that a "real man" would do whatever Trevor had mentioned. I had these rigid ideas that a "real man" only behaved in certain manner. Of course, now I realize that a "real man" is honest and takes care of his responsibilities, which is exactly what Trevor did, but at the time I just couldn't accept someone acting in ways that challenged my limits.

The next day I called him and he was quite short with me on the phone. I had fucked up and I knew it. So I started racking my brain trying to figure out what I could do to make it up to him and let him know I realized he wasn't being fake, but that was just who he was. As I milled over ideas, I knew I needed to truly let him know that I actually understood the creative and unique person he was—and to convey that was going to cost me a piece of my pride.

Urban Outfitters had just come out with a new over the shoulder backpack for men. It was very trendy and not many people had it—and that was right up Trevor's alley. When it comes to someone I love, I'll instinctually do whatever it takes, even if I don't realize I am in love at the time.

So I went to Urban Outfitters and got them to wrap up the bag and then gave him a call. Somehow I convinced him to let me come see him. We ended up meeting at the park close to his house. In the back of my mind I knew he still cared for me and if I could just show him I was sorry I could get him back.

When he got to the park, he was still upset. Whenever we went to a park, we always sat on the swings, and that's what we did this time. I started explaining how sorry I was and I told him that I knew he wasn't being fake. I apologized and handed him the bag; he opened the box and now it was his turn to smile. At that moment, I knew he knew I was actually listening to him and valued him and what was important to him.

JUST ME AND YOU

"IF YOU LEAVE her, I'll leave him. We'll pack our bags, don't say a word. Let's go far away, to another place. Let's hideaway. Oh, just you and me." Those are the lyrics to Destiny's Child song, "If You Leave." And that's exactly what we did one weekend. Trevor and I decided to drive up to Conroe, TX. On the drive we listened to Mary J. Blige's "Give Me You" as he laid his head in my lap. That night we stayed in a hotel and took turns intimately engaging each other all night long. The next day we got up and went to the Woodlands Mall. My initial lust had now officially turned into a form of love I had never been privy to and I didn't know what to do. I found myself doing things I thought I would never do with a man in public, like kissing in a movie theater. Hell, I don't even remember what movie we saw. I was beyond ecstatic that we were alone and away from everyone we knew.

Up until Trevor, I had never introduced any guy I had slept with to my mom. My mother was raised by a Baptist minister from Tennessee, and she believed homosexuality was a sin, so it was the last thing she would want for her son. Nevertheless, my mom was and still is the most important person in my life and I knew that if I let on that I was having sex with men it would break her heart. But the way I felt about Trevor was different than I had ever felt about anyone else before; just talking to him made me happy and just seeing him—well, I have no words to describe it. So I decided to introduce him to my mom because I wanted the two people who meant the most to me in the world to meet each other.

Of course, my mom didn't think twice about me bringing a new friend over to meet her. I had tons of friends she had met on various occasions and she always treated each of them like they were her own children. When we came into the house, my mom was in her traditional spot—in the kitchen, cooking. I didn't want to stay too long because my mom would start using her psychology and start asking questions about how we met or how he knew me and I didn't want Trevor to have to lie. I told my mom I was coming in to change clothes because we were headed out. This would be just enough time for them to get acquainted but not too acquainted.

In typical fashion, though, my mom doesn't allow anyone to come through our door without eating, especially if she is cooking. Mom offered Trevor some food and he tried to politely refuse. But he didn't realize that my mom can convince a person to eat who has just left an all-you-can-eat buffet. She ended up fixing Trevor a tuna sandwich and something to drink. By the time he was halfway through with the sandwich, I was ready to go. I gave my mom a quick goodbye kiss and we headed out the door. I was so happy at that moment because even though she didn't know he was the reason I was so happy, she had at least gotten to meet him. Whenever Trevor wanted to know how my mom was doing he would jokingly bring up the tuna sandwich.

NEVER CAN SAY GOODBYE

ALTHOUGH TREVOR MADE it clear to me that I was first in his life, what I didn't know beyond a shadow of a doubt was whether he truly loved me. He wouldn't hesitate to tell me he missed me or that he liked me. But while we were together, he never told me he loved me. It was a very clever power move on his part. While he demonstrated his love for me on several occasions via his actions, he never let the words come from his lips. As I look back, I realize it was his way of holding back the most intimate part of himself. He knew that saying the words "I love you" meant so much to me because I constantly told him that I loved him. Yet he knew that no matter how often I said those words, I could never give him all of what those words encompassed. Which is so ironic, because I've never loved anyone in the way I loved him, and I'm not sure I ever will. It was almost like forbidden love, which doesn't always equate to true love.

Looking back, it amazes me that Trevor knew me better than I knew myself at that point in my life. He knew, even when I didn't, that although I loved him, in the back of my mind I still wanted to be married with children. He realized what I hadn't: my spiritual convictions were preventing me from totally committing to him. The way he ended the relationship hit me like an eighteen-wheeler carrying a ton of bricks. The horrible moment is still etched in my mind like a permanent tattoo that can't be removed. I was sitting on a barstool talking on the phone in my mom's kitchen when Trevor educated me to the fact that I was waiting on Jeri to get married the way he was waiting on his boyfriend to get off drugs. I could hear the hurt in his voice, almost like he was crying but it was too painful to let out a sound. At that moment all the hurt he felt transferred to me. I couldn't talk, yell, scream, cry, or do anything but I felt an immense amount of sadness overtaking me; I had finally realized that he was absolutely right.

He taught me one of life's most valuable lessons: never sacrifice the true love you have for the perceived love you want. I thought I wanted to be with Jeri because we could have the "traditional" family. In reality, Trevor and I didn't have the "true love" shared between "traditional" families. My true love didn't come in the characteristic cookie cutter fashion. It came in a shape that I wasn't mentally, emotionally and, most of all, spiritually, ready to handle.

You're probably wondering why I didn't mention the sex between the two of us. When we were together I wasn't addicted to sex, I was addicted to him. While we had great sex in various places and at unplanned times, which made it that much more exciting, what I regret most about our relationship is that we never made pure love. Having sex is one thing, but making love with someone you are truly in love with is spiritual. There is absolutely nothing better than two people making love climaxing at the same totally encompassing moment. I had experienced it with Kim, but only yearned for it with Trevor. Because of his relationship with his boyfriend and my inexperience with same sex relationships, we never made love. They say everything happens for a reason. The only thing I know is one of my biggest regrets in life is that it didn't take place. The reality is it never could have. Why? Because I allowed myself to compromise my values by trying to establish an intimate relationship with another person's love.

ONE FOR THE ROAD

I HAVEN'T FORGOTTEN Trevor, of course, and I call him every year on his birthday. He taught me a valuable life lesson: knowing when to let go. (Maxwell's "Pretty Wings" does a very good job of reminding me, as well.)

It's hard for me let someone or something go which really brings me joy, but sometimes I'm forced to.

Chapter Thirteen
ATL—A TIME OF LONELINESS

In solitude, I was forced to confront who I had become.
Yearning to become the man I was called,
I look to You for guidance.
— Rock Bottom, A.D.

UNKNOWING PREPARATION

IN THE SUMMER of 2001, I made a very unorthodox decision to move to Atlanta, right after I had just moved to Nashville. I generally make very strategic and thought-out moves when it comes to planning my future, but this was the one time I made a decision on impulse and I quickly learned you can't plan everything in life. At that time, I didn't know all the ways that God was preparing me.

I was in Nashville working for my cousin, who owned a unisex salon. He heard from my dad that I had been working with some concert promotion companies in Houston and wanted to start a promotion company. So I left Houston and stayed with my cousin in Nashville in order to start Platinum Plus Promotions. I knew I had to be extremely careful because I didn't want to give any signs to the openly gay stylists at my cousin's salon that I was bisexual. If they found out, not only would my cousin know my secret, my entire family would know. Besides, my cousin was known as a ladies' man and, naturally, his good-looking cousin would have to be the same. While I was staying with him, we made a few trips to the strip clubs. He even paid for a female stripper, who had one of the best bodies I'd ever seen, to take me to the champagne room.

Most men would have jumped at the opportunity to be with a hot stripper in the champagne room. Not me. As I mentioned earlier, as I matured I had established some rules about sex. Sex rule number one: absolutely never pay for sex. Either a person wants you or they don't. Rule number two: never have sex with a woman you don't love. This rule evolved because of the relationship I had with my mom. While I could have random sex with a guy and not give it a second thought, I never wanted to hurt a woman emotionally the way my dad had hurt my mom. So when we got to the champagne room, all I did was talk.

Now that my cousin and I had "played" with the ladies, it was time to get to work. Platinum Plus Promotions' first major event was at the University of Tennessee in Knoxville. We hired rappers Trick Daddy, Trina, Ying Yang Twins and DJ Kid Kapri for the concert. Although it was a great accomplishment just to put on the event, it wasn't profitable and we quickly learned that you have to cater to the respective market.

Our next big production was in Nashville on a boat ride featuring the R&B artist Case. I was extremely excited about this event because the featured artist was living the exact lifestyle I wanted: he was making great money and performing all over the world. This event would be the perfect opportunity for me to get a firsthand account of how he had "made it" and to seek his advice on what I should do to get to the next level.

While I had access to Case during the event, the most helpful person was his manager. It became quite apparent that the manager was handling all the business aspects of his career and was the person who could actually get me connected. I talked to his manager about my music background and where I wanted to go. He heard me sing and told me that if I really wanted to move forward in the business, I would need to move to Atlanta. We exchanged contact information and he told me he would be willing to connect me to some people if I decided to move.

After seeing Case on stage living my dream, I knew I had to step out on faith and move to Atlanta. But I didn't have a job. Unlike all the other places I had lived in my life, I didn't know anyone in Atlanta, nor did I have any family there—or so I thought. It's amazing how God always provides what you need when He is working in your life.

PURSUING MY PASSION

I TOLD MY parents that I wanted to move to Atlanta and pursue my music career. One thing about a family as diverse as mine: if we don't have relatives who live in a particular city, we know someone who does. My uncle attended Morehouse College and had friends, the Thomases, who lived in Atlanta. In addition to my uncle's contact, Tracey Gordon, one of the girls from my church family group who was around my age, was in the Spelman-Georgia Tech engineering program. So I would not be totally alone in Atlanta.

I packed up my stuff and moved from my cousin's house in Nashville to a Microtel in Atlanta. It was really hard for me because there was no one around when I returned from the day. In tough times like these, I had to rely on the passion that fueled my music career to keep me focused.

After about a week of finally getting settled in the city, I sought out the Thomases. Mr. Thomas had a brother, Coach Thomas, who had retired from the Atlanta Public School System. Coach not only helped me get a job at the local school district teaching science, but he also rented me a room in his house until I was able to get my own apartment. This was one of those blessings I just knew only God could have provided.

Now that I had the basics taken care of, I needed a social outlet, especially if I was going to get into Atlanta's music scene. Tracey came to my rescue. Spelman College, which is located in the epicenter of the Atlanta University Center (AUC), has a student body made up of mainly African-American women.

Tracey was one of those supportive social butterflies everybody knew and loved. Being connected to her was like being connected to a personal Atlanta Yellow Pages.

I told Tracey that the only reason I had moved to Atlanta was to further my music career. Unlike other industries, you can't just decide you want to work in the music industry—you have to know someone. It turned out that Tracey had a girlfriend, Tammy, who was dating a big-time music producer, and she said she would introduce me. Tracey's friend would turn out to be the connection and blessing I needed.

While getting into the professional side of Atlanta's music scene was somewhat difficult, the scene itself wasn't really that big. There were a handful of major camps: LaFace (L.A. Reid and Babyface), Dungeon Family (Outkast), Freeworld (Dallas Austin) Patchwerks, Noontime, Sony ATV, and RedZone. The business is extremely competitive and cutthroat, yet all of these camps supported one another on some level, which was extremely rare.

Tammy was dating the head producer and owner of one of the major production companies, which had produced hits for Mya, Chante Moore, Sole, JT Money, Charlie Wilson and countless others. One of their biggest hits is on Beyonce's "I Am . . . Sasha Fierce." The diversity of artists, producers, writers, engineers and styles could not have been better.

Since I was a singer and songwriter, Tammy thought it would be best if I met one of the main writers in the camp. Unlike most of the people I had met in the industry, he was not at all arrogant and was in fact extremely cool and laid back. When I told him I wanted to be a singer/songwriter, the next thing he asked me to do was sing.

I quickly learned that if you want to get anywhere in the industry, you always have to be prepared. Time is money and money is time in the music business and the last thing you want to do is get a reputation for wasting people's time. You get one shot and one shot only.

After I gave him a few quick bars of a song, he told me that I sounded like Kenny Lattimore and that I might want to start some vocal lessons to strengthen my skills. He also said I could work as an unpaid intern at the studio. This was an opportunity I would never have gotten on my own and certainly not so quickly. God was working His magic.

With one foot in the door, I needed a vocal coach to take my skills to the next level. One day I was singing in the hallway at Grady High School, where I taught, and the school's drama teacher heard me. She introduced herself and told me, "You have a beautiful voice."

I thanked her and told her that I had moved to Atlanta to pursue a music career.

"Where is your church home?" she asked.

"I haven't found one yet," I told her.

She invited me to her church and told me that her choir director had major connections in the industry. In Atlanta everybody supposedly has connections in the industry, but I needed to find a church home so I thought maybe this was a sign.

Ravine Black was the choir director at Providence Missionary Baptist Church and she was ruthless. She didn't care if you were male or female, old or young, if you were singing your part wrong, she was on you. Her primary method of getting results was through intimidation. Unlike most prima donnas, she was actually qualified.

She had graduated from Spelman College with a triple major in voice, piano and organ. To double major in music is difficult, but to take on a triple major was borderline genius. When I heard this, I had no doubt where I needed to be—working with Ravine to hone my musical skills and singing in a church choir.

Attending church on a regular basis had been a staple in my life. I was inspired by the songs the choir sang, but the pastor's sermons were the most important part of service for me. A well-written, thought-out sermon was like hearing God speak. When I was a kid, my mom used to take notes and map out a preacher's sermon. Through that process, it was easy to determine which pastors were putting on a show and which were actually preaching God's word. Sadly, it seemed that a substantial number of preachers were just putting on a show. But not Reverend Dr. Greg Dooley, the pastor of Providence Missionary Baptist Church.

Only God could have led me to Providence, and He used my passion for music to do it. Of all of the churches in Atlanta, how is it that I was led to the one whose choir director had legitimate ties to the music industry and whose pastor had known both my parents? (They had all gone to college together.) When I first met Dr. Dooley, I introduced myself as A.D. Burks. He immediately looked perplexed and asked, "You aren't related to the A.D. Burks who went to Tennessee State University are you?"

I told him I was and he erupted with, "I know your dad!"

I knew that if he knew my dad, he probably knew my mom too because she was "Miss Brains" of her graduating class. Sure enough, he did.

MY WALK THROUGH THE WILDERNESS

FINALLY, I WAS somewhat settled in Atlanta. I had a teaching job, thanks to Coach Thomas; a social network, thanks to Tracey; an internship at one of the top production companies, thanks to Tammy; and a vocal coach and spiritual home, thanks to the school's drama teacher. Best of all, I found a quaint one bedroom apartment near Turner Field. At this point I felt like I was hitting my stride and well on my way to reaching my goal of becoming a singing star. There was just one major problem: I felt totally alone!

Beneath all this activity were haunting memories of events from my past. There is something about being secluded from all the noise of the world which allows God to talk to you and work on you. Even with all the success I had getting established in

Atlanta, I couldn't get over the fact I felt so alone. Initially, I told myself that I was homesick, but I knew that wasn't it because I lived away from home during college without a problem. Then I thought it was because I didn't have a significant other. I had dated a few girls but I really wasn't interested in any of them and, besides, I was focused on my career. No, it was something else and eventually I figured it out: I had been living a lie and I had been keeping a secret from my mother.

Once my parents were divorced and it became apparent that my mom was doing everything in her power to make sure I had the best life possible, I made a commitment to always tell her the truth. We shared everything with each other. Although I hated to admit it, she was my best friend. I told her everything—well, everything except that I had been abused as a child and that I had begun experimenting sexually with men when I returned home from college.

How do you tell someone who loves you so much, who's sacrificed everything she has for you, something which would hurt her so deeply? I didn't know how to do it and it was eating me up inside.

One night in particular I will never forget. I was in my apartment and I couldn't sleep. The fact I had been lying to my mom all this time had reached the breaking point and I finally hit rock bottom. Around 1:00 or 2:00 a.m. I had had enough. I called my mom and told her how depressed I felt. This was probably the worst thing I could have done because her natural instinct was to try to relieve any pain I was experiencing. She couldn't, though, because she was in Houston and I wasn't really telling her the true source of my pain. By the end of the conversation, we both were crying and she was telling me how much she loved me. I knew at that point, I was going to have to tell her.

God also led me to seek guidance from Dr. Dooley. A trifecta of reasons led me to him: he was a licensed professional counselor, he knew both my parents, and he was a pastor. I felt comfortable revealing my darkest secret to him, even though it was eerie knowing I was going to see him for counseling. My mom had counseled countless numbers of people at our house when I was a kid, and now after all this time, I was going to tell a counselor what I had strategically hidden from her.

I made an appointment with Dr. Dooley. As the session began, I felt extremely awkward. How was I going to tell this pastor that I had been having sex with both men and women? And on top of that, that I had been hiding it from my family? I was trying to find a nice rational and logical way to say it and his patience told me that he had all the skills of a great counselor. When I finally told him, he replied, "I already knew"!

I couldn't figure out how he knew. I thought I was extremely good at covering my tracks; nearly everyone I met in Atlanta would ask me about what girl I was dating. Was there some sign or characteristic trait I was giving off? So I asked him, "How did you know?"

He said, "I just knew. I could see it on you."

I had no doubt this was a man of God, and I knew he had the gift of prophesy.

Now that the "bomb" had been dropped, my mind and spirit felt at ease and we started discussing my childhood: my parents' divorce, my dad not always being there, the fact that neither of them knew, etc. Then we progressed to some of my past relationships and the spiritual ramifications of homosexuality.

Instead of him coming at me with the traditional church dogma that same-sex relationships were sinful, Dr. Dooley told me he was one of the more progressive ministers in the area. He went on to say that a gay couple had asked him to marry them and he said he would, but only if they attended marriage counseling sessions with him first. During those sessions he said it became apparent to them, not because of their spiritual beliefs, but because of their physical and emotional differences, that they shouldn't be married. This was a subtle, but very effective, way for him to illustrate to me his stance on homosexuality: he didn't think it was God's original idea of marriage. He ended the session by reassuring me that both my parents loved me and that they could handle me telling them the truth.

When I left, I felt so much better and knew I had to tell my mom the secret I had been keeping from her. But more importantly, I felt that the sexual sins of my past had been forgiven and that God still loved me.

THERE IS SOMETHING THAT YOU MUST KNOW

IT WAS THE spring of 2001, and I was scheduled to fly back to Houston for my birthday. Since it was spring break, I wouldn't have to take any time off from work. I thought this would be the perfect opportunity to tell my mom. Figuring out the right place and time to have the conversation was another issue. I knew that when I got home my mom was going to be excited to see me and we would have to catch up on everything that had happened since I left. So I didn't want to bring it up then. Nor did I want to tell her on the trip back to the airport because I didn't know how she would take it. I thought about what would happen if she had a heart attack or some other health crisis (she has had nine health-related surgeries since I was born, and has been near death more than once). I would need to be there. So I made the decision to play it by ear.

It was a great spring day outside, slightly breezy and not too hot, which was atypical for Houston. So I asked my mom to go to the park with me. I remembered how we used to go to the park in Tennessee when we would visit in the summer and how she loved it. Also, it didn't feel right to tell her at the house: it was our home and it felt sacred to me. My mom is very senti-mental and I could envision her replaying the conversation in her mind every time she was at the kitchen table or wherever the conversation would take place. It would be like returning to the scene of the crime.

We arrived at the park and I was racking my brain trying to figure out how to get this conversation started. My traditional direct and succinct approach to things wasn't going to work this time. I decided to take the irresponsible and easy route and blame my transgressions on someone else. My mom already knew, or at least suspected, that Jeri was involved in a lesbian relationship. I think she also knew deep down that Jeri was the one and only woman I truly wanted to marry and raise a family with.

I began by discussing some of the details of Jeri and her significant other's relationship and eased into how I started "messing around." Remember, I didn't want to lie to my mom, and at the same time I didn't want her to know too much. The more she knew, the more she would worry. I told her that when I got back from Grinnell I started going out with Jeri to some of the gay clubs and things sort of progressed from there. Her immediate response was one of shock and she started to blame herself.

"I had no idea," she said. "What didn't I do when you were growing up? I tried to expose you to several Godly men so you would have plenty of father figures. I supported you playing sports and everything I could possibly do!"

She started crying and I did too. I knew she had done everything humanly possible to make up for my dad not always being around when I was a kid, but the reality is: a woman can't be a man.

We both continued to cry, but I made sure to reassure her that she had done everything she was supposed to do. The "problem" wasn't what she had done or had failed to do; the problem lay with her ex-husband—he hadn't stepped up to the plate to be a father. I didn't have to tell her the reason I initially slept with some of the men: I was looking for a man to love me the way I thought a father should. She already knew that.

Now that I had done most of the talking, she began to pummel me with questions. It was worse than I could ever have imagined. Her biggest concern was my health. In her mind, the majority of AIDS cases were a result of men having sex with other men. A few men at our church, some of whom were married to women but were sleeping with men, had died of AIDS; one of her distant cousins in Tennessee was living with HIV. So her first question was, "Are you all right?"

I reassured her that I was fine and that I had been using protection. (In reality, I didn't always use protection and God had kept me from becoming a statistic.) The next thing she wanted to know was whether this was a phase or a permanent lifestyle choice. I told her the reason I was able to have this conversation was because this behavior was a part of my past and I was completely done. At that time, it was an accurate statement. I hadn't been involved in any sexual relationships with men since I left Houston.

My mom reiterated that she loved me and that everything was going to be all right. While I was glad I had finally told her my all-consuming secret, the fact remained that she would never look at any guy I brought home the same way again. Ever afterwards she would scrutinize them, unconsciously and subconsciously, and wonder about the true nature of our relationship.

REACHED THE OTHER SIDE

BACK IN ATLANTA, things were much better now that my burden had been lifted. I decided to participate in the annual Bronner Brothers International Hair Show. Since I could dance, the producer of the show made me the lead dancer in one of the spotlight performances. I would be dancing with two other girls to a remix of Toni Braxton's "Spanish Guitar." A friend of Tracey, Glenda Bloomfield, helped choreograph the performance, which was so hot because the two girls were basically fighting over me during the number. It was a visual reminder of a seductive threesome and I loved it.

The hair show marked a new beginning in my life. I decided during rehearsals that I was going to cut my shoulder-length curly hair. It was my way of saying that I was leaving all the past behind and starting anew. The hair show allowed me to make some great friends, both male and female.

You just click with some people in life, and Glenda was one. She had moved to Atlanta from Houston, as I had, and we ended up being spiritual soul mates. We had almost everything in common and there was nothing about her which got on my nerves. I couldn't have asked for a better friend in the world.

I completed my demo and continued to work at the studio, and I began to realize that there were only three ways to make it in the music business: (1) sleep with someone, (2) have a family member who was in the business, or (3) have your own money. So in 2002, I decided to come back to Houston and work on option number three. Before I packed up and moved back, Glenda surprised me with a going away party. I was so shocked because all the friends I had made in Atlanta were there. I felt so good and what it did for my spirit was beyond anything I could express.

Chapter Fourteen
WELCOME BACK

Even though I tried to run, I couldn't hide.
What I thought I left was still inside
Patiently waiting to be reinvigorated
While I fooled myself thinking I had eradicated it.
— You Can't Run, A.D.

PAUSE

LOSING TREVOR WAS the first time I had truly experienced a romantic loss. Anonymous sex was the drug that seemed to pacify the pain. Since I couldn't get the adulation I craved from the one person I truly wanted it from, I reveled in the temporary adulation of other extremely attractive people. I felt out of control and at times I felt as though I wouldn't make it to thirty. I decided I had to stop. The best way to yield not unto temptation was to get rid of the porn I had purchased in Chicago—my main trigger. I took the tape to work, ripped it up, and tossed it in the trash.

I got a clean break from the sex addiction cycle when I moved to Nashville. It's amazing what an addict will do to maintain appearances; you're constantly trying to live a double life. The good thing about trying to save face in front of my family was that the desire to fulfill my sex addiction slowly started to diminish. So when I moved to Atlanta, I didn't even seek out my sexual triggers. As soon as I got back to Houston, though, I quickly slipped back into the bad old sexual habits. It all started with a trip back to the Sunday Circuit.

OLD HABITS ARE HARD TO BREAK

Shawn Long, my good friend and "play brother," was celebrating his birthday on May 17th. He was going to start the celebration at LaStrada and go from there. My close friends know I'm big on birthdays, so saying no wasn't happening. Once I arrived at LaStrada, it was all downhill from there. The excitement of the club and the fact that people were giving me the sexual attention I craved made the temptation so strong it felt like I had never left the scene. In no time, I slipped back into the hell I promised myself I would never return to: feeding the addiction. It was the newness and the excitement of sex to which I was heavily addicted, and being away so long made it even more tempting.

Wednesday through Sunday, I returned to partying. But unlike the first time when I would go out to dance and enjoy myself, this time I focused primarily on establishments where I was guaranteed to find sex partners. After hooking up with a countless number of anonymous sex partners, to my surprise, I ran into a guy who looked just like George Michael. The "Faith" video immediately started playing in my head when I saw him. We were at JR's on a Sunday night and after checking him out a few minutes to see if he was with anyone I decided to make my move.

"How's it going?" I asked.

With an unassuming smile, he responded, "I'm fine! And you?"

"I'm good," I responded, and in a split second the attraction between us was sealed.

Although it was evident from the look on his face that he wanted me to fuck the shit out of him, he wasn't about to give it up that easily. For me to get the goods, I was going to have to put in work—real work. A challenge was right up my alley.

Mr. Genuine was about to turn forty. I had never seen a 40-year-old guy who looked so young. And this would be the first time I ever considered talking to someone who was that much older than me (I was in my late twenties). After a few probing conversations and deep discussions, I determined that Mr. Genuine was a spiritual and genuinely wonderful person who had been hurt by men just like me before.

Finding a man who engaged in sex with other men and who made God a priority in his life was extremely rare. Besides being spiritual, he was authentically kind, often to his own detriment. Selfless people always give of themselves, yet they seem to receive so much grief in return for being themselves. I was always curious to know how openly gay men reconciled their sexual desires and lifestyle with their family. He said he always prayed for God to take away his sexual desires for men so he could please his mom. The prayer wasn't answered, but in time his mother and family eventually accepted him.

Most of the guys I had been with were fairly masculine and had been with women or a woman at some point in their life. But they preferred men or a combination of both sexes. For the first time, I realized that for some people, like Mr. Genuine, sexuality wasn't a choice. They were actually born homosexual. While I had the option of choice, it wasn't that cut and dried for everyone.

No matter Mr. Genuine's innate sexual desires, he was a great person who people liked and easily fell in love with. And just like most sweet people, he had a weak spot for bad boys. Opposites attract, but for Mr. Genuine they did more than attract, they left unforeseen damage. His last relationship had left him in both emotional and financial turmoil. That would have been enough for me to say, "no more guys, I'm headed back to women." For him, it wasn't an option. Instead, he had erected an invisible wall as protection, which was understandable. My challenge was to take it down, brick by brick.

Sex addicts are the best manipulators on the planet. We quickly determine what it is a person values most and we give it to them. Most of the time, we don't even give it to them; we just give the illusion that we will. Whether it's excitement, companionship, support, or what everyone wants most of all—love—we make sure we supply that particular need. As soon as we get what we want and are ready for the next adventure, all bets are off.

That's exactly what happened with Mr. Genuine and me. I gradually broke down what some might have seen as an impenetrable wall and touched his heart. While I honestly had good intentions, I wanted him to be able to love again, and I genuinely had feelings for him, I ended up integrating myself into his family life as if I would always be there. I led him to believe that we might live together and have a happily-ever-after story. In reality, those eventualities were far from plausible. What I did, the way I set him up, was despicable.

What was really second nature for me was finding another prospect while I was out touting my current one. There's nothing more appealing to single sex addicts than seeing two attractive people together and one's flirting with them. It's like a piece of forbidden fruit we are just salivating to get a taste of. We don't think through the logic of it: if one member of the couple is flirting with someone else, then they'll certainly end up doing the same thing to whomever they happen to end up with.

One night I was at a non-official party for an MBA conference and I had decided to bring Mr. Genuine along. By this time, I had already mentally and emotionally checked out of the relationship. I was just stringing Mr. Genuine along because I hadn't found anyone better to pique my interest. That was until I ran into Mr. Materialistic. As I was working the room, networking and introducing Mr. Genuine to different people, I noticed that a well-dressed guy kept staring at me.

I had to quickly and cunningly devise a plan to work my way over to him without Mr. Genuine tagging along. Not wanting to be blatantly rude and disrespectful, I conveniently excused myself to get a drink while Mr. Genuine was engaged in a conversation. Seconds after I headed in Mr. Materialistic's direction, he introduced himself.

"How's it going?" he asked, and then told me his name.

"A.D. Nice to meet you."

We quickly chatted with each other. I got his business card and was back standing next to Mr. Genuine in less than five minutes. Not wanting to waste any time now that I had the number, I had to do my duties as a local celebrity and make my grand exit by telling everyone goodbye and what a pleasure it was to see them.

After we left, I wanted to drop Mr. Genuine off early, so I needed to come up with a believable excuse. Since I was getting my MBA at the time, I told him that I had some work I had to do and that I needed to get some rest. While all of that was true, my additional plans included meeting up with Mr. Materialistic. With a quick phone call, I found out where his hotel was and I was making my way to the Sheraton in less than an hour.

Mr. Materialistic was extremely intelligent. With both an accounting degree and a MBA, at twenty-five he was already working right under the CFO for a major international restaurant company. When the company's SEC filings went out, his name and signature were included. With all that knowledge, I knew this was someone I needed to learn a few things from. So Mr. Genuine had to go. Like the selfish sex addict I was, I broke the heart of another person who truly loved me and would have done anything to see me happy.

I had picked up and dropped Mr. Genuine like he was a disposable napkin, and my close friends gave me major grief. While I knew they were right, I was focused solely on my desires. I didn't want Mr. Genuine anymore and Mr. Materialistic had the financial knowledge I sought. And like most sex addicts, with a flip of a switch, I could turn my feelings on and off for a person. But with Mr. Genuine, I actually felt some remorse. He was such a nice person and for me to come along and turn his world upside down was totally unfair. The fact that he has forgiven me and that we have remained friends is a true testament to the person Mr. Genuine is, rather than what I deserve.

With Mr. Genuine out of the way, I could focus on Mr. Materialistic. Our fall semester break rolled around and I had planned to go to New York with the Finance Club to visit the New York Stock Exchange. By this time, Mr. Materialistic had gotten a job to head up a new division of a national flower company and was moving to New York. So he asked if I would fly to Greensboro, where he lived, and help him drive up. Once I assessed the pros and cons of the opportunity, I realized the cards were stacked in my favor: I'd get to see him in his element; I'd have a place to stay while in New York; and there's nothing like a road trip to find out who a person really is.

The trip up was cool because we had the same musical taste. I also found out that he had a few connections in the music industry. But once we reached The Big Apple, I got to see the real Mr. Materialistic—he was a selfish, materialistic egomaniac who couldn't take any dick. As a sex addict, I could temporarily overlook Mr. Materialistic's selfish and materialistic attitude, but he was starting to get on my nerves. For one thing, he seemed to have a litany of complaints the first time I tried to penetrate him when we were having sex. It really was no fun and it made me seriously reconsider spending any more time with him.

After we arrived and got settled, I wanted to meet up with my girl, Nasha Mina, who lived in the Bronx. I had met Nasha, who was originally from Ghana, at Grinnell. With a sweet genuine spirit to match her amazing voice, she was like family to me. The plan was to pick up Nasha in Mr. Materialistic's car at a Manhattan train station, go out to eat, and then do some shopping. But then Mr. Materialistic decided he needed to get his car washed. Nasha had already gotten on the train, so I couldn't call her to tell her we'd be late.

Because Mr. Materialistic was so selfish and so concerned about his BMW being clean, Nasha wound up sitting at the station for over thirty minutes waiting for us. I called her cell phone and left her a message to explain what had happened. But by the time she got the message, nothing could be done. Of course, I was pissed because my biggest pet peeve is wasting time. And I especially hate when someone wastes my friends' time.

When we finally met up, Nasha was understandably livid. Mr. Materialistic tried to mollify her by offering to pay for lunch. Neither Nasha nor I was impressed by the gesture and she not-so-politely let him know. Still, since she wasn't one to hold a grudge, she kindly showed him how to navigate the shopping district he so eagerly wanted to visit, but I was done with Mr. Materialistic. Of course, in a way, Mr. Materialistic hadn't done anything worse than what I had done to Mr. Genuine. There's nothing like karma.

GOD BLOCKED IT

AFTER THAT EPISODE, it was back to the cycle as usual: watching porn, finding new sex partners and not getting involved. It got so bad that on a given night, I would call one sex partner, hook up, and then go out to the club and find a new person with whom to have sex. When addicts get so far gone in the addiction, they start getting sloppy and behaviors they think no one is noticing start to become quite apparent. You never know who is watching and, luckily, I had true friends who were.

I've heard that God gives a warning before destruction comes. And my warning came unexpectedly. I had been clubbing and decided it was getting late so I needed to find someone to fuck. I headed to the Mining Company to see what I could find. Right before I walked in the door, Shawn called my cell phone.

"What's going on? You out tonight?" I shouted over the noise of the club.

"Where are you?" he asked.

"Uh, about to go into Mining Company."

"Boy, it's late. Go home."

"Nah, I'm cool. I'm just going to run in and I'll be out."

Then he said it again and commanded, "Go home! A.D., listen to me. Go home!"

After he said it the third time, I realized God was telling me through Shawn to leave or I might never be able to get myself out of what I would get myself into. There is no doubt in my mind, given the road I was traveling, that if Shawn hadn't called me that night I would have ended up having unprotected sex. And given the warnings God had given me before about having unprotected sex with men, this might have been the night I contracted HIV.

THE PERSONAL TRAINER

GIVEN MY LEVEL of sexual attraction toward Latin men, and the experiences I had had with them in the past, the gym became my one-stop-shop for finding new Latino sex partners. The most physically attractive one was The Trainer who was originally from Mexico City. This was 2003. I had quit teaching and started graduate school at Rice University to work on my MBA, so I would train either in the morning or right before the after-work crowd got there. I had seen The Trainer during my workouts training a frail-looking man who was probably in his late thirties to mid-forties. This particular client exuded a certain level of feminine energy; he was somewhat passive but not a flaming queen.

The Trainer was a client's ideal personal trainer since he had the body you would do anything to get. If he told you to do 1,000 squats, you would do it because all you had to do was look at his physique—perfectly symmetrical with each muscle clearly defined—and think, I want to look like that. His muscles had a good amount of volume, but they weren't too large or defined with veins popping out everywhere, the way most professional bodybuilders looked. He had a cute face with pink lips and a boyish smile; he also had an accent and a lot of charm. On top of that, he had one of the best pairs of legs and the nicest ass I'd ever seen.

I noticed a couple of little mannerisms: for example, he would maintain eye contact longer than straight men do, which let me know he probably messed around with both men and women. That was the cue for my sex addict to come to the forefront and take control. The next day, I saw his client and asked him, "Where's your trainer?"

"I only train on Monday, Wednesday, and Friday," he said. "Why? Are you interested in him?"

Realizing I had been busted, I smirked as I explained, "Yeah, he's in great shape, and I'm sure he can give me some suggestions for my calves."

I think I noticed an eye roll in there as he mumbled, "Yeah, I'm sure."

I didn't want to lie and pretend I wasn't interested, but I also didn't want to give the impression I was like the rest of the sex addicts in the gym. The next day when I came in, they were training and The Trainer was doing lunges down the hall near the water fountain. Since he wasn't an official trainer at this gym, he worked out as he trained. I figured that word had gotten back to him that I had asked about him. So I thought it's now or never.

As I approached the water fountain, he gave me his signature smile while lunging and holding a 50-lb. dumbbell in each hand. After grabbing a quick sip, I worked my way over to him and when he completed his set I said, "Looks like those lunges are working well for you," and laughed.

He smiled and said in his sexy Latin accent, "Yeah, they're the best workout for your legs and glutes."

Once I heard his response and saw that smile beam across his face, I knew I was in. (Got 'em, coach!) I kept spitting game and he was playing right along with it. One thing led to another and I was getting his number—and not for a training session. I told him I'd give him a call so we could hang out.

While I had been sexual with models and other gorgeous people, I had never been with a trainer, especially one with a body like this. What I had yet to realize was that when you don't play by the rules you lose the game.

I called him that Friday, which was way too early, but I wanted to strike while the iron was hot. (Not a good idea because it made me look like I wasn't in control. To be a successful sex addict, you must, at all costs, remain in control.) I suggested he let me pick him up and we go out for dinner. He said, "Cool. I just got back from the gym. Let me get ready and I'll call you."

All I could think about was how good the sex was going to be that night. I dressed to make sure I looked like I had just stepped out of a GQ photo shoot, and then I put on some of my most erotic cologne. But then it seemed to take him forever to call me back. He finally called and gave me the address to his apartment, which was in an expensive complex off Woodway. When I got to his place, he let me in and went back to getting ready. My eyes immediately went to the shag rug on the floor near the fireplace and the screws in my mind started turning. (Oh, yeah, baby!) After about five minutes he came out in this very metrosexual outfit—a fitted shirt with jeans that were so tight they looked like they'd been painted on. But there was no denying it looked sexy as hell. Those quadriceps and ass were stretching the hell out of that denim. And like the McDonald's commercial jingle says, "I'm lovin' it."

We got in my car and I asked him where he wanted to go and he suggested Barnaby's because of the healthy cuisine. Normally I'm the most decisive person when it comes to food, but when I had a trainer sitting directly across the table from me it made things a little bit awkward. So I used it as a conversation starter to get to know him a little better. He went on to tell me when to eat carbohydrates and when not to. He really knew his shit and I had to admit I was impressed (but I was even more infatuated with his body).

After our meal came, he questioned, "What made you ask me out?"

"Because I saw something that I was interested in."

"Usually people are afraid to approach me. I like the fact that you weren't intimidated," he explained.

And that's when I knew I had to get back to running the show and stop being excited about the fineness sitting in front of me. "I'm not most people," I said.

When we finished our meal, I grabbed the check and told him, "Let's get out of here."

Once we got back to his place, it was on, or at least I thought it was going to be. Walking through the door I instinctively wrapped my arm around his waist, grabbed the ass that had been talking to me all night and planted my lips on his. We worked our way to the bedroom and he came out of those clothes. Seeing his naked body in all its glory left me spellbound. How could one person's body be so perfectly fashioned? From head to toe, his was the best male body I had ever had the opportunity to get sexual with (until Santiago).

I lay in his bed licking his nipples and caressing his silky smooth skin, while he played with my penis; I was trying to work my way inside him, but he wasn't having it. I was a little surprised given that we had gone this far, but I figured that maybe he didn't want to give it up on the first night. We ended up jacking each other off and then he asked if I wanted to use his shower. Most of the guys I had messed around with just offered a warm wet towel, so of course I accepted the offer. In the process of me drying off, he told me he was getting sleepy and he had to train someone early in the morning. Since it was late and he was a trainer, I believed him. I quickly threw on my clothes and left.

My sexual appetite hadn't been completely quenched, so I decided to go to "The Strip" to see if I could find another piece of ass. The more I fed the addiction, the more I wanted sex. As I was coming out of one of the clubs, there he was—the man whose bed I had just been in. I was shocked; I had actually believed his "I've got to train a client in the morning" story. But as they say, all is fair in the sex addiction game.

I saw him a few more times at my gym, but I didn't get the real story on him until I started working out with my friend Henry a year or so later. Henry had a wide range of professional and non-professional athletes he trained at a personal training only fitness facility. We were working out and The Trainer brought one of his clients in. He gave me his cute smile as always and said hello. When he finished his session he left and that's when all the information was spilled.

Another trainer and Henry let it be known that The Trainer was a "kept man."

"I wouldn't let another man stick his dick in my ass for just a Crossfire and an apartment," Henry told the other personal trainer.

I didn't want to believe it, but then again, it was pretty obvious that his work as a personal trainer wasn't paying for The Trainer's lifestyle. I asked nonchalantly, "What do you mean?"

Henry went on to say some guy in Miami was taking care of The Trainer and he would fly him out whenever he wanted him. While he was definitely fine enough for that to happen, I never would have guessed that was the situation.

There was probably a little jealousy on Henry's part, because most of those trainers at that gym were looking for a sugar mama or daddy. Personal training can be lucrative, but it's such a fickle industry in Houston. Besides, The Trainer was definitely the most attractive of the bunch.

UNFATHOMABLE PASSION

As ALWAYS, I quickly put that sexual experience behind me. During this period of my addiction, obtaining the "perfect body" both personally and figuratively though sex partners was my main goal. It was sort of a way to validate my worth. I had to look the best and be with what our society considered the "best."

One afternoon I was working out at my regular spot and I noticed this Latin guy on the elliptical machine. I'll call him Mr. Passion. He appeared to be slightly older than me, but he had these amazing legs. I'm always drawn to a great pair of legs. As I quickly surveyed the rest of the package, I discovered the abs and upper torso were nice as well, but his legs were his true asset. Now his face left a little to be desired, but his ass and skin tone more than made up for it. He had my absolute favorite skin tone—a golden bronze hue, which is so rare, and only a few Latinos have.

During my initial assessment, I concluded he was probably gay, but could pass for straight in certain environments. As I continued my workout, I made sure to keep him in view to get a better feel for his personality and mannerisms. He seemed quite jovial and approachable, which could be both a good and a bad thing. Good in the sense that having a friendly personality made it easier for me to get into his pants, and bad in the same sense because it also made it easier for other people. Even as a sex addict I was picky. The last thing I wanted was to fuck someone who everyone had been in. It may seem like a contradiction in terms, but when you're always hooking up you have to be extra-vigilant about STDs.

After I finished my workout, I took a shower and we just happened to meet in the sauna. Well, it really wasn't that much of a coincidence—a great sex addict always plans his moves. There were other people in the sauna, and I wanted to give the appearance that I was interested but without letting everyone else know. I said hello in a casual but covertly flirtatious manner. He told me his name, but he responded in a way that let me know he had absolutely no clue I was trying to flirt. Not wanting to blow my cover, I left shortly afterwards and decided to wait for another opportunity.

Since I suspected he was gay, I further assumed he would be on "The Strip." I went out that Friday night and as I was driving through the area I saw him crossing the street from one bar to the next. Most people usually bar hopped from JR's to the Mining Company, but the atmosphere in the two establishments was totally different. JR's was well lit with a clientele of typical metrosexual and mainstream men and women, while the Mining Company was dimmer, with a more rugged and seedy crowd. Both spots hosted strippers, but you were more likely to see people engaging in some salacious sex act in the bathroom of the Mining Company.

Since I wasn't the biggest fan of the Mining Company, I headed straight to JR's to see if I could find him. Meandering through a crowded maze of people, I couldn't find him to save my life. Finally, I saw this guy I assumed was a friend of Mr. Passion's.

I walked up to him and asked, "Aren't you a friend of Mr. Passion?"

"Yeah."

"I thought I saw him tonight."

"Yeah, he was in here but he went over to Mining Company. Are you interested in him?" he asked.

Not wanting to give away too much, I said, "Maybe. He seems cool."

As our conversation continued, it became quite evident this guy was interested in me. Looking me over thoroughly he said, "I've seen you at the gym a few times. And then he introduced himself."

"I'm A.D."

We talked a little while longer, but I was trying to cut the conversation short so I could go find Mr. Passion. I hopped across the street to the Mining Company and Mr. Passion was nowhere to be found. Pissed because it was late and I couldn't find the ass I was looking for, I went back over to JR's. The same guy was still there, so I went back over to talk to him.

He said Mr. Passion was probably gone, which meant he had already hooked up with someone for the night. The more we talked, the more attractive Mr. Right Now became. He didn't have Mr. Passion's well-defined body; he was muscular but he had a layer or two of fat surrounding the muscle. What he did have, though, was great conversation—this guy was no dummy.

The next thing I knew, I was fucking Mr. Right Now at his three-story townhouse. I hadn't exactly planned it, but you know what they say, "I didn't mean to have sex; my dick just fell inside this nice beefy tight ass." We ended up going out a few times and having sex a few more times and that was it. Remember: the only reason I met him was because I was looking for Mr. Passion.

A few weeks later at the gym I ran into Mr. Passion, and I had to seal the deal. So I went up to him while he was working out and let him know I was interested. He was totally shocked I messed around. "I thought you were straight," he said with an adorable but bewildered smile.

"I'm bi," was my conniving answer. This hot tamale was smoking and I couldn't wait for an opportunity to get a taste.

As we kept talking I could see he was definitely attracted to me. "I've been checking you out, but I didn't say anything because I thought you were straight. You've got a great body," he said.

"Nah, you're the one with the hot body."

As the attraction between us kept escalating, he mentioned that he lived around the corner and usually rode over with his roommate, who was still working out. Not wanting to miss this opportunity, I offered to give him a ride, which he graciously accepted.

When he said he lived right around the corner, he wasn't lying. He could easily have walked the two and a half blocks from the gym. Once we were inside his apartment, we made small talk for five or ten minutes until his roommate arrived. Mr. Passion introduced me to a pasty steroid-injected guy I'd seen at the gym a hundred times. I played cordial and grinned as I said hello.

"I'm going to take a shower," Mr. Passion yelled to his room-mate. Then he looked towards me and said, "Come on in."

I was thinking to myself, Yeah, baby, I'm about to get some of that ass. We walked into the bathroom and Mr. Passion started undressing. Of course, I was getting a slight erection at that point, but I didn't want to come off like all I wanted to do was fuck him, no matter how true it might have been. I instinctively grabbed his ass and started playing with it. He gave me his gorgeous smile and said, "You like that, don't you," as he grabbed my dick.

"Of course!"

"Good, because you won't be getting any just yet," he teased as he jumped into the shower.

I was mad as hell because I was standing in the bathroom about to get Blue Balls and the person I wanted to fuck the shit out of was in the shower next to me. But he was making me play his game and I was actually enjoying it. There is nothing more sexually exhilarating to a sex addict than a challenge from another sex addict. Each addict is trying to see who's going to make the other give in first.

So we played the cat and mouse game for maybe a week or two. Each time we would hang out, our interaction would get a little more physical. Mr. Passion knew I wanted him sexually and he also knew I was the type of person who persevered when he wanted something; I wasn't going to stop 'til I got what I wanted. This just played right into his game. He started giving the impression he wanted more than just a fuck buddy. He must have known that as soon as I got the goods, I would be gone. It definitely wasn't his first time around the block. What I eventually came to realize was that he wanted someone to take care of him, but, like my mom always says, "I don't take care of grown men."

That first time at his apartment, when he went to take a shower, we first walked into a bedroom, which I assumed was

Mr. Passion's, but in actuality there were two bedrooms—one belonging to one roommate and the other to a third roommate, a woman. Mr. Passion, it turned out, was sleeping on the couch. The first question that comes to mind: why is a forty-year-old man sleeping on a couch?

It didn't matter what night of the week it was, I always knew I could find Mr. Passion on The Strip at either JR's or the Mining Company, sometimes with friends and other times by himself. Whether he was alone or with company, the common denominator was alcohol.

Normally I would have lost interest as soon as I found out he was an alcoholic, since I really didn't drink. And it was clear that he was looking for someone to take care of him, which didn't sit right with me (the only people I planned on taking care of were my future wife and kids). Even with all that baggage, the sex addict in me wouldn't let him go. It wasn't like he was the finest thing out there, and I had had better. But more than anyone I had ever been with Mr. Passion exuded passion, and I loved a challenge.

Mr. Passion was a very touchy-feely guy and so was I. Whether he was shaking a stranger's hand, or hugging a friend, you could see his inner warm spirit radiating out to greet people. In bed it was another level. By this time in my sex addiction I had been with plenty of people. I had experienced the entire sex spectrum from the lows of fucking someone and not ejaculating, to sex which was so good that semen came uncontrollably gushing out. Yet I had never experienced passion to this extent before. It's hard even to put it into words. He knew how, when, and where to touch me. Whether it was a soft caress or a firm grip, he had my body wanting to explode, and that was before ejaculating even came into the picture.

I'll never forget the first night he stayed over at my apartment. The sexual tension that had been building between us was so palpable that before I even got the front door closed we started kissing. There are people who know how to kiss and then there are people who make you think they invented a new form of French kissing. There was so much intensity behind his kiss, it made me feel like there was no other person in the world he wanted to be with at that moment; and there was no one else I wanted either. It may sound like a cliché, but he knew how to take intimacy from being just sexual to almost a spiritual experience.

As we made our way from the front door to my bedroom, all I could think about was how much I was going to enjoy placing my throbbing penis into his perfectly sculpted round ass. Grabbing his shirt and throwing it on the floor, I immediately went to erotically licking and playing with his nipples, as he started to softly moan in pure pleasure. While he worked his shoes and socks off, I aggressively labored with his buttoned-up jeans to reveal his thong.

I had never been into underwear until this moment. His 2(x) ist thong looked like a bikini brief in the front, but when he turned around, instead of going straight up it split in two and made a triangle. I had never seen a three-prong thong before. It was absolutely beautiful and it reminded me of when I had bought lingerie for Kim and she kept it on while we made love. And that's what almost happened that night. Strapped up, I strategically pulled the centerpiece of the thong to the side and pleasurably worked my way in.

Just when I was about to really get into my groove, Mr. Passion stopped me. "It's starting to hurt," he complained.

"Let's use some more lube," I suggested.

Somehow he weaseled out of letting me get back in and suggested I just hold him. I was so dumbfounded I didn't know what to do. He knew he had me, and he was playing me like a Julliard-trained violinist. All I could do was wait for another concerto.

Normally, I would have been livid and decided to just take him home; yet the passion I had just experienced wouldn't let me. It was probably equivalent to the feeling that drug addicts get when they take a first hit of something. Once they get that initial taste, they want more. And I definitely wanted more. While we lay in bed with our bodies intertwined, I totally took pleasure in feeling his skin against mine—soft yet toned. At times he would wake up in an inebriated state and whisper, "A.D., I love you!" Those words sure were convincing, and I was inclined to believe them, but given that he said them when he was still drunk, I couldn't be sure.

I later came to find out that most, if not all, of the night had been an act. While the passion we experienced that night left me contemplating how I could get more, my analytical side remembered that this was someone who wanted to be taken care of. The quickest way to see if Mr. Passion was legit was to give him a little space. The only way sex addicts can go without it is if they truly love a person, and even then they may slip. So I let a couple of days pass and, sure enough, I found him kissing another guy in a bar. A few months down the road, he tried to get together. I went back and forth with him a couple of times throughout the year. But the fact remained that we both knew each other's M.O. He wanted someone to take care of him and I just wanted his sex. No check or checkmate; we'd have to call this one a draw.

Chapter Fifteen

BATHHOUSES—A SEX ADDICT'S CRACK HOUSE

An animalistic nature overtakes my being
Enabling the seduction of your emotional, physical, and
mental essence;
As I manipulate, penetrate, and obliterate with complete
disregard.
– The Beast, A.D.

YOU'VE PROBABLY HEARD the saying, "Never take a crackhead to a crack house." Well, the same could be said about taking a sex addict to a bathhouse. Once inside, they won't want to leave and they'll keep coming back to get a bigger and better "fix" than the one they had before. The more they feed the addiction, the worse it truly becomes. And before they know it, things have spiraled out of control. The reason I know is because it happened to me.

THE VERY FIRST TIME

IT'S AMAZING HOW addictions can escalate exponentially. Something as small as going out to a club (which becomes a trigger) multiplies and the next thing you know, you're strung out on that drug called sex. I'll never forget the first time I went to a bathhouse. I hadn't planned on going. To be honest, I never really knew about them, much less where they were located. But all that changed in a matter of a few hours.

It was during the summer of 2003 on a Friday or Saturday night when I went to South Beach, one of Houston's most popular nightclubs for lesbian, gay, bisexual, transgender and sexually curious "straight" individuals. South Beach was located in Montrose, a neighborhood equivalent to West Hollywood in Los Angeles or the Castro District in San Francisco.

Once inside, I did my normal walk-through to see who and what all was going on in the club. Unlike the clubs I normally frequented, South Beach played more house, techno, and trance music. The deejay was probably one of my least favorites, but then again I wasn't looking for sounds that night. After I found a nice spot to settle into, I noticed this couple "cruising" me. While I was used to people hitting on me individually, being "double-teamed" by two people in their version of a committed relationship was something totally new.

Being the sex addict I was and loving the attention I was getting from two people simultaneously, I decided to go along with it and see where it would take me. When I think back, I really must have been horny because these two were not the "eight and ups" I was used to dealing with. One was probably a six and the other was a six and a half, maybe a seven on a good day, or should I say a bad night. But when you're a sex addict, you're always looking for new sexual experiences—the "next level," so to speak— and I knew this was one I hadn't played.

Adding another layer of excitement to the game, I made eye contact with them both and decided to move locations to see if they would follow. I went into the bathroom and they made their way in as well. While I had absolutely no intention of doing anything in there (getting caught having sex in the bathroom was a quick way of landing yourself in jail), it let them know I was down for some potential action.

I walked back out of the restroom and the Top (the more masculine one) came up to me and asked my name. When I met strangers and didn't yet know what the extent of our interaction would be—anything from a one-night stand to something a bit more long-term—I would tell them my name was "D." He told me his name, which I forgot as soon as he said it, and mentioned that he and his boyfriend thought I was extremely attractive and wanted to get to know me. As soon as the boyfriend saw I was taking time to converse, he approached me and said, "How's it going?" while looking me up and down.

By this time, I knew I had these two exactly where I wanted: ready to compete to see which one would get to suck the cum out of my dick and swallow. Yes, it's brash, but that's what my mindset was then. Still, I didn't want them to think it would be that easy to get a taste. So I made sure my conversation was short, not too abrasive, and somewhat alluring. I left them and made my way through the club again to guarantee I hadn't missed anyone else who might grab my attention. The thought of having sex with this couple kept creeping into my mind.

In less than thirty minutes I was back in their line of sight. I gave the Bottom (the more feminine one) a slight head nod and he came scurrying over like a bitch in heat. He told me he would love for me to fuck him while his lover watched.

"Is that right," I said nonchalantly. It was important to maintain the impression that this type of thing didn't faze me. The key was to always remain in total control. Sex fiends loved it and there was no doubt in my mind these two were indeed sexually uninhibited.

The Top quickly made the trek over to us and suggested we get out of there and go somewhere we could set things off. As we made our way through the packed dance floor to the front door, my adrenaline was pumping, my heart racing. And my only thought was: how fast was I going to make each of them come? Once we got outside the club, we arranged to get our cars and meet up in front of the club, at which time I would follow them to the next destination.

Looking back on this incident, it startles me to fathom how out of touch with reality I had become. They could have been leading me to an undisclosed location where I could have been robbed or even killed. No one would ever have known because at this time I never let any of my friends know I was going out to these clubs. But I was so entranced with the idea of quenching my sexual thirst that I was willing to follow them anywhere. I figured that if the situation came to a point where I needed to defend myself, I was strong enough to take them both. Still, I was no match for a bullet.

I followed them for less than ten minutes to a parking lot in Midtown. We parked, crossed the street and went into the bathhouse. As we did, my adrenaline kept pumping but it wasn't because of excitement anymore—it was pumping because of anxiety. There was no telling what could happen and what was waiting inside.

We entered what seemed to be a holding room. There was a locked door to the right side and in front of us was a thick bulletproof partition made of glass or plastic with a desk attendant behind it who wanted to see some form of identification. The couple showed their IDs and the attendant pulled out their records from the file. Since they had been there before, they had already signed the necessary paperwork for entrance. I, on the other hand, had to take time to fill out the card, which asked more information than I really wanted to disclose: name, address, etc. Since I was required to give my driver's license as a primary form of identification, the information had to be accurate. I noticed the camera behind the partition was facing directly toward us. I tried to keep my head lowered to avoid having my face clearly visible. The absolute last thing in the world I wanted was to be on tape at a bathhouse.

After I had the paperwork and identification requirements taken care of, it was time to pay. You could purchase a one-time pass, which included a locker and towel, or you could get a room for a certain number of hours or the entire night. I'm not exactly sure how the room pricing went because I wasn't paying, but it did include a towel as well. The couple had agreed to pay my way beforehand so I waited for them to decide. They decided to pay for a room and a one-time pass for me. Whatever the total amount was, they ended up being short a couple of dollars, so I handed them a five and got back the change, and then the attendant buzzed us in.

We strolled past a workout area, which had an aggregate of outdated exercise equipment and free weights. The establishment had the word "Spa" in its name, so I assumed the gym was part of the cover-up for being a health facility. In addition to the less than extravagant fitness area, there were lockers and restrooms on the first floor. The lockers were numbered and the keys given at the desk had a number which matched the corresponding locker. In an effort to prevent patrons from losing the keys while they were getting their groove on, a bracelet was attached.

There were other people in the locker area, some coming and others going. As soon as I walked in, they started flirting. "Are you just getting here? I was about to leave but I'll stay," someone said. I didn't want to be rude so I just smiled, but I didn't give his comment a second thought. I didn't have to worry, though; the Top quickly spoke up and said, "He's with us!"

Still somewhat nervous, yet excited about the two asses I was about to hit, I found my locker and began to undress. You would have thought Klymaxx's "The Men All Pause" was playing when I took off my shirt. Everybody started staring. The Bottom looked at me and gave that, "ooh, this is going to be so good" gaze. Since I was getting all this attention from just taking my shirt off, I quickly took my shoes and pants off and put my towel around my waist to keep all the dick watchers from getting too much of a view.

One definite positive about the place: there were tons of free condoms downstairs. Barefoot and in nothing but a towel, I followed them up the stairs where the rooms were located. I was bombarded by several guys passing by, giving me flirtatious stares as they tried to get me to hook up with them. Not knowing what lay ahead, I stayed close to the couple. At the top of the stairs, I noticed a large room with a big projector screen in the corner, playing porn. In the hallway, the private rooms appeared to form a maze. Initially, it seemed like there were endless pathways and hallways in every direction, making it easy to get lost and discombobulated. Plus, the music seemed conducive to lulling you into a trance-like state.

Unlike the downstairs areas, this floor wasn't lit well at all. The majority of the light was generated from the individual rooms' crevices and openings. Passing by a room where the door was slightly ajar, I quickly figured out that the only light was coming from the porn videos playing in the rooms. I also noticed there was a guy lying face down, ass up, on a bed in the room. As we passed other rooms with their doors shut, I could hear banging and the moaning and groaning of people getting fucked. Some were even yelling, "Fuck me! Fuck me! Fuck me harder!" There was something about hearing a grown man begging in a deep voice to be penetrated—the more I heard, the more I became aroused. My heartbeat was racing: it was like I had entered the devil's playhouse and could now act out all the illicit sex my mind could conjure up.

After we had passed what seemed like a countless number of rooms and turned down a couple of intertwining hallways, we arrived at the assigned quarter. As the key turned and door unlocked, I knew it was show time! You hear how entertainers turn into different people once they hit the stage. Once that door shut, I morphed from A.D. to "D," an uninhibited Beast who didn't play when it came to blowing out a person's back and brains during sex. Unlike A.D., the Beast wasn't concerned about a person's feelings, spirituality or all the other characteristics that made him a child of God. The Beast was the addict at his pinnacle.

Some might explain it as an out-of-body experience, but for me it was an out-of-mind experience. It was as if my mind had been possessed by someone else whose sole purpose was to make these people come to a point, both literally and figuratively, where they lost total control of their mind, body and soul. Unlike some sex addicts who just want to fuck a person, nut and move on, my obsession centered on making the other person reach new heights of orgasm and beg for more. And that's exactly what happened that night.

I placed my key on the nightstand as the Top broke out the condoms and flipped through the channels and found a good station to watch on the TV, which was perched above the bed next to the door. He made his way to the bed and positioned himself behind the Bottom, who had assumed the traditional position of placing his feet under him while balancing on his knees. As the Top aggressively penetrated him, he reached over to me and started caressing my arms and chest. I kept one eye on them and the other on the screen because the people in the video were more like the eight and ups I was accustomed to. In an effort to get the Beast aroused to the state where he could perform at his maximum, I needed to mentally place myself in the porn film with those actors. This sounds both conceited and vain, but it was the reason why the couple had propositioned me in the first place. They were looking for a fantasy and for me to give it to them I had to take on that persona.

While the Top was working it out, the other partner was eagerly anticipating the moment when I would enter him. I could tell he was one of those bottoms who liked it rough, so I would have to really be physical with him. As the break came in the back-and-forth motion between them, I hurriedly put on a condom and worked my way inside. The Bottom was thoroughly enjoying it, as I forcefully grabbed his ass and rammed my throbbing penis inside him, not caring if he needed any additional lube.

"Yes! Yes!" he moaned. His partner stared in amazement as I moved with a rhythm that mimicked a trained porno star. Within minutes, the Bottom's body started twitching involuntarily and as he let out one final moan, he shot his load to the other end of the bed. The look on his face was one of true ecstasy.

The other partner, obviously not wanting to miss out on what he had just witnessed, assumed the same position as I changed condoms. His anus was tight, so I wasn't able to just shove myself inside. I had to get some lube and patiently work my way in. Once I was inside, he made a petition for me to take it easy, but I wanted to make sure he felt the exact same thing his lover had. It became quite obvious, though, he couldn't take it like the other one could, so I eased up a bit, but not to a point where he felt totally comfortable. He needed to know I was definitely back there.

His partner began kissing and caressing my back and arms. Feeling somewhat jealous, the Top grabbed him and repositioned him so he could get his dick inside. I'm on one end fucking the Top and the Bottom is on the other end, getting fucked. I loved it. The next thing I knew, both of them came, and I was watching the TV, wishing I was banging the guys on the screen instead of these two.

When the Top went to the shower area to rinse off, the Bottom was going on and on about how good the sex was. He even wrote his number down on a scrap of paper.

"Isn't that your lover?" I asked.

"Yeah, but anytime you want to do something, I'm available," he responded. I took the number even though I had no intention of calling. His partner came back and the Bottom went to shower. Before the door could close, the Top asked for my number. I asked him the exact same question and his answer was just as callous.

"We're together, but I wouldn't mind getting with you!" Not wanting to break up an already unhappy home, I quickly gathered my things and made my way to the shower without giving my number.

As I was showering, a handsome, well-built guy walked in. I said hello and tried to see if I could feel him out, but he promptly nodded and left. I immediately began wondering what other types of men I could find there. I was still horny, hard, and I hadn't come yet. I dried off and then went to explore. There were several people pacing the hallways, trying to find someone to hook up with. Wanting to get a true assessment of all my options, I initially passed by some of the people I was interested in. It also gave me a chance to get a better grasp of the floor's layout.

There were a couple of rooms set up for group sex located throughout the floor. One room was totally dark and had no door. There were people in there I couldn't see, but I could definitely hear what they were doing. I could hear glutes slapping against pelvises, interspersed with moaning and groaning. As soon as I walked in, hands reached out to touch and grab my whole body, and I got out of there as quickly as I could.

Even though I was driven by an addict's need for sex, I was very uncomfortable with the idea of being the "bottom," the one who gets fucked. For me, that was a very vulnerable state and when I was acting out the role of the Beast, I needed to feel all-powerful.

Another spot located on the opposite end was dimly lit, yet there was enough light for me to make out a person's face standing near me. In this area there was a raised platform with a separate room that had a swing. Needless to say, all kinds of sex acts were going on in there. The fact the space was so open and well-lit made it less attractive for me because I didn't want spectators to see my face.

As I walked the hallways, I started to snap back to reality and realized I might need to make my exit soon. I passed up the couple I had come with and they tried to get me to come back for another round, but I politely declined. The dilemma I still faced was that I had not come yet. So I started to look for another person I could hit quick and get out.

But it was not to be. As it got later and later, the more attractive people had already started leaving. With nothing left but fives and under, I had to make an executive decision to leave without getting my nut. It was a hard decision, but I wasn't about to lower my value by having sex with someone I didn't find remotely attractive. If I got a reputation for having sex with less than a "certain caliber" of people, I would be ostracized from local celebrity sex status. Although only a few people in the gay community knew with whom and where I had sex, rumors proliferated like an epidemic. So I had to make sure I personified the reputation I wanted to create.

I made my way back downstairs to the locker room to put on my clothes and retrieve my personal belongings. When I looked at my cell phone I was flabbergasted at the amount of time that had passed. It was well into the next morning and as I crossed the street to get in my car, I could see that the sun was about to rise. While I had entered the bathhouse with nothing but anticipation of what sexual fantasies I'd be able to fulfill and experience, I left with a deeper level and another layer of sexual addiction I didn't know how I'd be able to get rid of. And as drug dealers say, "The first one's free, but the next one's going to cost you!"

I'm nowhere near an expert on the origin of bathhouses, but it appears they originated in Greece and transformed to our modern-day sex free-for-all here in America. Whoever established the remixed version must have been a sex addict. Only an addict would consider putting a bunch of horny testosterone-addled men together in one place. It was like a sanctuary for all sex addicts to convene and indulge in a most "unsacred" act. At that time, I might have tried to convince myself that I hadn't yet opened Pandora's Box, but after my first trip to the bathhouse, any illusion went out the window. I knew beyond a shadow of a doubt that the box had been ripped open and I was headed straight towards the center.

WHAT'S DONE IN THE DARK

I'D BECOME QUITE confident that my rendezvous at the bath-house and my undiagnosed sex addiction were solely my own little secret. What were the chances I would see anyone I knew? Ultimately, I became cocky and arrogant, like most sex addicts, and convinced myself that it was nothing more than harmless consensual sex among adults. No one would ever find out. But as they say, what's done in the dark will surely find its ugly way into the light.

One night I was feeling very restless, naughty and horny, so I decided to swing by the bathhouse. Each time I drove up to the parking lot, I would get that nervous feeling about going inside. Should I go in or should I go home? A mental battle would commence in my head. It was as if I had an angel inside telling me not to go in, but the devilish monkey on my back kept reminding me of the indescribable pleasure that awaited if I only crossed the street. At times I would tell myself, It's late, go home, because I knew if I went inside I'd be sacrificing several hours of sleep. On this particular night, my sex addiction had reached a point at which I was unable to resist the temptation.

Since this wasn't my first time at the rodeo, my information was already on file. All I had to do was show my driver's license and pay the locker fee. It's amazing how once the foundation is laid for feeding a sex addiction, it becomes easier to come back and get more. I quickly changed in the locker room and rushed upstairs. As I meandered my way through the halls, the last thing I expected to see was the first thing I saw: someone I knew.

At first, I thought, it can't be. But the more I stared, the clearer it became that I had come upon Bleu's cousin. The egotistical snob in me thought, what is that fat fuck doing in here? It's easy to be judgmental when you don't want people to be privy to your dirty laundry. Plus, he was one of those messy queens who, as soon as they find dirt on someone, they spread it like wildfire.

In a slight panic, I instinctively turned down another hall so he wouldn't see me. I tried to make a mental note of exactly where he was located, in an attempt to avoid crossing paths with him. But we ran into each other shortly after my initial sighting. I tried to save face, because I knew he was thinking, what is he doing in here? I played it cool, nodded my head and said, "What's up?" as I walked by. Coming to the bathhouse wasn't about finding someone willing to have sex with me. It was all about having uncommitted anonymous sex with as many attractive people as I could find. But for others, it was about finally having the opportunity to engage in sex, because the fact remained that they couldn't get anyone else outside of the bathhouse setting. The common denominator was that we were all looking for something or someone to make us feel better about ourselves and our current situation.

I was convinced that running into Bleu's cousin was just an isolated event and that there was no way I would see anyone else I knew. WRONG! Later that night, walking through the labyrinth looking for my next conquest, I saw the church's new organist. He was somewhat attractive with a slim build. There had to be some justification for me seeing two people I knew in one night. Or was God trying to tell me something?

Since I sang in the church choir, he immediately recognized me and smiled. When we reached a point where we were close enough to speak, he said, "You didn't see me in here."

"Don't worry," I responded.

Our paths crossed a few more times throughout the night. And while I could tell he wanted me to fuck him, I wasn't about to cross that line. Sometimes it makes a lot more sense not to engage in an experience. I couldn't imagine sitting in church watching him play the organ and knowing I had made him come. And he'd be looking at me wanting me to do it again. Just say no!

The next time I ran into Bleu, he informed me in his slightly chastising way that his cousin had seen me at the bathhouse. "What were you doing there?" he asked. I came up with some lame excuse and Bleu saw right through it. If

Bleu knew, then Jeri knew. How do you explain to a woman you want to marry someday that you visit bathhouses so you can fuck as many people as you want? Yet this was the same woman who had a bet with Bleu to see who could have sex with the most people in a single month. Luckily, Jeri didn't win the bet, nor did she address my bathhouse situation. I made sure to avoid that particular bathhouse in the future.

Chapter Sixteen
BOTH ENDS OF THE SPECTRUM

The insatiable lure of sex addiction
Has no predisposition when it comes to:
Age, gender, orientation, race or religion.
—*No Preferential Treatment, A.D.*

Birds of a feather flock together—nowhere is this saying more true than among sex addicts. Naturally, I surrounded myself with the best of them on both ends of the spectrum. I had two very close friends during the prime of my addiction: one who was more into women and the other who was more into men. They both could have had any man or woman they wanted, including me, at that time. And one actually did.

TROIS PREMIERE

It was August 2002 and I had recently moved back home to Houston from Atlanta. I attended the special screening of the movie Trois 2: Pandora's Box—there probably couldn't have been a more appropriate event to spot a fellow sex addict. The film was a sequel to Trois, and just like the prequel, Pandora's Box had its share of erotica and borderline porn scenes. Tyson Beckford was the poster boy for the movie. After the viewing, Rainforest Films sponsored an after party at Club 7, which was on the ground floor of a building where my singing manager rented an apartment. Monica Calhoun and a few of the other supporting cast members were flown in to promote, but Tyson was nowhere to be found. Luckily, there were plenty of female and male aspiring model types dancing to the blaring pop and hip-hop songs that evening.

Like a typical addict, I made my way around the room, checking to see who I knew and who I needed to get to know. Some of the women were pure natural beauties who wore minimal makeup, while others had piled on enough makeup for a week's worth of photo shoots. Since I was a face man, I started by checking out the faces, and then moved on to the more titillating mammary glands. No itty bitties for me. I didn't know how size conscious I was until a few of my homeboys informed me that I had never dated a girl below a "C" cup. The big jugs were out that night, which was not surprising given the industry execs in the room. But it was the legs that were really grabbing my attention. The skirts were sky high instead of thigh high, and it's hard to beat a pair of legs in stilettos that terminate into a beautifully sculpted gluteus maximus. I knew it was going to be a good night.

After making a few rounds and posting up near the bar, since I wasn't a drinker, I saw a being of pure perfection out of the corner of my eye. I have an internal radar detector for beauty and fineness and it was registering CODE RED. I did a complete body scan. Lightly brushed honey skin tone, check. Gorgeous face with hazel eyes, double check. Muscular build, check. Oh yeah, it was completely flawless. Notice I said "it." For me to have said "he" would have meant I saw him as a person. No, sex addicts have a tendency to view people as nothing more than objects and I was definitely guilty of that.

The club was dark so I couldn't get the full picture, but there was no denying the fineness, even from afar. If we had been in a more conducive setting, I would have immediately made my way over. But this wasn't that milieu so I kept my distance and tried to block the thought out of my mind. Besides, there were plenty of fine women in the room. If we were meant to meet each other, we would.

INTRODUCTIONS

MOVING BACK TO Houston from Atlanta turned out to be an unsettling transition. I was twenty-five and floundering, deep in the process of trying to find myself after my concerted attempt to make it in the music industry hadn't gone as planned. Any sense of structure and normalcy was a rarity, and this created quite a conundrum for an addict looking for an escape. One constant had been working out. After playing the workout partner merry-go-round for a few months, I finally started training with a guy I'll call Mr. Military. At the time, he was training for a bodybuilding show and had just begun teaching grade school after serving in the military. Since I had been using my chemistry degree to substitute teach while I pursued my music career, we clicked.

One afternoon I came into the gym and Mr. Military was warming up on the stationary bike, which was our normal pre-workout routine. Seated next to him was a guy in a light gray hooded jumpsuit. Mr. Military introduced us and I immediately recognized him from the Trois 2 movie premiere party.

He told me his name was Quinton McKnight, or Q for short, and I was immediately intrigued. I didn't want to come on like I wanted something from him, but at the same time, I wanted to make a connection. The addict in me desired a physical connection, but that need quickly waned once we talked. Much to my surprise, we made a genuine connection, and over the next few months we grew to be as close as brothers.

Since I wasn't looking for a long-term relationship during the deepest part of my addiction, I tried to avoid getting into them. It allowed me to do what I wanted, when I wanted and I didn't have to answer to anyone but myself. There was a group of people I would see regularly out at the alternative bars and they would constantly ask me why I wasn't with anyone.

"I just haven't found the right one," was my patent answer. They would go on about how I was too attractive and nice not to be with anyone. But what they didn't realize was that in the back of my mind was a desire to get married and have children, while in the forefront of my mind was the simple thought, I want to fuck the finest thing I can lay my eyes on. I was straddling the fence, which resulted in me being alone at times.

On the night I met Rico, I was feeling very horny and alone, so I decided to go to a bar and find a piece of ass for the night. At this stage in my addiction, I had learned all the ropes and knew exactly what to say and where to go to get anyone I wanted. It was all about perception and I had mastered the art.

Jeri Jones told me when I first started going out, "you are the shit and you can have any man you want." The scary thing was that I believed her and it gave me a level of confidence which couldn't be touched. The more masculine and street I looked, the easier it was for me to go in for the kill. Dressed in my ruff-neck gear—baggy pants, Timberland shirt and shoes—at Jeri's recommendation, I was determined to hook up with the finest thing in the place.

After making my initial scan, I made a counter-clockwise loop around the bar to check out who was in the place. If a person didn't have a model face and muscular physique, they didn't get a second look. It was all about business that night. I was ready to get down and dirty and I didn't have time to waste on anyone who wasn't able to get me instantly aroused. As I made my way through the building, I realized that things weren't looking too good. Nothing but average and less-than-average people. Then finally, when I made my way back to the front, sitting on a barstool at one of the small tables was the "10" I had been craving.

I knew I had found the one: short dark curly haircut, tightly fitted v-neck t-shirt that showed off his long muscular upper torso and large developed chest, and a pair of nicely fitted jeans, which conveniently hugged his subtle round ass and long muscular legs. Although he was taller and bigger than me, I wasn't about to let that deter me from reaching my goal. The way he was dressed led me to believe he liked dick, but his build led me to believe he might also like ass. I'd have to talk to him to get a better sense of his preference. So I slid into the open seat across from him and introduced myself. He said his name was Rico. I couldn't place his accent, but he later told me he was from a small country in South America; I had no clue where it was located. But I knew it wasn't in North America and I knew they'd produced one hell of a specimen.

We sat there playing the "are we going to fuck tonight?" game; he offered me a drink as he went up to the bar to get another one for himself. I declined and used the opportunity to check him out further. He was a few inches over six feet with a killer body, and I was ready to go the distance to get a taste of that ass. When he came back, he was ready to go to the next stage of the game, so he asked me if I wanted to go to Club 1415. It was a club right up the street, which wasn't open regularly, but when it was, the parties were amazing. I jumped up and said, "Let's go!"

He was parked closer to the bar than I was, so I drove around and followed him. When we got there, we quickly noticed the extended line outside the club, a sign that it was probably packed. We made our way to the entrance where both the person checking IDs and the one collecting the entrance fee began to flirt with the both of us. Rico's nonchalant response let me know he was used to being hit on, but he remained focused on getting to know me.

Inside was a slightly different crowd than I was accustomed to, so I quickly took note of the ethnic diversity but stayed focused on the task at hand—getting into his pants! On the patio we talked a little more and it became obvious that each was ready to see what the other had to offer physically. Given the amount of alcohol he had consumed, he needed to go to the bathroom. I followed, both out of necessity and also because I wanted to see what he was working with. Taking turns using the restroom in the same stall was such a turn on.

All I could focus on were his large muscular legs and tight ass in those jeans, and yes, the package was right.

Enough foreplay, it was time to take it to his house and seal the deal. On our way out, I ran into my friend, Shawn Long. Normally, I would have taken time to really talk to him and find out how things were going. But I was on a mission and didn't want to miss the opportunity I had been waiting for all night. I quickly introduced the two and let Shawn know I would call him later.

Rico lived nearby and as soon as we hit the door, it was on. We were already near the pinnacle of sexual arousal, so we went straight to his bedroom, broke out the condoms, and got to work. The sex was remarkable and this was the first and only time I had ever fucked someone who wore a cock ring. When I saw it, I knew I was working with a freak —a person who was sexually uninhibited.

The next morning we got up and took a shower together and that's when I realized how mesmerizing his body truly was. I discovered that he was one of his country's premier athletes and had come to the States on an athletic scholarship. But he had also managed to get an accounting degree. Some of the best sex addicts I know are also some of the most intelligent people. They'll never let on that they have an addiction, yet in the prime of an addictive cycle they're accomplishing professional goals others could only dream about.

It was rare to find brains and beauty in one person, so I ended up falling into lust with Rico and had to find a way to make sure our liaison was not just a one-night stand. My inner sex addict had finally met its match, and I was determined to see where this relationship would lead. At the same time, taking time to invest in a real relationship with a man went against all of my moral and spiritual upbringing.

JUXTAPOSING THE ADDICTS

WHILE I WAS in the midst of forming a purely sexual bond with Rico, Q and I were forming both a brotherly and a spiritual bond. Q and I did everything together, whether it was working out, going to the club, or delivering furniture for his stepdad's business to get extra money; that is, we did everything except sleeping with guys. I hadn't told him about that part of my life. It got to the point where he had a key to my car and I had a key to his apartment and truck. He would introduce people to me as his brother, which was exactly how I felt. My close friends would ask all the time if we were fucking. I kept explaining that our relationship had become what I had been missing once all my boys from Grinnell College had left.

As close as we were, I slowly became aware of traits most people would never be privy to unless they truly knew Q. He was an undercover sex addict. The porn collection he kept at his apartment was quite substantial. One afternoon, an older neighbor of his who was moving stopped by and added an entire box to the collection. This was one of my first clues I had a fellow sex addict on my hands. Another clue: almost every time we went clubbing he ended up with a new girl to have sex with. I can't fault him for being attractive and having women constantly swooning over him, but sealing the deal with a different one each night was a sign of a true sex addict.

But what amazed me most about Q was his ability to pray. I had grown up in the church, and my grandfather was a Baptist minister, so I had heard tons of people sing, preach and pray. Every now and then I would hear someone pray and I could feel the Holy Spirit in the place.

I'll never forget when Q prayed for my mom during one of her many leg infections. He started off with "Father God," and went to church. The prayer was so sincere and heartfelt, both my mom and I were almost moved to tears. There was no denying Q was given the gift of prayer. Eventually, though, his gift was overshadowed as he gravitated toward his sex addiction.

I was clubbing with Q on one side of the spectrum, and visiting the bathhouses with Rico on the other. After our first few sexual rendezvous, it was obvious that the two of us weren't going to be able to maintain just a sexual relationship. We were two sex addicts who liked to be in control. But we always had a good time when we hung out, so I thought maybe we could be friends. Becoming true friends with a sex addict after you've initially been intimate is extremely rare. The relationship was based on sex. After the sex is done, what's left?

When I compared Q and Rico, besides being sex addicts, they were polar opposites. If someone were to look at these two people on paper, it would have been impossible to determine which one was the sex addict. Rico was well-educated, had a bachelor's degree, and was working on his master's. Q was street educated and a bit of a hustler. Q didn't have any children (at the time), while Rico had a daughter who lived with her mother in Georgia. Rico was also financially stable. As he was working his way up the corporate ladder, he was saving his money for a down payment on a house, which he ultimately purchased. Q, on the other hand, was moving from job to job. I can't count the number of jobs he had been through since we met. Yet Q had a close relationship with God, a common thread among all of my friends, except Rico, whose faith in God was questionable at best. I tried multiple times to get him to go to church, but he would always make an excuse or say he could have church at his house.

While I was unsuccessful in getting him to the Lord's house, he was quite successful in getting me into the devil's house. One night, we were hanging out on The Strip and he suggested we go to the bathhouse in midtown. Everything in my being was telling me not to go, but R. Kelly's song was playing in my brain: "My mind's telling me no, but my body, my body's telling me yeah." So I gave in and went. Once inside, we played a game to see who could fuck the most attractive people. His taste was similar to mine, so if a person wasn't attractive, nothing was going down. But we had turned up there on an off night. The pickings were quite slim and I'm not sure if I even had sex that night. I should have followed my first thought and I would have been able to avoid wasting so much time.

SECRETS

SPEAKING OF WASTING time, Q was religious about clubbing. If it was up to him, we would have gone out every night. It got to the point that if I went out to a party without him, everybody would ask, "Where is your brother?" Because of his looks, almost everybody knew him. I had to be careful that we didn't run into guys I had seen at some of the alternative clubs, especially the unattractive ones. I had been able to maintain one image in the alternative scene and a mutually exclusive image in the straight scene, and it took a lot of work. Several unattractive openly gay men lived to "out" attractive undercover men because we wouldn't give them the time of day.

There was a guy I'll call Mr. Gossip, who was about five or six years older than me and who worked out at the gym where Q and I trained. He had a nice muscular build, but I hadn't really noticed him before because he wasn't my type. One night I went to a bar close to The Strip and it happened to be a night when the club's male strippers were performing. Mr. Gossip walked up to me and said, "You're Quinton McKnight's brother." I hadn't known that he was playing on both sides of the fence and the fact that he approached me and used Q's full name shocked the shit out of me. One word came to mind: BUSTED! Right then and there, I had to figure out how I was going to handle him, because I hadn't told Q everything about me yet.

I responded cautiously. "Yes."

"Does he know about you?" was his next question.

"I haven't told him yet," I said. We ended up getting into a conversation, one way longer than I wanted, but I had to make sure he wasn't going to run back to Q before I could discuss this sensitive topic. The best way for me to neutralize the situation was to determine what, if anything, Mr. Gossip had to lose by me knowing his secret. Apparently, Mr. Gossip was, like me, playing both sides, and he didn't want everyone to know his business. During the conversation, he mentioned that he was in real estate development, which I was concentrating in for my Master's at Rice University, and he gave me his business card. But I saw right through that. He wanted to fuck, which was never going to happen.

After that night, I started seeing Mr. Gossip out more and more and I still hadn't told Q about my other sexual escapades. I hadn't told him because I knew that Q could become extremely violent in an instant; I had seen him inflict physical pain and it wasn't a pretty sight. Because he was so attractive, he had to fight a lot because other guys were jealous of him. He had learned that it was either fight or flight, and he chose to fight and win. My biggest fear was that someone I had slept with or someone who knew I also slept with men would come up and say something in front of Q. There was no doubt in my mind that he would have knocked the shit out of them because he would have assumed they were lying on me. Like a true brother, Q was very protective of me.

To prevent that from happening, I finally decided to tell him. Finding the words to tell someone who loves you and you love that you sleep around with the same sex is extremely difficult. My first thought was, if I tell him will he stop being my friend? Next and worst of all: Did he think I had gotten close to him because I wanted to sleep with him? These were two of my worst fears, but I've always found when my intentions are honest, the truth sets me free. So I finally decided to man up and tell him that I had been sexual with men. He took it well and told me that when he was taking some pictures for modeling, one of the photographers had tried to come on to him and he had to set him straight. It was a relief that my secret was finally out and that I didn't have to hide anything from Q anymore.

VIDEO STORE HOOK-UPS

WHEN I RETURNED to Houston, finding an adult video store was as easy as finding your local Walgreens—they were on almost every corner. With names like 24 Hour DVD Rentals, Smoke Shops, and Adult Video Store, they stuck out throughout the city like a woman's nipples on a cold Iowa day. Still, the ultimate challenge was finding the right content. For me to find my favorite types of porn—group sex between guys and girls and orgies—I had to go to the spots that had more of an "alternative" selection. Where better to get that type of selection than your neighborhood gay video store?

Q-Video was located right behind Club 1415, where Rico and I had hung out the first night we met. There was a two-panel swinging chain link fence on the street, which allowed access. Parking was in between the video store and the club, which obstructed the view of customers going in and out. This was great for me since privacy was my primary aim whenever I was doing something I wasn't proud of. But all that privacy went out the window when you rented a video: Q-Video required a driver's license for rentals. The cost of buying one of those videos was five times the amount of renting one. Plus, I quickly learned that after I had watched a video once or twice, I was ready for something new. The lustful nature of porn keeps its fans always wanting more, which fed right into my sex addiction.

It wasn't uncommon to see people hooking up at adult video stores. There was a 24-hour video store a block down from LaStrada on Westheimer, which had viewing rooms, in addition to selling and renting porn. There was ample parking and whenever I saw several cars parked in the front and on the side street I knew someone was probably fucking inside. This spot was so hot that men, women, and transvestites hung around at night waiting to pick up clients.

There was definitely too much action going on at that video store, so when I chose to rent porn, I would go back to Q-Video. But that didn't mean I would be able to avoid people trying to hook up with me. I guess people automatically assume that if you're in an adult video store, you want to hook up. While sex was definitely on my mind at the time, my standards were so high that most people didn't meet them.

At times, I would go through a cycle where I would rent two videos back to back. Whenever that occurred, the cashiers on duty would immediately take notice. After turning in the first rental, I started browsing the orgy collection again to find another flick. While thumbing through several of the binders, I noticed the cashier was staring at me, but I didn't think anything about it. Finally, I found the one I wanted and approached the checkout counter. As usual, I had to show my ID. When he returned it to me, he started flirting.

I put out my hand for my change, and he put it in my hand, and then stroked my palm with his middle finger. In total, it was probably less than two seconds, but I found it quite strange. With the rental in one hand and my change in the other, I gave him a smile, said "thank you," and left.

I was familiar with the different looks people would give to let you know they were interested, but this hand thing had me bothered. Since Rico was a regular at the video store, I thought I'd give him a call to tell him what happened.

"Oh boy, he wanted you to fuck him," Rico explained.

Still puzzled, I said, "What do you mean?"

Rico educated me to the fact that if someone intends to convey their desire to have sex with you in a discreet way, they'll rub their middle finger in your palm. It was definitely discreet, because I had no earthly idea what it meant.

BIENVENIDO A MIAMI

IN BETWEEN THE summer of my first and second year of business school, I decided to go on vacation to Miami with Quinton for the Fourth of July, 2004. Being part Creole and part Trinidadian with hazel eyes and a body builder physique, he was the ultimate chick magnet. Although neither of us had been to Miami before, we knew it would be filled with beautiful women. Stepping off the plane, we could feel that this place had a different vibe from any other city we had been to before. There was something in the air, and it was the smell of sexy bodies. Once we got settled, we found out that several beautiful people from New York usually came down each year for the Fourth.

And beautiful they were. I don't think I've ever been to a destination in my entire life, whether nationally or internationally, with so many breathtakingly gorgeous women and men in one place. I mean, these women could easily have been featured in Sports Illustrated.

The guys were just as cover-worthy as the ladies. Men's Fitness could easily have done a photo shoot on the beach that weekend. A handsome face, slightly toasted skin, a well-defined six-pack, and bulging biceps equals winner in my playbook.

We went to Bayside Marketplace, an indoor-outdoor mall, on the Fourth, and I literally stood in one spot and did a slow 360-degree turn and saw someone stunning at every single angle. With the diverse Latin culture prevalent throughout the city, plus the added Afro-Cuban influence, these were probably the most beautiful people in the world. And the best thing about it was that with our exotic features we fit right in.

Now with all this fineness in one location, you know there had to be some great sex going on somewhere. While I hate quoting the Bible for purposes other than building God's kingdom, the verse "Seek and ye shall find" sums it up perfectly. In Miami, though, we didn't have to seek. It just came rushing up to us. As we were walking down Ocean Drive in South Beach, I would have sworn there was a billboard above Quinton's head with an arrow pointing that said "Touch my chest." Girls were coming out of nowhere just feeling him up. I didn't mind one bit because he introduced me as his brother and the next thing I knew, they were squeezing my biceps.

The freakiness didn't just stop on the street, it extended onto the beach. I was chilling in the ocean, enjoying the water, and I turned around and saw this girl running through the water. She just happened to be topless with two guys and another girl next to her. If the residents were this free out in the open during the day, I could only imagine what they would do behind closed doors.

We stopped in a delicatessen shop for lunch and while we were looking over the menu, I noticed a flyer on the ground with a gorgeous half-naked Latin man on it. Upon closer inspection, I realized that the flyer was for a bathhouse. Not wanting to be obvious, I knelt down to tie my shoe and picked up the flyer, sliding it into the pocket of my swimming trunks.

At that time Quinton and I were very close. I mean, we were closer than all my boys at Grinnell. And there wasn't anything within reason I wouldn't do for him. While I had told him I had slept with guys, I had not disclosed my excursions to bathhouses in Houston. Some things are better left unsaid.

I had already decided to go to the bathhouse and once I made a decision, it was a done deal. If the people were as half as good-looking as the ones on the beach and on the flyer I would once again be in "sex heaven." But getting there wasn't going to be easy task. Since Quinton didn't know anything about my plans to go to the bathhouse, how would I find enough time to slip away when he was otherwise occupied?

The opportunity came that night while we were clubbing. We wanted to get into Club Bed, but we had to wait outside in line. The doormen were trying to get the line to start wrapping around, so they were only allowing women and guys they personally knew in. Quinton and I were both impatient people and our frustration level was rapidly mounting. Then a group of guys from the Upper East Coast made their way near us and started complaining about the wait. The bouncers could not have cared less, but a promoter from the neighboring club came up to them and said, "With the number of people in your group, I'll walk you right in if you buy our champagne package." Quinton quickly befriended the alpha male in the group and within a couple of seconds we were counting how much money each of us needed to pay to get in.

Once inside the club, a waitress escorted us to the VIP section with a bottle of champagne and glasses already set up. You would have thought we were up and coming stars the way everyone was fixated on us. A group of girls immediately descended on us. The music was jamming, we were having a good time and, best of all, Quinton was totally occupied. He had new friends just in case something jumped off, and a harem of women to keep him entertained. This was my prime opportunity to make my way to the bathhouse. Still, I had to give the appearance that I was there even when I wasn't. So I picked up my phone like it was ringing, pretended to be talking, and with the other hand I tapped Quinton on the shoulder and pointed towards the exit.

As soon as I got out the door, I rushed down the street. Since I had been planning to go to the bathhouse, but didn't know exactly when the opportunity would present itself, I had memorized the streets earlier that day as we drove. But I needed to confirm the exact directions based on my current locale, so I called the number on the flyer. The attendant said I was right up the street and that was music to my ears.

Keep in mind that I had started out on the crowded boulevards of South Beach and then descended to the secluded back streets and alleys. Again, anything could have happened. I could have easily been shot or killed and Quinton would have had no earthly idea where I was. But I wasn't about to let anything or anyone stop me from reaching my goal. This demonstrated the true extent of my addiction: it was escalating to pure insanity, and all logic and morality went straight out the window. Nothing was more important than getting the next high.

Unlike the bathhouse in Houston, which was in a freestanding commercial building with a "gym," this bathhouse was actually a former residential house. When I entered the front door, I received a warm greeting from the desk attendant. He said he didn't remember seeing me before and asked if this was my first time. I hesitantly told him yes. "Well, you picked a great night because we're pretty packed tonight," he explained.

If the place was packed, I knew it was going to be a good night. Since the building used to be a two-story house, the bedrooms had been converted to private fuck rooms for guests. Like the bathhouses in Houston, you could rent a room for a certain amount of time, which wasn't on my to-do list. My one goal that night was to stick as many fine people as I could and get back to the club without Quinton knowing where I had been.

Since my time was short, I had to quickly scout out the place and determine whom I would hit first. As I made my way through the house, I noticed a door leading to an outside patio. There was a Jacuzzi and a picnic table in this section. Immediately behind that was another outdoor area which was covered up. Apparently, these public places served as the designated group sex spots.

A few guys in the Jacuzzi were making out and there were other people sitting outside on the picnic bench talking. I made my way over to the back area, which was covered by a dimly lit canopy. This was the hot spot for the house. There were about five or six guys of various nationalities engaging in all kinds of sex acts. When I entered and walked past the draping, all eyes were on me. A short stocky Caucasian guy promptly spoke up and asked my name. Going straight into character, I told him,

"D." He went on to let me know that he was mine for the taking. I was still trying to get my bearings and see who else was in there; then I saw a medium built African-American guy who was fucking another guy look in my direction and give me a smile.

There was a whole lot going on and I needed to get things under control fast before I became the prey – I wasn't afraid of getting raped, but I couldn't be 100% certain. After this Latin guy propositioned me to knock his back out, I pointed towards the black guy and told the short stocky white guy who was still enamored, "I want him to fuck you before I do." This would give me an idea of what exactly Short and Stocky was willing to do, and how much work I would need to put in to let everybody know I was definitely the person who should be orchestrating this orgy. He happily obliged and I got to see firsthand how much dick he could really take.

Watching the first guy banging the shit out of him, I knew I was going to have to come hard or not at all. The competitive ego-driven part of me wouldn't let anyone out-fuck me that night. So I eagerly awaited my opportunity, and so did he. As soon as the first guy finished, I strapped up and watched as Short and Stocky bent over, spread wide and placed his hands on a box or something to brace himself. I went in like there was no tomorrow. Taking it like a true champ, he started uttering, "Fuck me, D. Fuck me like that. Yeah! Give me that dick." Having to watch my rhythm before I ended up climaxing before I wanted to, I eased up a bit, then went back full throttle.

The black guy, who had just fucked the guy I was banging, looked at me and said, "I like that ass." Ignoring his comment, I kept right on without missing a stroke. But he wanted to make sure I heard him, so he decided to place his hand on my ass, letting me know he wanted to fuck me. I immediately moved his hand to signal it wasn't happening. Around that time I became more aroused and so was the ass I was hitting. Within a few seconds his cum shot out and I pulled out to release mine. He told me I was one of the best fucks he'd had.

Now that I had experienced my first true orgy, I needed to get back to the club before Quinton started looking for me. I threw on my clothes and ran out. Before I could make it out the door, the desk attendant stopped me and handed me a pass to come back the following night for free. I thanked him and hurried back to the club. As I checked my phone, I realized that Q had called, so I knew I had to hurry.

I got back right at the time the club was letting out. "Where have you been?" were the first words out of his mouth. I told him I had been outside on the phone talking to Norma, a high school classmate. Quinton knew she could talk and it was a legitimate alibi. He was slightly inebriated and he went on to say he had been looking everywhere for me in the club. But I played it off and told him I had been outside and he must have missed me. Feeling somewhat guilty about lying, I let the thought quickly fade away as I focused back on the orgy I had just masterminded. At this point I was deep into another sex cycle and I had a pass to go back tomorrow and indulge some more.

The following night, my path to the bathhouse was much smoother. After we left one club where the rapper Fat Joe had dropped in unannounced, the deejay quickly threw on "Lean Back." Q found some chick he wanted to hook up with. This was our last night in the city, so I knew he would be occupied most of the night, if not the entire night. I dropped him off at her hotel and broke out the GPS to lead me straight to another helping of the intercourse that was so vividly emblazoned in my mind. Although parking in Miami wasn't as easy as it is in Houston, the bathhouse was located in a residential section, so it was rather convenient.

Strolling through the house, I realized there wasn't going to be the same level of action as the night before, based on sheer numbers alone—it was already past midnight and maybe a third of the clientele were currently there. But I wasn't about to leave without finding me a hot ass to get up in. The best place to find someone was going to be the patio. Everybody seemed to make their way out there at some point during the night.

While I was checking out the people in the area, I found a seat near the Jacuzzi and decided to settle in until the right person walked by. It was similar to watching the National Geographic Channel. I was like a lion waiting in the bushes ready to pounce on the next unsuspecting attractive prey. Suddenly, an emaciated-feminine short Latino guy approached me and started flirting. Now I don't have anything against feminine men, but they are typically not my type.

"Hey papi, what's your name?" he said.

"D," I said rudely.

"Oh, you're sexy, why don't we go somewhere?"

"Thanks but I'm waiting on someone."

But he wasn't about to let it go and he started laying it on thick, and my patience was growing shorter and shorter by the second. Looking at him again, something about his appearance just didn't look right, but I couldn't put my finger on it. It was quite eerie.

I was dismissive of his advances, and he finally got the message I was sending and left me alone. Relieved, I took a deep breath and went back to patiently waiting. So much wasted time for someone so impatient, but this was my last night in Miami and I was certain this would be another night of firsts. Then the emaciated guy was back, desperate and frustrated. He approached me one final time and said, "How much?"

I couldn't believe what he had said. "What?"

"How much do want me to pay you to fuck me? I'll pay whatever," he pleaded.

The thought of being paid to have sex with someone fed my attention-seeking ego to another level, but the idea of being a prostitute made me feel dirty, both spiritually and emotionally. Rule number one: never pay for sex. Never take money for sex—that was a rule I hadn't yet created because I had never been in that particular situation before. That inner voice inside would not let me entertain the thought for more than a second. "I don't do that," I said angrily, and walked away.

The manager must have seen the guy propositioning me because when I passed him, he said, "Be careful about making out with people in dark places. You never know what they have." Right away I knew what he was saying. That guy was HIV positive. To think that I could have had sex with him and ended up the very thing I abhorred: a statistic. Yet even in the midst of my sin God was able to let me know; not only did He save me, He gave me a second chance.

But that didn't serve as a warning to me to leave at that very moment: my addiction wouldn't let me go. So I ended up doing what I thought I'd never do: a pity fuck. The manager was attracted to me and I felt grateful that he had informed me about the other patron's health status, so I said I'd make his night. Only an addiction would drive me to bang a person I wasn't attracted to. While it did make his night, I felt almost as bad as if I had taken the money. Right then and there I made a promise never to do that again. And, thankfully by grace, I haven't.

Nine Inch Nails has a song titled "Closer." "I want to fuck you like an animal" is the song's most recognizable phrase. Several people assume that's the name of the song. Although it isn't, the phrase accurately describes what my sex addiction was doing to me and the people I engaged. Whenever I hear that beat drop, I immediately envision some of my many experiences at various bathhouses. The lyrics at the beginning so vividly describe what I was doing to countless people: "You let me violate you, you let me desecrate you. You let me penetrate you, you let me complicate you." On the other hand, the last line of the song, which was sung at one of their live concerts, "You get me closer to God," couldn't have been further from the truth. Each time I fucked those people "like an animal," I felt the farthest from God. Yet He hadn't moved. But I had.

GROUP SEX

RICO HAD BEEN telling me that a guy he knew wanted to experience a three-way and Rico thought I would be the perfect person to join them. I'll call him Mr. Ready. We headed to Mr. Ready's apartment and things started off a little weird.

Mr. Ready wasn't really my type: he had an average face with a toned but not truly muscular body. But Rico was definitely fit, so one out of two isn't bad when it comes to a threesome. All I had to do was focus on one while I was fucking the other. We sat down on the couch with Mr. Ready in the middle and I opened one of his coffee table books, one with a display of nudes. While thumbing through the book, I noticed Mr. Ready had unzipped Rico's fly and was giving him some oral pleasure. Mr. Ready was wearing some tight jeans and I enjoyed the view of his nice round ass staring back at me. One thing led to another and we all headed for his bedroom.

After Rico and I took turns trying to see who was going to fuck Mr. Ready the best, we called it a draw and Rico hit the shower. While he was cleaning up, Mr. Ready didn't waste any time letting me know how much he had enjoyed our session. He went on to say how he loved my body. I appreciated the flattery, but in the back of my mind I was thinking, I hope he doesn't think this is going to happen again. A couple of weeks later, Rico called me up and said Mr. Ready had been asking when we might come back over. Since I wasn't interested in another repeat performance of that trite tryst, I made up an excuse.

Yet the experience of group sex was extremely enticing and I welcomed almost any opportunity in which I could engage in threesomes and other types of group sex. But then I encountered the most disrespectful form of group sex: a bunch of guys running a train on a woman at a bachelor party Q and I attended. A friend of ours, who is in a well-known fraternity, invited us to a suite on the Westside of Houston.

One room had a bunch of guys sitting around drinking and watching the game, while people kept coming in and out of the other room. After a quick peek inside, I realized that a guy was having sex with a girl and the others in the room were waiting in line for their turn.

I had heard about guys running a train on a woman, but to see it up close and in person was another thing. To say I was nervous would be an understatement. There were so many emotions running through me, I didn't know what to do. The God in me was saying, "This is wrong. You have more respect for women and you need to leave." But the sex addict in me was saying, "You've never done this before. Join the guys and be a 'real' man. You need to stay and play."

Needless to say, Q was all into it. His radiant smile let me know that this wasn't his first time at the rodeo. As I stood watching two guys on this one chick, it was like I was on the set of a porno having an out-of-body experience. These were some true heavyweights when it came to sex. One guy was pounding the shit out of her from the back while she was giving head to the other. After they shot their respective loads, she was on to the next ones. She took a brief reprieve to take a sip of her drink of choice, Crown Royal or some type of whiskey, and then she was back at it.

The longer I watched, the more nervous I became and my shakes started to get the best of me. Q, on the other hand, was anxiously awaiting his turn at bat. In addition to all the peer pressure, all I could think about was why this woman would allow herself to be used as a sex slave for what could be an unlimited amount of men she didn't know and had never met. Although the guys were using protection during penetration, any type of STD could have been transmitted during oral sex. All those thoughts kept flooding my mind and while I had definitely been in more risky sexual environments than this, the sheer volume of men on one woman didn't sit right with me. So when it was my turn, I froze up.

As she started to perform fellatio, I couldn't get erect. No matter what I tried, nothing seemed to work. I couldn't believe this was actually happening—me not being able to achieve an erection! I could always get it up when it came to women. But then again, when it came to women, it was always about some level of intimacy rather than just sex. I made love to women and fucked men. That was my unconscious and unstated rule. And trying to break it that night wasn't happening, no matter how much pressure I was under or how much embarrassment it might have caused. My mind, body and soul knew it was wrong.

With everyone in the room watching, after a couple of minutes of her still trying to get me aroused, I stopped her, got up and told her I just wasn't feeling it. The theory that sex first starts in the mind was clearly evident at this moment. Embarrassed, I walked into the other room like a little dog with his tail between his legs. No one said anything about me not being able to perform, but I knew they were thinking it. I don't know why, but it was as if I had to prove something. Maybe it came down to the fact that I had never pledged and wasn't a part of the fraternity. I ended up feeling so much guilt for participating I didn't know what to do. Instead of being a real man and saying that it was wrong and refusing to join in, I went into groupthink mode and only added fuel to the fire.

Between the three-way with Rico and the train at the bachelor party, I finally realized that sex addiction didn't have a preference and my life was getting out of control. But it wasn't like I could go tell anyone. What would I say? Hey, mom, dad, Jeri, I have a sex problem, and I need some help. That wasn't going to happen. I had to keep pretending because people thought of me as the perfect son and friend. Relatives and neighbors always complimented my parents on how successful I was. Yet I was living a double life in total misery with no "logical" way out—because I didn't know what was at the foundation of the addiction.

Chapter Seventeen
ONE MORE TRY

Mentally, physically and emotionally I'm being pulled
Back and forth, left and right;
And finally a momentary halt.
A halt but not the exit I so desperately seek.
—Disillusion, A.D.

EVEN THOUGH I had no clear way out, I decided that I could at least take a step back and evaluate what I was doing with my life and what I really wanted out of it. Fast forward a couple of years to 2006: I had finished grad school and decided I needed to give it one last chance with Jeri. It was either now or never because I couldn't go back to where I had been. The key was going to be getting Jeri away from Satin and every other potential influence to see if we actually could be a couple.

It took a lot of work, convincing, and money on my part but I needed a definitive answer or I would never be able to move forward. With a little help from her oldest sister, I got Jeri to go to Las Vegas with me on Martin Luther King weekend. Since Jeri was a coach, she always had to be at some tournament. Luckily, this holiday was celebrated on a Monday, so no games were scheduled. She agreed to go at the last minute, so I booked the flight and hotel and we were off.

Our schedules were totally opposite and we lived on opposite sides of town, so we rarely had a chance just to get together by ourselves. When we got to Vegas, we had an unforgettable time. It reminded me of when we were little kids and I'd run over to her house and stay all day and vice versa. Once we found out we could get free tickets for dinner, a show and $150 if we went on a tour, we were all over it. The salespeople just knew we were going to purchase a timeshare. After the third salesman failed to convince us to buy, he asked, "Well, what did you two come for?" In unison we replied, "The gifts!"

To this day, we still laugh about the timeshare experience. We took the money and tickets and thoroughly enjoyed ourselves in Vegas. While we were there, it was obvious that we worked well as a team and could be a great power couple. More importantly, this was a woman I would love for the rest of my life.

Yet one main ingredient was missing: sexual chemistry. While I had it for other women and she had it for other men, when it came to romance between us, it was non-existent. We spent two nights in a row in the same king-sized bed and nothing happened. The answer I needed to know but didn't want to accept had been delivered. As a matter of fact, the only intimacy between us happened when we got back on the plane to go home. Jeri leaned over, thanked me for a wonderful trip, and gave me a kiss on the cheek.

When we got back, Jeri's older sister told me, "I thought y'all were going to Vegas to get married!"

MRS. RIGHT NOW

FACED WITH THE reality that Jeri wasn't going to be the future Mrs. Burks, I started contemplating possibilities with a high school friend who let me know in every way imaginable that she would gladly step up to the plate. Norma Usher was the perfect wife on paper. She willingly put me first, was active in her church, loved kids, music and cooking, and was everything I would want my wife to be. And more importantly, she let me know she didn't care what man approached her, it was all about me. I had some very attractive friends and she didn't give them a second glance. On top of that, my mom loved her because they were two peas in a pod. What else could a man ask for?

Norma and I started unofficially dating. One of Jeri's sisters had a Super Bowl party and I decided to bring Norma along. Unlike the Independence Day episode with Miss Petite, Jeri already knew Norma so I didn't have to worry about her reaction. But something did happen, and it was something I couldn't have foreseen.

I brought Norma in and introduced her to everyone. After we had grabbed a bite to eat, Mr. Jones came over and gave me the green light. Several years had passed since the Miss Petite fiasco, and Mr. Jones knew how I felt about his daughter, so he was letting me know that Norma was a true keeper. He could see the amount of love she had for me. When I look back, I see now that he was trying to tell me to stop waiting for Jeri and be happy. But there are some lessons in life I just had to realize on my own.

While Mr. Jones had come to the conclusion I needed to move on, Jeri's grandmother hadn't. When I made my way over to the condiment station, Granny asked, "Baby, who's that girl? I thought you and Jeri were together."

"Granny, your granddaughter doesn't want me," I said sheepishly.

Then, in a voice loud enough for everyone to hear, Granny said, "Well, you didn't take this one to Las Vegas!!! Why'd you take Jeri if you didn't want to be with her?"

It happened so fast and without warning, I couldn't think of anything to say. Thankfully, Jeri's mother came over and diffused the situation while I quickly made my way to Jeri's two brothers-in-law for some reinforcement. I made it out without my ego too bruised and battered, but the reality was that Granny knew what we youngsters didn't: you can't fake who you truly love. And the reality was I wasn't in love with Norma, no matter how hard I tried to make myself believe that I was.

While sex was a no-go with Jeri, it turned out to be problematic with Norma, too. We were definitely intimate, but I knew once I had sex with someone, they usually became hooked and I knew that if I had full intercourse with her, she would never be able to move on. The last thing I wanted was for her to wait for me like my mom had for my dad or like I was waiting for Jeri.

So where did this leave me? I realized that if I kept up this addictive cycle, I would never be able to have the family I really wanted. Something had to change or I would never be able to experience true happiness, which was the one thing in the world I wanted. The problem was that I was going about it in the absolute wrong way.

Then I had THE DREAM.

Chapter Eighteen
THIS WAY OUT

The prodigal son, I had become;
Deliberately and defiantly veering off course.
Yet patiently You called me
Then I finally sought the One.
—The Answer, A.D

WHEN IT CAME down to navigating my way out of the cycle, I was utterly hopeless. On several occasions, I had promised myself that this was the last time. But it never failed: I'd soon be right back where I started. Sex addiction had become a way of life and I was a functioning sexaholic. Covering my tracks, avoiding complete disclosure, and putting on a good face among family and friends when I was hurting deep inside were just things I had to do. Yet when God spoke, I heard His voice and I had to listen.

A NEW WORLD ORDER

As I MENTIONED earlier, God spoke to me in a dream. I had awakened from that dream with a strong sense of the potential humiliation I could have brought on my mom: she had invested so much time, money and effort in raising me, and it scared me to think that she might have to endure ridicule for having a son who was a sex addict. I was so jarred by the dream and its aftermath that I had to meet with my pastor that same morning. During our meeting, he confirmed what I already knew: God was definitely speaking to me. Our conversation gave me a new confidence: if I wrote a book about my experiences, it could help countless people in similar circumstances.

Now that I had been given the message, the hardest part began: figuring out a way to get out of the addiction and move forward. Sex addiction had become my life: I had skillfully crafted an environment in which almost everything around me was set up to feed my addiction. Destruction of my contrived world might mean destruction of me. But I was able to look back on the times in which God had brought me through: I had had unprotected sex with both women and men without becoming HIV positive. Maybe I was in a place where I could start over and have a clean slate. I began to see that allowing things to continue in the way they had been was no longer an option.

Getting rid of my triggers—porn tapes and DVDs—was first on my to-do list. There was no way I would be able to get out of my addiction with access to porn at my fingertips. So the collection I had rebuilt had to be thrown away. Although it was only four or five DVDs and a couple of tapes, it only took a couple of minutes of viewing any one of them to get me ready to act out again.

Next, I had to make a conscious decision not to frequent The Strip. The bars and clubs were my scouting territories. If I didn't find a new piece of ass that piqued my interest, I was more than likely to run into an old piece that did. So I tried spending my weekends with friends or at the straight clubs instead. If I didn't make a concerted effort to plan ahead, I could easily fall into the habit of going back.

The hardest part of my plan was not attending house parties and gatherings thrown by people I knew. In my view, not showing up to an event I am personally invited to is rude. Those closest to me knew that if they personally invited me to an event I would make every effort to attend. Sadly, I had surrounded myself with people who hosted events that kept me in my addictive cycle. So what was I supposed to do? I couldn't exactly say, "Thanks for the invite, but I'm trying to get out of my sex addiction, so I'll be unable to attend." I usually ended up telling people I had plans or saying I'd do my best to make it but I was really busy right now.

While this plan seemed like a great idea, it really didn't work that well. Often it served only as a Band-Aid for a much deeper wound because I didn't yet understand the source of the addiction. I would get frustrated about not having a sexual release and I'd slip up. But the frequency and duration wasn't what it had been before the dream.

LABOR DAY 2009

BIANCA HARRIS AND Alice Roth were two of my closest friends from business school. We had spent so much time studying together we were like family. After business school we all stayed in touch and would occasionally get together when they had to travel back to Houston. Bianca had moved to Washington D.C. to work as a consultant and Alice had moved to Dallas to work at a non-profit.

Labor Day was coming up and someone suggested we all get together. They knew as soon as the suggestion was made, I was ready to purchase my ticket. For the past couple of Labor Days I had been going to New York for the U.S. Open Tennis Tournament, but I said I could make an exception to see my girls. Bianca's former college roommate had married a guy who had just finished his MBA from Rice, and they were going to drive down from New York. I wouldn't be the only man and we would have a house full of Rice University graduates.

The weekend was a blast. Bianca had events set up for each day. From visiting various restaurants to club outings, we were enjoying every moment. When it was time for the couple to head back to New York, we caravanned and stopped in Philly to see my boy Hector from Grinnell and his girlfriend.

Since we were in separate cars, Alice, Bianca and I were

able to talk freely about relationships. I had informed them of my addiction prior to the trip so they were concerned about how things were going. It was during this conversation that Bianca mentioned she had been going through counseling and suggested I might want to seek some as well.

Initially, I was set against it. "What can they tell me that I don't already know? Besides, my mom's a licensed professional counselor. I've seen her counsel countless people," I said dismissively.

"That's true, but she hasn't counseled you. And she doesn't specialize in sex addiction," Bianca replied. She went on to mention she had had some great success from her sessions just from looking at things in a different way.

Analyzing my situation from a different perspective was something I definitely needed to consider. The fact remained that I still didn't have the family I so desperately wanted. And although I had stopped having anonymous sex, I still had other addictive urges and had slowly rebuilt my porn collection.

In Philadelphia, Hector and his girl took us to one of the best Philly Steak shops and guided us through a tour of the Liberty Bell. It was so refreshing to see that he was doing well while working on his doctorate.

On the drive back to D.C. that evening, I carefully considered taking Bianca's advice about getting some help. It wasn't so much that I was afraid or that I was worried about the stigma associated with counseling. It was the possibility that it wouldn't work and I would have wasted all that time and money. Then again, I'd never know until I tried.

SEX THERAPY

Finding a qualified sex therapist wasn't like finding a regular counselor. Only counselors with a Certified Sex Addiction Therapists (CSAT) designation have been trained to handle patients with addictions related to sex. While most licensed counselors may believe they're qualified to treat sex addiction, that is not always the case. I'd learn later that even those with the certification aren't always proficient.

I worked at a Fortune 100 company which subsidizes mental health treatment, so there were few barriers in terms of cost. I did some research to determine who had the best qualifications. There was one therapist who was nationally acclaimed for sex addiction but female. I thought it might be better to find a man with similar credentials, since he might have a better idea of what I was experiencing.

Finally, I found a male therapist, Dr. Not the Right Fit, whose office was two blocks from my building. During the first couple of visits we were sort of feeling each other out. At the start I informed him that my mother was a licensed professional counselor so he could get a grasp of what he was dealing with. Since my mom and I are so close, I'd picked up on several of her psychology skills, frameworks and methodologies, which usually resulted in me being a good judge of intellect and character. I wasn't getting a great feeling, but I wanted to go into the sessions with an open mind. That was until he said, "I think you're bipolar."

Immediately, I thought this isn't going to work. I did at least try to entertain his line of thinking for a minute. So I responded by saying, "I don't have the vast mood swings associated with the disease, nor have I ever tried to kill myself."

Dr. Not the Right Fit went on to say that there was a range to the disorder and some people stayed on the high end predominantly. While I agreed there was a range, I didn't feel I landed anywhere on the continuum. But this was the first or second session, so I wanted to give him the benefit of the doubt. By the time we reached the tenth session and he had to provide a rationale for continuing my treatment, he said, "Well, I guess bipolar disorder isn't it."

At that moment, I knew this was going to be a long road and I understood why certain patients think counseling is useless. Nonetheless, I had seen the results of my mom's work and realized I might be able to get something out of it, but with Dr. Not the Right Fit I realized that I would have had to do a lot of his work for him.

Dr. Not the Right Fit used Dr. Patrick Carnes' books: *Facing the Shadow* and *Out of the Shadows* as my main resource for treatment. Dr. Carnes is considered the expert in the field of sex addiction. When Tiger Woods went through his ordeal, he was admitted to Dr. Carnes' treatment program.

The books were extremely helpful and I would recommend them to anyone dealing with sex addiction. In Chapter Three of *Facing the Shadow* there is a section which discusses courtship disorder and the ten types. Dr. Not the Right Fit noted that I would jump from Steps Three and Four (flirtation and demonstration) directly to Ten (intercourse). This was a major revelation for me to be able to see in print what I was acting out.

Another prominent part of my treatment required that I attend group meetings with fellow sex addicts. The meetings basically follow the same 12 Step Program established by Alcoholics Anonymous (AA). The meetings are designed to be a forum for sex addicts to openly discuss whatever they want without judgment. Typically, the meetings start with attendees collectively acknowledging that they have a sex addiction problem and then the floor is open for monologues. The topics of the monologues range from how a person acted out to how a person maintained their sobriety.

I found the meetings frustrating because no crosstalk was permitted. My frustration mounted when someone would deliver a story and I would feel as if I could offer certain solutions that might have helped them. After the meeting was over, we were more than welcome to discuss what people had said during the meeting, but by then there were too many stories to keep track of.

But the main reason why I chose to stop attending the meetings was because I felt as though I was being exposed to new ways of acting out. The meetings require that the information discussed in the meeting stay there, so I will honor that request and not give specifics. The problem was that I would hear of things I hadn't tried sexually and be tempted to act out. I made the decision that this line of therapy wasn't holistically beneficial to me and I needed to stop.

The opportunity presented itself when Dr. Not the Right Fit was planning a trip overseas. He informed me that he was going to Russia and would be gone for a couple of weeks. I knew this would be my perfect chance to end our sessions without having to deal with an unwanted line of questioning. So I told him that I would schedule an appointment when he got back.

Dr. Not the Right Fit called a few times after he returned and I would let it go to my voicemail. I finally called him back and told him I wanted to take a break.

THE FOUR-STEP PROCESS

WHILE I BELIEVE counseling can be extremely beneficial, it's not for everybody. For some people, the cost can be prohibitive, but it can also be detrimental if administered by unqualified "professionals." After my less than ideal experience, I strongly suggest addicts who are considering counseling find someone they have both faith and confidence in. It might take going to a few different therapists, but if your gut is telling you no, don't stay. Dr. Not the Right Fit might be a great counselor, but he was not for me.

Nevertheless, I was able to gain some valuable insight from him and for that I am grateful. After going to the sessions for six months, I spent some time reflecting and I realized that it was the following four steps which ultimately led to my initial breakthrough.

STEP ONE

REESTABLISHING MY PERSONAL relationship with God and growing closer to Him was paramount. If I did this, I knew everything else would fall into place because He, not my addiction, would be leading me.

Before I could get back to getting closer to God, I had to first make the decision that I had truly had enough and that I wanted to change. No one could make this choice for me— not my mom, my dad, my close friends, not even God. All sex addicts are given free will and until we make the decision that we are ready, willing, able, and committed to change, nothing will. Taking that first step is extremely difficult, because as humans, we are creatures of habit. I had been in the habit of going to clubs, video stores, bathhouses and bars looking for my next sex fling. But the time finally came when I had to say enough was enough.

STEP TWO

WANTING TO CHANGE was great and a step in the right direction, but Step Two required me to enter the phase that all sex addicts abhor: abstinence. We sex addicts believe that to forgo indulging in sex is a complete impossibility. Yet for the addictive cycle to be broken the main ingredient had to be removed until a new pathway for healthy sexual intimacy could be established.

Not having sex with anyone was brutal, but with abstinence comes a change of mindset. When I knew that having sex was no longer an option, I was able to once again commence the process of breaking the addiction. Plus, my stint in Atlanta, when I had gone a year and a half without having sex, had shown me the benefits. Abstinence meant I could not go down my long list of contacts I could turn to: "in case of emergency, break." I was forced to find another way to deal with problems. And the best way to handle them was to seek guidance from God.

STEP THREE

AFTER I MADE the decision to change and remain abstinent, I had to walk the walk, not just talk the talk. So Step Three involved a change in my typical environment. Unlike when I moved to Nashville and was forced to stop clubbing to keep my family from finding out my secret, this time I had a self-imposed restriction from going out and fulfilling my sexual desires. Instituting a STOP GAP into my stream of consciousness was extremely difficult.

How does a man who grew up as a spoiled only child tell himself NO? It goes against my nature and all laws of selfishness. But it had to be done if I was going to be able to get out. By placing myself in those tempting environments, I was bound to end up feeding the addiction. I had to remain committed to avoiding clubs and certain parties because I knew that once I was there, the cycle would begin again.

Changing my environment also meant distancing myself from certain people and leaving some of those I truly and deeply loved behind. This was probably the most challenging part for me; given that I am an only child, once I make a true connection with someone it's painful for me to turn my back on them. I've had friends do unjust things to me on more than one occasion, but I've allowed them back in my life because no one is perfect. If God had given me a second chance, then I had to do the same.

Yet this time it was different. God was calling me out of my addiction, and that meant that I had to let go of certain people indefinitely—or at least until I could get better control of myself. A friend like Rico is a good example: he's so entertaining, upfront and honest, but I knew that he could easily persuade me to go to places where I would end up breaking my vow of abstinence. For that reason, I had to draw a line in the sand and keep my distance. Friends and associates would call and say they hadn't seen me in a while. While everything in my body wanted to say, "Yeah, let's hang out," I knew I wasn't strong enough yet. So I'd be honest and explain to them I was trying to change my life.

That wasn't what they wanted to hear. For some, when I told them I wanted to stop clubbing and get on the path to my destiny, they thought I was saying I was better than they were. It didn't take long for the gossip they were spreading about me to get back. What was hurtful was the idea that my "friends" were spreading lies about me when all I was trying to do was become a better person. Everything happens for a reason and I was quickly able to see how genuine some of these "friends" really were. A true friend only wants what's best for you, even if it means they have to give you space or let you go.

STEP FOUR

WHEN ONE DOOR closes, another opens, and that's what led me to Step Four—establishing a supportive network. While it hurt to see people I loved and called friends spread such lies in regard to me trying to better myself, it made it easier to gravitate toward people who had my best interests at heart. Real friends like Sarah and Mitch were truly heaven sent. I could go to them about the struggles of trying to remain abstinent and during those times when the desire to give up was overwhelming, they wouldn't let it happen. Instead, they were always willing to lend an ear or deliver some encouraging word.

Of all the steps, Step Four is the most crucial and is often neglected when it comes to seeing a true breakthrough. I needed someone with whom I could have full disclosure and not have to worry about being judged or ridiculed. I needed someone I could be accountable to and call when I was thinking about going to rent a porn video. Someone who

would tell me, "You've come so far. Don't turn back now."
And I definitely needed a person during those times when
I felt absolutely alone. There aren't enough words I can say,
write, type or think to stress how important it was to establish
a supportive network of people I was able to trust.

ENTER THROUGH THE NARROW GATE

THESE FOUR STEPS enabled me to break my addictive sex
cycle: (1) making the decision that I wanted to change and
reestablishing my relationship with God, (2) taking a vow of
abstinence, (3) changing my environment, and (4) establishing
a supportive network. Of course, having a four-step process
might seem easy, but the reality is that there's absolutely nothing further from the truth. I didn't just wake up one day after
the dream or therapy and say, I'm going to do these four things
and I'll be fixed. It took years to get to the point where I am
now and I'm still moving forward.

The good news was that the sooner I proceeded in the
direction of heading out, the quicker I was able to get there.
Yes, I had setbacks. Yes, there were days I wanted to give up.
And yes, there were days I abandoned all four steps and did
what I knew I shouldn't have done. But the good thing was
that I had established a workable plan which enabled me to get
back up and move forward.

The reason I moved forward was because of my relationship
with God. This one relationship was instrumental in formulat-
ing my way out. I was blessed to have been raised by a family
who knew the benefits that came when a person allowed God to
lead his or her life. All of that was irrelevant until I went down
the road of seeking to know God for myself. By picking up the
Bible, studying alone and allowing Him to speak to me directly, I
was able to decipher how to get out of my sex addiction.

I gained strength from verses like Psalm 103:10: He has not
dealt with us according to our sins, nor punished us according

to our iniquities. This verse reminded me that no matter what all the naysayers in church or in the club were saying, I was forgiven of my past sins and I could find my way out of my addiction. Furthermore, who were they to judge me? As Luke 6:41 asks: Why do you look at the speck of sawdust in your brother's eye and pay no attention to the plank in your own eye?

For me, it was a monumental step forward to realize that people were going to talk both positively and negatively about my attempts to get control of addiction. I didn't have to place any significant value on that; instead of focusing on what others were saying I chose to meditate on what God was saying. Isaiah 30:21-22 says: Whether you turn to the right or to the left, your ears will hear a voice behind you, saying, "This is the way; walk in it." Then you will defile your idols overlaid with silver and your images covered with gold; you will throw them away like a menstrual cloth and say to them, "Away with you!" Instead of my idol being made of silver or gold, it took the form of lust in flesh and bone. But I had heard the Voice that scripture mentioned and I was yearning to say, "Away with you, addiction!"

By now you have probably noticed that I've tried to avoid using the words "free" or "freed" when discussing my sex addiction. That's intentional. Humans are preprogrammed with preferences and sometimes those preferences can result in addictions. For one person it might be alcohol, for another, drugs, and for me, sex. Whether those preferences change or not, what can definitely be altered is how you allow those preferences to affect you and how you react.

If I allow my sexual desires to consume me, I'll regress into my addiction. Conversely, if I stay focused on my plan and manage my responses, I'll progress toward my destiny. Thus I try to steer away from saying I'm "free" or have been "freed" from my addiction because I know that if I don't keep various situations in check, I could easily slip back, as some addicts do.

Chapter Nineteen
DON'T LOOK BACK

It's the past.
Leave it there,
Or it will never leave you.
—Moving Past the Past, A.D

Of all the things I've learned and experienced during the recovery process, the one thing I know for sure is this: looking back and reflecting on the fun and excitement I had during my addiction leads me right back to the place where I was addicted to sex.

COMPARATIVE SEX

Being a recovering sex addict is hard because so many images around us are focused on sex. These images solicit us to look back on some of the best sexual experiences we've had. My addict mind could easily recall every minute detail of some sexual encounters. And by doing that, I was setting myself up for failure.

I was heading to church one Sunday and Dr. Dana Carson, one of the local Houston ministers, was on the radio with a message titled "Crappy Relationships." He explained why so many relationships aren't working. One of the main reasons, in his opinion, was because we jump from one sexual relationship to another and start having comparative sex. I couldn't agree more.

I had created a Top Five list of the Best Sex and Lovemaking of All Time and when I would engage in sex with someone new, I would always subconsciously compare the new person to those on the list. This was dangerous on so many levels. I wasn't allowing myself the opportunity to enjoy the intimacy between myself and the new person, and I was keeping the sexual experiences in the past in the forefront of my mind. When the current experience didn't measure up to a previous level of sexual ecstasy, I would immediately move on to the next person. And if the present experience exceeded those earlier ones, I would obsess and do whatever it took to get another helping.

Often it was to my own detriment because that person had no emotional or spiritual attachment to me. Once a recovering addict can ascertain that sex is not just a physical act but a spiritual one, he will be able to stop having comparative sex. But like most things, that's easier said than done.

PAST PARTNERS

As soon as I made the decision to move in the opposite direction of my addiction, all sorts of people associated with my addiction started materializing in my life. I could be doing my regular workout at the same gym, and I'd run into someone.

For instance, one time as I was working out at my regular time, I saw one of the guys from the couple I had fucked at the bathhouse. Just like that, all of those thoughts and memories from the past started flooding my mind.

Then I ran into Mr. Six-Pack at the gym, the guy who had cleverly deceived me with a picture of his abs on the internet. I thought to myself, what is he doing here? He doesn't even live on this side of town. We spoke, caught up, and that was it. While I have no doubt that he would have loved for me to take him back to the new enclosed separate showers and give him some of the same stuff I'd given him on his desk back in the day, I wasn't about to give him any indication it was an option.

In addition to past sex partners popping up during my workout hour, I would run into booty calls I hadn't seen in years while out or at friends' birthday parties. I ran into a guy from my high school, after I had been committed to leaving the past behind. The fact that he was one of the people on my Top Five list made things quite difficult. As soon as I saw that cute smile gleaming across his face, all I could think about was how this dance company leader/choreographer knew how to work his ass both on the stage and in the bedroom. To make matters worse, it was he who had decided to end our relationship, not me. My ego wanted both revenge and some more of that beautiful ass, and the combination was too tempting to resist.

What I should have done was leave what had happened between us years ago in the past. But no, I had to remind him of what he had given up. I couldn't resist, and we were back in the sheets like it was yesterday.

While the sex was good, I had finally had enough and realized that I was just using him for sex. I wasn't ever going to be committed beyond my addiction, but it seemed that he was growing deeper emotional attachments. So I let things between us just fizzle out. Not because of the intensity of the sex, but because I knew I needed to move forward.

MOVING FORWARD

HERE IS THE long and short of it: basically, it all boiled down to how I chose to respond to the various situations which came my way. I could choose to act on them, realizing as soon as I did that I'd be back at square one. Or I could choose to refrain. For a person who hates wasting time as much as I do, just the idea of regressing instead of advancing was and is a great motivator. By making the conscious decision not to act on the temptation and to stay focused, I'd be further along in reaching my goals and true purpose in life.

Again, I have to refer back to a fundamental law of physics: two things cannot occupy the same space and time. So I'll never be able to receive the person God has for me as long as I'm looking back. That lingering gaze in the rearview mirror is what the devil uses to keep me from seeing what's right in front of me. More importantly, I end up missing what's passing me by, which is exactly what I need.

For me, there is one key way to avoid getting caught up with looking back: stick with the Four Steps. It's essential that I have a plan in place to deal with potential temptations, and that means I have to be honest with myself. I know what tempts me: watching porn, seeing people on my Top Five list, and running into past random fucks. But I have come too far to let my past hinder my future. It's mandatory to remind myself: Your sobriety won't last if you keep looking in the past.

I knew without a doubt that God had put me on this earth for a purpose, and it wasn't just to have sex. The longer I stayed focused on those sexual desires, the longer it would take me to reach my goals and fulfill my destiny.

During the process of focusing on this book, I had to press reset. That meant getting back to my original settings, back to the way I was uniquely designed. I needed to focus on what I really felt about life, not what my mom, dad, sister, brother, wife, cousin, uncle, aunt, husband, boss, neighbor, best friend, enemy, society, church, media, or any other person thought. I listed each of those to make you think and to remind all of us that there are so many outside influences in our lives. How can we really hear what God—who lives inside us—is saying?

The good news is that every day I'm alive is another opportunity to get it right. I keep reminding myself not to take life too seriously. Dealing with any addiction is truly a process. There are periods when I'm moving forward and nothing can stop me, and then there are times when I unintentionally and intentionally resort to earlier behaviors. The key is how I deal with the temporary setback. Do I sit there and feel sorry for myself? Or maybe even get pulled further back into the addiction? NO! The best thing I can do is press the reset button and not look back.

Part Three
THE DELIVERED

Chapter Twenty
REUNION & HEARTBREAK

If you willingly place your love
In my hands to have and hold from this day forward
I'll love you from now until forever.
—*A Promise I Can't Keep, A.D..*

1.6.12

CHRISTMAS AND NEW Year's went by and I still hadn't heard back from Santiago. But I didn't think much about it because I knew I was busy as all get out and he had a wife and son. I was trying to reconcile dating Santiago with my Christian values: not only was I having sex with a man, I was also seeing someone who was married. But one thing about feelings—you can't turn them off and on. Yet I was sure that Dr. Xana Bynum, my new therapist, would have reminded me that it's not always best to act on those feelings. I had just started seeing her in December of 2011, so it had only been a month.

It was the first Friday of 2012 and I was off due to my 9/80 work schedule. While I'm technically off from work, I'm never really off. My to-do list is unending and I had to swing by my mom's house to help her. Earlier I had planned to go to Ra Sushi for happy hour with Rem and Shawn. Whenever I got together with friends for happy hour it usually turned into an all-night affair.

That evening at my mom's house, I was standing near the barstools talking to her and I got a text from Santiago. He wanted to know if we could get together around 8:00 that night. I went from zero to sixty in about one second flat. Of course, I replied. Now I had to figure out an alibi for ditching the guys early. So I called Jeri and asked if she would be home later that evening. She said that she would be and I now had an alibi in place.

Communication among the guys got mixed up regarding the exact time to arrive at Ra, and only Shawn and I got there on time. When Rem met us, things were winding down at Ra, so the next stop was Cyclone Anaya's, a Mexican restaurant in Midtown which was closer to my house. When we got to the restaurant it was packed with the usual Friday after-work crowd. I said hello to a few people I knew and when I sat down I realized it was 7:45 P.M. I sent Santiago a text to see if he was headed to my house. He said yes, but he wouldn't arrive 'til 8:15.

Now it was time for me to put on my best Oscar-nominated performance so I could slip away. I had told them earlier that I was going to hang out with Jeri so they wouldn't be surprised when I left. Still, when I got up abruptly from the pub table, they kept trying to question where I was going. The performance was a complete debacle. My true friends always know when I'm up to something.

I rushed home, arriving just before Santiago got there. When I opened the door to let him in, he was holding a bottle of Chilean wine and his smile was irresistible. Normally he would drink the 1800 Silver Tequila Reserve I had, but he would typically be coming from the club. Within seconds of closing the door, we were kissing like we hadn't seen each other in over a year.

There was just something about him that totally did it for me! It probably goes back to what Dr. Bynum says about me wanting what I can't have and pushing what nourishes me away due to my relationship with my parents.

As we're walking up the stairs he asked, "Do you love me?"

"Of course, do you think I would be going through all this if I didn't?" I replied.

I had made up my mind that since I loved him our relationship wasn't going to be just sexual. My plan was that instead of immediately giving into our peaking libidos, we were going to take a ride in my drop-top for a night on the town, but I was sadly mistaken.

"No, papi! I don't want to go," he said, putting his foot down. He was a masterpiece of a man, but he was married and unavailable.

"We're getting out of here. Put on this jacket," I demanded.

"No, papi, I just want you and me lying in your bed."

"We always stay here. We're getting out tonight," I commanded.

"Come on, please," he purred, seducing me with his body language and a pout.

And just like that, I gave in. I couldn't resist the temptation, since I hadn't seen him in over four months. He was the only person I really wanted to have sex with, and for someone who struggles with issues of sex addiction that was saying a hell of a lot.

He went over and opened the blinds that obstructed the view of the sliding balcony door in my bedroom. He stood there, his body so beautiful in silhouette, and I remembered the last time we had had sex on my balcony; it was just past 2:00 A.M. and any of my neighbors or drivers on Interstate 10 could have seen, because the balcony faces both the street and highway in my urban townhouse community of West End.

Illuminated only by the moon, Santiago wasted no time in stripping naked. He then walked over to where I sat on the edge of the bed and unzipped my pants. And it was on.

After he came the first time, we went downstairs and finally opened the wine he had brought. I'm usually not a red wine drinker, but this time I gladly made an exception. We headed back upstairs for round two.

"I can't stop kissing you. You're so beautiful," he said.

"I don't want you to." I looked directly into his eyes. "You were the only reason I went to the club," I whispered.

"Everybody keeps telling me that, but I don't believe it," he snapped.

"It's true. If you weren't in the club I wasn't coming." I stepped out of his embrace and said, "I've got something I want you to hear."

I grabbed my laptop and impatiently waited for YouTube to pop up, and then typed in Ne-Yo's "The Way You Move." I wanted him to hear the line, "if you ain't in the club, I ain't coming." That song had become the soundtrack of my affair with Santiago. I had fallen in lust and was helpless to its whims.

"You're my kryptonite," I said, as he smiled and laughed, knowing he had me under his spell.

"Don't fall in love with me," he said pointedly.

I felt he was warning me, but it was already too late. After I played him a few other songs, he played Romeo Santos and Usher's duet "Promise." The lyrics are in both English and Spanish, so I could only make out about half of the song. Yet the chorus said it all: "I'll give you my heart, girl, but you got to promise. Promise to hold me, touch me, love me, way past forever."

He moved gently toward me and sang Toby Love's "Llorar Lloviendo" directly in my ear with his tongue flicking my earlobe and inner ear. The whole thing was in Spanish, so I had to look up the lyrics the next day. I was amazed to see how vulnerable he was being without me even knowing it, because he knew I didn't know enough Spanish. It was the most intimate moment we'd shared and I was finally able to get his birthday out of him: June 23. The same day as Jeri Jones, the woman who might someday bear my child.

But then my beautiful dream came to a crashing halt. At the conclusion of round two we headed for the shower and he told me he couldn't stay. I was so disappointed: I had just got him back but now he was leaving before I could thoroughly enjoy him. Could the moment have been any more bittersweet?

After four months of no contact and five months of not seeing him, as soon as I get him back in my bed, he's out before the night could even end. I started questioning: am I fucking him or is he mentally fucking me? It must have been both. Although my body wanted to keep tapping his ass, my mind and soul kept longing for his unwavering love.

Once he left I called Jeri to see if she was still up. She said she was so I rushed over to her house where I shared the remaining wine he had brought with Stephanie, Jeri's girlfriend, and gave them all the intimate details of what had just transpired. Of course Jeri was happy for me and Stephanie gave me some tips on how to see him again: she thought that because Jeri and he shared the same birthday they also had similar personalities.

Two days later I sent Santiago a text in Spanish asking when he was going to finish what he'd started, because on the night we had been together I had never come. His response, "Lol. . . . . okay soon bro soon. I like u Spanish. .!!!"

Maybe this was karma: I had fallen in love with someone unavailable and now I was just like all those people who had wanted me so badly. It didn't matter—I was in a state of blissful insanity with no motivation for getting out.

THE CHALLENGE

WHILE I THOROUGHLY enjoyed Christmas with Megan, my mom and all my friends, the excitement and passion I felt with Santiago made everything else seem insignificant. It doesn't take long for reality to set in with me, so I knew this blissfully insane state of mind I was in had to end. And after the Friday night I had just had, I knew I couldn't continue dating Megan. It wasn't fair to her.

Dr. Axelrod, who had been my never wavering mentor, had suggested several months prior to this incident that I see Dr. Xana Bynum. She was a colleague of his and he informed me that he had gone through counseling at the prime of his medical career and it was the best thing that could have happened.

Dr. Axelrod shared with me some concerns he had about the book I was writing. His biggest concern was that I was being "too selfish" by writing about my own life, if in fact my intent was truly to help people grappling with the effects of sex addiction. At that time, I was going through final edits with my first editor and was preparing to self-publish. My mom had read the final draft and was adamant about me not publishing. She knew that Dr. Axelrod had a big influence on me and she thought he might be able to talk me out of it, so she called him. She wanted the three of us to meet and talk in her living room.

"Dr. Axelrod, thanks for taking your time to met with us," she began.

"It's my pleasure. A.D. has a special place in my heart because he reminds me of me."

"Well, I've asked you to come because I can't seem to talk any sense into him," my mom said. "He doesn't seem to realize that now is not the time for him to release his book. I could see if he was married. But what woman is going to want to marry him after this is out?" I could see how frustrated she was and could read the genuine anger in her body language.

"The woman that God has for me," I snapped.

"You're giving the people at your company a stick of dynamite," she continued. "You've worked too hard to get to the level you have reached for it all to come crumbling down behind this book being out. Very few men at your age and color are making the money you are. You are so blessed and you don't even know it."

Dr. Axelrod had not said a word since his opening statement, but I knew he was listening intently and taking everything in. Besides, when my mom's talking it's hard for anyone to get a word in. Over the years, I've learned where her "pauses" are and I can get my points in.

"Where is this spirit of fear coming from?" I demanded.

"You raised me to be fearless. You said you worked and saved as a single parent like you did so I wouldn't have to take anything from anybody. Now you're trying to take that away from me. I can't believe you're trying to get Dr. Axelrod to talk me out of publishing my book. You say you're a Christian, but where is your faith?"

I knew my last statement was as low as I could get, but I truly felt my mom was attacking me and I had to bring out the big guns for her to see. While I understood that she thought she was protecting me, I felt that she was actually making this about herself.

After my last comment, Dr. Axelrod had heard enough and decided to break the verbal onslaught going on between us. "Let me just say this: it's obvious this woman loves you more than anything in the world. It reminds me of the relationship I had with my mother. For you to sit here and refuse to receive what your mother is telling you borders on being disrespectful. She didn't call me behind your back and ask me to talk you out of publishing. Rather, she just asked that I meet with you two. I'm going to support you whether you publish the book or not. And I'll be there supporting you whether the book's a success or you fall on your face. But you really need to consider what she's saying."

I respected Dr. Axelrod so much: he was 80 years old and so venerable in his wisdom. But I knew that the main reason my mom didn't want my book to come out was because she was worried about what her friends and fellow church members were going to think and say about our family.

"Well, I appreciate and love you both but I'm moving forward. This book isn't about me, it's about all the other addicts that are out there who have no source of hope," I said.

My mom is not one to give up easily. "Can't you just work with some local kids or something instead?" It was her final, desperate plea.

At that point I was furious that she would even suggest such a limited option. "No, I've got to do this!"

Since we disagreed on how I would proceed with publishing, we couldn't reach a compromise. And that was how the conversation ended. It was late and I had to get back to my side of town, but first I wanted to make sure Dr. Axelrod made it home safe, so I followed him home.

After our talk, Dr. Axelrod kept after me about making an appointment. He would continually ask me, "Have you gone to see Dr. Bynum yet?"

I kept pushing back, telling him, "She can't tell me anything which would stop me from putting the book out."

"Are you scared to go?" he asked in a challenging tone.

"I'm not scared! I just see it as a waste of time."

"Well, it's definitely not a waste of time. I went through counseling at the prime of my medical career. And it saved my life. I dare you to go."

"Since I respect you, I'll think about it."

There was no doubt in my mind that Dr. Axelrod had my best interests at heart, so I finally called my company's benefits department to see what I needed to do to set up an appointment. Luckily, all I had to do was show up and pay the co-pay. Given that the process was so easy, I figured it must have been a sign.

When I got to Dr. Bynum's office, I was surprised to see it was a home office. The entire first floor seemed to be dedicated to her practice. There was an ample waiting room with chairs. The adjoining room was set up like a receptionist area. Off that room was a hall with a bathroom and the actual "treatment" room. Since the home was older, I could tell this room previously had been a bedroom, with the old style push-up windows and thick baseboards.

Hanging above the "dreaded couch" was her diploma, which certified her as a licensed psychologist. What immediately struck me was the similarity between her name and my mom's. They both have distinctive first names; they both had the same number of letters in their first name, and the same first letter in their last names. My mom was also a licensed psychologist. It had to be more than coincidence.

Given my natural aversion to sitting on a couch at a therapist office, I intentionally sat in one of the chairs. When she entered the room, she had a pen and a new patient file in her hand to do an initial assessment. Dr. Bynum was a petite African-American woman who wore glasses and had a natural hairstyle. She introduced herself and I could tell right away that she was quite professional.

"Hello A.D., I'm Dr. Bynum. What brings you here today?"

"Dr. Axelrod thinks I'm being self-centered by publishing my book because I'm making my book about me instead of focusing it on helping others. So I'm here only because he thought I needed to come and I respect his opinion."

"Okay, tell me more about this idea that you're being self-centered."

"Well, my book is about sex addiction and my mom doesn't want me to publish it. She says she doesn't want me to put it out because I'm giving people at my company ammunition to destroy me. But I think she is more worried about her reputation and what her family and close friends are going to think. Like you, she's a licensed professional counselor. She has a doctorate in education, as well.

"All her friends have come to her for advice and counseling through the years, for both themselves and their family members. Everybody always viewed me as the perfect child because I was successful in school and in life. My past and current success is definitely due to the way she raised me and the sacrifices she made as a single parent.

"She probably feels that if the book is released, my reputation and hers would be damaged, but, honestly, I could not care less. She didn't raise me to live in fear. Besides, there are so many addicts that I ran across when I was in the prime of my addiction who need to know there is hope and a way out."

"Okay." She continued to write notes while listening intently.

I wanted to see how skilled she was as a therapist, so I started throwing tons of information about myself at her at once—from my parents' divorce, to my strained relationship with my father, to my bisexuality—and like Neo in The Matrix, she caught it all.

"You're good!" I told her. "I'm not like most of your patients, huh?"

"Yeah, most of my patients come to me because they want help, not because someone else referred them. Well, time is up. I'll need a couple more sessions before I can make a thorough diagnosis. But I'm going to need you to help me figure out the right questions to ask, because you use intelligence as a defense mechanism," she explained.

She's brilliant, I thought. I was sold. Not only did I respect her level of intelligence, I was deeply impressed that she could hear all the things I wasn't saying.

THE SECOND TIME AROUND

THE SATURDAY MORNING following my "reunion" with Santiago, I was scheduled to see Dr. Bynum. I had been in therapy for just over a month and this session couldn't have come at a better time. Prior to this meeting, I had already told her that Santiago and I had talked on December 22nd. I plopped down in her chair with a loud sigh of relief. My internal moral compass knew I couldn't keep dating Megan with the feelings I had for Santiago and especially after the night we had just experienced. I needed Dr. Bynum to confirm that my compass was right.

"Hey, Dr. Bynum," I said with a mischievous smile.

"How are you doing? And what's that smile about? What did you do?" she asked.

"What makes you say that?"

"Cause it's all over your face!"

"Well, Santiago came over last night."

"Enough said," she said, and then cracked up laughing. I really appreciated her at that moment: she had proven to be a true professional, but she also proved to be a real person. We could laugh at what some might consider mistakes and analyze them for what they really were—expressions of what I really wanted deep down inside. The problem was that I was at times taking the wrong path to meet my goals. I wanted to be loved passionately and to give love passionately, but it couldn't be coerced or forced. And with Megan, that's exactly what I was trying to do.

"So I've got to end things with Megan."

"Definitely. She doesn't deserve to be led on like that. Besides, you're doing an injustice to yourself as well. Although you like her, I don't hear any of the passion in your voice when you describe her versus when you describe Santiago."

"Yeah, but on paper, she's exactly what I would want to have the family I so desperately desire. I'm still not sure she's not the one God has sent. At the same time, if I could do what I did last night, I have to let her go."

"Exactly! So when are you going to do it?"

I took a quick mental break, momentarily glancing at the black tower lamp positioned behind Dr. Bynum's chair.

"Well, she and some friends are coming over tonight. I guess I'll have to do it then. But it's going to hurt her so bad. I already broke up with her once and here I am doing it again."

"Would you rather just keep stringing her along?" She asked this loaded question with a dumbfounded look on her face.

"No."

"You can do it," she assured me with a pleasant smile.

"Thanks, Dr. Bynum."

"Let's get you scheduled for your next appointment."

When I left there, I knew I was going to have to hurt Megan, but I decided it would be better to do it now than keep living a lie. So that evening everybody came over and we watched the DVD of Adele's live concert performance in England. Could there have been a more appropriate foreshadowing than a song like "Rolling in the Deep" or "Someone Like You"?

As we watched the concert, I couldn't help but notice the seating arrangement—it spoke volumes. Megan was sitting by herself on a barstool and I was sitting on the couch with my other friends. After my friends left and it was just Megan and me, she said, "Well, I'm about to head out."

"I need to talk before you leave."

"What's going on?"

"Let's sit down." Trying to find the words to let someone go are never easy, but having to do it twice was much harder.

Although I knew she deserved to know the real reason why I was ending things, because I was in mad love and lust with Santiago and had slept with him the night before, I couldn't bring myself to say those words. Plus, I'm not sure it would have been the best thing. Telling someone who is obviously in love with you that you're in love with someone else isn't always beneficial, especially when that someone else is of the same sex. The last thing I wanted was for her to question her womanhood. She was a beautiful lady inside and out. I just wasn't in love with her.

"I can't keep going on with our relationship."

"What do you mean?" She looked shocked as she distanced herself from me, no longer making eye contact.

"You are a wonderful person, but I'm just not feeling it and I can't keep forcing myself to pretend things are one way when they aren't."

In pure agony, she said, "You aren't fighting for us. I just wanted you to fight for us."

She ran to the bathroom and shut the door; I could hear her sobs through the door. I felt so bad, but I knew it was for the best. When she came out, I could see how angry and hurt she was. I didn't know what to say to comfort an uncomfortable soul, so I said, "I'm sorry."

"Don't!" she said as she headed for the door. I couldn't think of anything to counter—I really understood her pain.

Chapter Twenty-one
REMAIN OPEN

What we're taught and what we've bought
Into might not always be right.
What we're experiencing and what we're feeling
Now just might not be wrong.
—*Openness, A.D.*

THE AWAKENING

I HAD RELEASED Megan from the idea that I would one day marry her and have a family, but I had to work on how I might actually start a family with someone I loved. Discussing the situation with my therapist was helpful, but I still needed to get some spiritual insight into my situation. I knew I needed to talk to my non-judgmental, ordained, spiritual confidante Ammon. I had disclosed to Ammon my never ending desire to marry Jeri, and explained that I wanted to have kids with her. I have always been able to trust Ammon and it's partly because he's so level-headed; it's also clear that he always has my best interests at heart. He could have written off my plan as ludicrous, since I wasn't in love with Jeri; I only wanted to marry her so we could have children. Ammon was even privy to the wedding proposal fiasco, but when I let him know how conflicted I was about all that was going on with me at that moment, he suggested we all sit down together and talk.

While I'm always game for having a thought-provoking discussion about ways to enhance my quality of life and my relationship with those in my life, I wasn't sure Jeri would be up for having such a discussion with someone she didn't know. The advantages I had on my side were that she really wanted to have a baby with me and that she loved me unconditionally.

I had no idea of the extent of that love until the day we all got together.

Coordinating all of our schedules was more difficult than I originally imagined, given that we're all in different professions, but I was able to organize a Monday lunch meeting. The most convenient place for us to meet was the IHOP in Meyerland. Jeri would be coming from the south, Ammon from the north and I would be driving in from downtown, which was located east.

They both arrived before me, but Jeri didn't know Ammon so she met me out front. We hugged and walked into the dining area. Jeri quickly spotted Ammon and said, "I think that might be him over there. He looks like a pastor."

I proceeded with the formal introductions and they started chatting. They're both extroverts, so any onlooker would have thought they had known each other for years. While I wanted to give Jeri enough time to get comfortable with him, I knew we all were on a time crunch, so we needed to get the ball rolling. At this point, I thought that Ammon was going to try to convince Jeri to marry me, but I hadn't explicitly asked him to do that. Ammon began by saying, "We're here to discuss the relationship between the two of you."

With the IHOP menu still in her hand, Jeri said, "I love A.D. like a brother. There isn't anything I wouldn't do for him. I was even willing and am still willing to go through with the whole marriage thing, just to make him happy. But I'm in love with Stephanie."

"Knowing that he wants a traditional family and you can't give him that, what would you suggest to him?" Ammon asked.

With a clearness of mind and intensity in her face and eyes I had never seen before, Jeri said, "By marrying me he would be settling. He likes everything to be perfect. But that's not life. The other day he asked me whether I would be there if he was dying. I told him, of course I'd be there. He's got two hands. I can hold one and the person he's with could hold the other.

He bases his relationships on whether the person can give him a baby. He needs to just relax and allow himself to fall in love, no matter whether the person is male or female. We can still have a baby either way," she explained.

I was struggling to process a concept I had never been able to imagine before this moment. I was in a state of shock, confusion and joy all at the same time.

It was at that moment when I finally awoke and realized I had been duped. From birth I had been taught that a man and a woman fall in love, get married, and have a baby. Any other way wasn't what God ordained and if you deviated from this model there were eternal consequences to pay. Going to hell for not following the model the Bible established was my greatest fear.

Yet when Jeri so vividly displayed her unconditional love for me, which didn't include any sexual nature, it reminded me of the love God showed for us when He sent Jesus to die on the cross for our sins. God is all about love! The love Jeri was offering was not only deeply touching, but it was also freeing. In a thirty-minute conversation she had given me the freedom to fall in love and still have the family I had forever longed for. For that I will never be able to thank her. And for that moment of awakening, I will never be able to thank Ammon, and most of all, I cannot even begin to express my eternal gratitude to God.

NO HAPPY VALENTINE'S DAY

JERI HAD GIVEN me the freedom to fall in love with anyone and still have children with her—in one stroke she had changed my life, and that change allowed my feelings for Santiago to grow deeper. The way he made me feel was something I hadn't felt since Trevor. All the excitement and anticipation of seeing him led me back to the place of wanting to have sex only with him. While this is an ideal place for a recovering sex addict to be, it's not ideal when the other person is only committed to a spontaneous sexual relationship.

Sex is one of the most intimate—if not the most intimate— experience shared between two people. But it takes a lot more than just intercourse to be completely satisfied. I personally need a relationship that has all the passion Santiago provided, along with the daily interaction of a true mate.

It had been several weeks since the last time Santiago and I had sex and I was extremely frustrated. The texts I sent him went unanswered and I found myself becoming angrier each day. Although he told me and showed me sexually that he loved me, the reality was that outside the bedroom he was a phantom. If he didn't contact me or if I didn't run into him, we didn't communicate on a regular basis.

In the back of my mind, I had to remember he was separated and not divorced. But the biggest reason he wasn't available was his son—he loved his son more than anything. One night we were lying in bed, which was the only time I could get into that brilliant mind of his. There is a euphoria that happens after sex that allows you to let down your guard. I knew if I wanted to understand the true Santiago I had to act fast on this fleeting window of opportunity, so I immediately started to glean information.

"So what do you want from me?"

"Nothing!" he said nonchalantly. "I enjoy our time together."

His apparent neutrality was so paradoxical. While I loved the fact he wasn't just trying to use me, I hated the fact that I couldn't have him when I wanted him because he didn't want or need anything from me.

I continued to probe. "Well, what do you want out of life?"

"I get up in the morning and go to work for my son. He is my life."

The fact that he loved his son so much made me want him and love him even more because it showed how much he valued family. But it also reminded me of what it was like for me when I was his son's age—three, about to turn four. I felt as if my father didn't love me.

Santiago worked for his wife's brother, went to school, and took care of his son during the week. That left him very little time for himself, much less me. He was also separated from his wife, and I knew deep down he wouldn't do anything to put his relationship with his son in jeopardy. While it hurt, I couldn't blame him because I would have done the same thing if I had been in a similar situation.

Valentine's Day arrived. We had seen each other the Sunday before, but I really wanted to have dinner or at least hear from him, so I sent an e-card expressing my love. The system which delivers the card alerts the sender when the card has been viewed. I hadn't received an alert, so after a few hours I sent a text to determine if he had gotten the email notification. No response.

It's nearly impossible to find something more emotionally draining than being ignored by the one you love. In order to relieve that pain I did the worst possible thing: I reverted back to my old habit of acting out. I went out and found a guy similar to Santiago and fucked the shit out of him. While the sex was good, I knew it was just sex because my heart belonged to someone else. I was able to stop after that one incident, though.

A few weeks after that, Ammon suggested we get together for dinner and catch up. I was definitely looking forward to it since we hadn't had a chance to talk in awhile.

When we got to dinner, we exchanged our typical greetings and asked about each other's family. Then he wanted to know what else had been going on and how I was really doing. I mentioned work was getting on my nerves as usual and then I went into all my relationship issues with Santiago. I told him about how disappointed I was about the Valentine's e-card going unopened, and mentioned that I had hooked up with a guy for sex.

I could see right away that Ammon was completely shocked by my confession. His eyes were wide and he seemed bewildered. "Are you back in your addiction?"he asked. The question was so jarring I had to take a moment to assess whether in fact that was the case. When I think back to the prime of my addiction, I think of being in a place in which my entire life revolved around finding the next sex partner. And I knew that at this time I wasn't constantly or strategically seeking out sex on a daily or weekly basis.

After stumbling and stuttering for a minute, I was finally able to relay to Ammon that I didn't think I was back in my addiction. Rather, I had had a moment of weakness precipitated by the fact that Santiago did not reciprocate my love in the way I wanted him to. Instead of continuing to seek out multiple episodes and individuals for uncommitted sex, I had willingly and purposefully put a stop to it.

The biggest realization from my conversation with Ammon that night was that I had allowed my desire for a relationship with Santiago to become my world instead of God. My misplaced desire made me susceptible to slipping back into the behavior of the addict. A great clarity came over me then: I knew that as a recovering sex addict and more importantly, as a Christian, I had to make sure then and in the future that I wouldn't allow anyone or anything to become my world.

WHY DO I LOVE WHAT I CAN'T HAVE?

IT WAS TIME for another appointment to see Dr. Bynum and after what I had been through with Santiago, and Ammon's question about whether I was back in the addiction, I knew this would be an intense session.

"So how are things going?" Dr. Bynum asked.

"Not that great. Santiago and I hooked up the Sunday before Valentine's Day."

Dr. Bynum nodded and said, "Oh."

"I went out and bought him a present. After giving it to him, we had sex and he left."

The blank look on Dr. Bynum's face conveyed to me she wasn't surprised. However, she maintained a non-judgmental demeanor.

Looking her directly in the eye, I continued, "Although I knew he couldn't be with me on Valentine's Day, I sent him an e-card expressing my passionate and faithful love for him and asked if we could have dinner. He never opened the email to get the link to read the card. So in my frustration I hooked up with this Ecuadorean guy who reminded me of him."

I tried to be slick as I slid the last part in. Taking every word in, Dr. Bynum peered over her glasses and said, "Keep going."

"We had sex on two different occasions, but that was it. When I sat down with Ammon the other night to catch up and discuss what had been going on, he suggested that I might still be engaging in addictive behavior."

Although I was going a 100 miles per hour to make sure I told Dr. Bynum everything, I took a slight break and looked up at the clock to make sure I had enough time left before I continued. "I reassured him that I wasn't. If I were, I would have been having sex with multiple guys to handle the pain Santiago was generating."

"So how are you feeling about things now?"

"I'm pissed. I found someone I'm passionately in love with, but I can't truly have him. Why do I love the ones I can't have and why can't I fall in love with the ones who love me?"

"A.D., this is a classic case of over love and under love. When you were a child, your mother gave you over love and your dad didn't love you enough, which is why you go from extremes. You will push away the people who love you and cling to the ones that don't. The prime example is a child who is full and his parent forces him to clean his plate. On the other hand, you have a child who is starving and he eats rocks to get the sensation of being full."

When she gave the analogy of the child and food, everything started to click in my brain and make sense. Even as she was speaking, I was still experiencing this opposite extremes of love from my parents. My mom was still cooking my food for me every weekend and making me her world, whereas my relationship with my father hadn't progressed to the level where I felt I could truly trust or depend on him. I'd hear from him every week or so.

Dr. Bynum continued, "You are going to have to find a relationship where you can find middle ground."

"You're right," I said. "Megan represents my mom—loving me unconditionally. But just like my mom, I push her away because I know I can get her to do whatever I want. On the other hand, Santiago doesn't love me unconditionally because he's really not in a position too. Yet I'm clamoring for that unconditional love. And the reality is that, like my dad, he will never love me like I need him to." As I was speaking, I was slowly starting to internalize these thoughts.

"So when was the last time you had a relationship where you weren't trying to manipulate the other person?"

"Probably back in college, with Kim. I wasn't trying to control her. We just loved each other—it was such a great place. But I haven't been in that space since."

Dr. Bynum was absolutely right. I had been going back and forth from being in relationships where I would unconsciously try to push the person away, although their unconditional love for me would make them stay. On the opposite end, I'd smother a person I was totally infatuated with, who didn't really love me but gave the illusion and fantasy of love. And what was truly sad was that this cycle had been going on for over ten years and I had absolutely no clue.

"Well, maybe it's time you start getting back to the middle. I've also noticed that you don't really care about pleasing people who don't know you—like at work. Yet with the people who truly love you—your mom, Dr. Axelrod and close friends—

you take on this people-pleasing persona. Which in turn causes you to behave selfishly in other areas. So you go to extreme lengths to please, but when things become too draining you revert to being self-centered and self-absorbed. And you're using sex to act out."

"Sex becomes my release when I get frustrated and can't get things in my world to go the way I want."

"You're people-pleasing because you're afraid the people who truly love you will no longer love you once they find out who you really are. If they knew you could fall in love with a man and be happy, you're afraid they'll stop loving you."

"You're absolutely right."

"It seems to me that you have two options: either stop lying by omission or find coping mechanisms to deal with the anxiety, because everybody isn't going to be able to handle that information and you're not going be comfortable letting everyone know. What are some things you can do creatively to relieve the anxiety instead of using sex? For you it needs to be physical."

"Well, I could start back singing in the church choir."

"That's good. What else?"

"I love dancing. That would give me the physical outlet I truly need."

"Good, give me something else."

"Well, writing is always good."

"There you have it. You've now created some tangible coping mechanisms for when things get chaotic, instead of going out and finding a new sex partner to get a temporary release."

"Easier said than done! There is theory and then there is reality."

"You can do it. Look how far you've come. This is also the time when you have to rely on your faith. Are you still reading your scriptures and meditations?"

"Not as consistently. That's probably the reason I'm anxious. I'm not trusting God to lead me. When I step away from the Source, my power is gone."

"Well let's try those and see how things work out," she concluded.

Dr. Bynum had discovered plausible solutions for problems which I had been dealing with for over a decade. Thank God Dr. Axelrod had suggested I visit her. Still, this was an enormous amount of information for me to process and it would certainly take more time for me to internalize and actualize. But now I had a point of reference to build from.

ROOT CAUSE

NOW THERE IS one great reason for all of us to look back at the past and that's when we're trying to determine the root cause of an addiction. As I've said, at the core of any addiction is pain that hasn't been addressed. The source of that pain can be buried so deep it takes years to uncover it.

For many people, myself included, both traditional and non-traditional methods of counseling help to understand addiction, but I suggest letting God guide you to the help you need. He always has the answer, we just have to be still and listen.

For me, the main source of pain stemmed from my relationship with my parents when I was a teenager. After the divorce, my mom tried to over-compensate me with love and affection that my father did not and could not provide. Once I became an adult, I sought the type of love I thought my father should have given me through sexual encounters with men. After I realized that those two types of "love" weren't the same, it was too late—the addiction cycle had taken root.

Moreover, I had created a fantasy that Jeri and I would one day have the family I so desperately wanted. Instead, I needed to discern that marriage is a sacred spiritual bond and Jeri was not who God had ordained for me. The mate God has for me isn't someone I can pick and choose, but someone He has to anoint. Ultimately, I have the choice to accept or deny that person.

Everything goes back to free will and choice. Either we can accept God's plans for us or we can choose to do things our way. I can't blame my mom, my dad, or Jeri for my addiction. I am solely responsible for the choices I made. Certain factors and forces facilitated those choices, but they were still my choices. Once we as addicts come to this realization, we can let go of our addiction.

Chapter Twenty-two
YOU'RE NOT IN CONTROL

The more I push , the more I force , the more I fight,
The more anger and frustration I feel.
The more I willingly release, the more I patiently wait, the more I
freely give,
The more I realize I'm not in control.
—Control, A.D.

THIS TIME IS THE LAST TIME

THE SUNDAY BEFORE Valentine's Day was the last time I had seen Santiago. Although Dr. Bynum had given me coping mechanisms and I was slowly getting back to building my relationship with God, I still missed Santiago. Yet he hadn't texted or called and he still hadn't opened the email with the link to my Valentine's Day e-card.

I have a hard time letting things go when I don't get my way, even when I know they aren't what's best for me. Why would I want or settle for a relationship which wasn't fulfilling or building me as a person? It must have been the addiction taking on a new form. My masochistic streak led me back to the bar where we had met even though he hadn't been or worked there in almost a year. I was doing the exact thing Proverbs 26:11 states: As a dog returns to its vomit, so a fool repeats his folly (NIV).

Since I knew what his car looked like, I circled the parking lot to see if he was there. After my initial look, I didn't see his car but I decided to stop in anyway. When I went in, I ran into an old friend from high school out on the patio. He was a regular at the bar and also a fan of Santiago's. They hadn't slept together but he would always say, "That's my man." My friend would have died if he knew Santiago and I had had the passionate sex he always talked about wanting with Santiago.

After my high school friend and I took a few minutes to catch up, I heard someone say, "Well, there's a blast from the past. How have you been doing?" Normally, I wouldn't have paid attention, but since there were only a few patrons out on the patio this beautiful March evening, all I had to do was look over. It was Santiago!

Just the sight of his face instantly brought back every emotion imaginable—first happiness, then elation, then excitement. I was overwhelmed just to see his gorgeous smile again. Then anger, hurt and bewilderment crept into my mind as I thought about why I hadn't heard from him. He had been sitting at the outdoor patio bar before I arrived. I hadn't seen him: his car wasn't in the parking lot so I hadn't expected him to be there. And I couldn't really see him because my sight line was blocked by a heavy-set lady in her late forties and a drunken man around the same age.

When our eyes met, it was just like the first night—pure magic—and then he smiled.

"How have you been," I asked, trying not to let the others know I had slept with him just a month ago.

"I've been good. I'm here with a couple of friends," he said as he motioned to the two people who had initially blocked my view.

Our conversation was immediately interrupted by his number one fan, my high school friend. "Yeah we haven't seen you in a minute."

"Yeah, I've been busy with school," he responded.

If I was going to set things up so that we could spend the night together, I knew I needed to cut this conversation short. Luckily, the large woman interjected and asked Santiago to help her get the drunken man to the car. After I watched him assist the man to the car, I waited to make sure he was coming back in. Once I saw that he was, I quickly made my way inside to get some distance between myself and my old friend.

Inside the club was getting crowded and the strippers were in full bloom. But there was only one ex-stripper on my watch list. After he spoke with a few of his friends and adoring ex-customers, we made our way to each other.

"So I'm going to your house?" he asked.

Without hesitation I responded, "Of course."

As we were walking out, I wondered where his car was parked since I hadn't seen it when I first got there. He was so cunning: instead of parking where he usually did when he was an employee, he had parked half a block up in an abandoned lot. I hadn't seen his car because it was blocked by two trucks. Once again, what was right under my nose was out of my sight.

While I drove to my house my mind was racing: how could I allow this to keep happening? Here was the man who wouldn't return my email or texts, even an email that expressed my unconditional love for him. Yet as soon as I saw him, none of those omissions mattered. Then again, he didn't have to leave the bar and go with me. He came with me because he wanted to. And maybe that was the reason I loved him unconditionally: he played by his own rules, the same way I did. He couldn't be bought, manipulated or controlled. Santiago did what Santiago wanted and I respected that and subconsciously admired it.

When we got to my house it was Passion 505 instead of Chemistry 101. The taste of his lips, the touch of his body, and the passion with which we made love was all I needed to feel complete at that moment. Nothing was more exhilarating and intense than having him force my rock hard penis into his tight moist ass—except for the moment when I made him climax. The release he got was all it took for me to get what I really wanted: to feel loved. It was also my opportunity to get the truth.

"So why didn't you return my text and check your email?"

He laughed, "What are you talking about?"

"I sent you an email and text on Valentine's Day. You never opened the email and you didn't respond to my text."

"I no check my email," he said in his broken English. Although his English was great most of the time, occasionally he would utter phrases which would remind me he was still learning.

His answer wasn't good enough for me. I went into control-freak mode, pulled out my laptop, and requested he check his email so he could see what I had written. To appease me he did open the email and to my surprise he had hundreds of unchecked messages. The sight of those unread emails was bittersweet because it showed me that he wasn't lying, but it also made me realize I was nowhere near his top priority and never would be.

After he had proven why the email hadn't been viewed, I wanted to know, "Then why didn't you answer my text?"

"We don't have that type of relationship."

His words hit me like a hammer shattering glass. They were so shocking yet so true. In my mind, I felt that since I was giving him what he wanted sexually, he should be giving me what I wanted: him.

As he continued, the truth made things even clearer.

"My wife texts me and I don't even respond."

Okay, A.D., I told myself—this is a reminder that he is married. "So why did you marry her?"

"Let me tell you how she got me. I would be at work and she would call and ask if I was hungry. I tell her yes. Sure. She would stop what she was doing and drive all the way over to bring me food. After we got married, she tried to control me and I'm easily controlled but I no like that."

It was sinking in: if even his wife, the mother of his child, couldn't get a response, how could I even imagine that I could make him do what I wanted?

"So what do you want?" I asked.

Without any hesitation, he said, "Nothing!"

"I can't keep doing this. I love you too much. We've got to stop."

"Well, if you stop it's on you. You are a nice guy and I enjoy coming over here."

It was hard to be mad at him because he was still lying in my bed with that after-sex glow and his body felt amazing nestled in mine. Yet when reality hits, not even great sex can change things.

"If I hadn't run into you tonight, you wouldn't be over here."

"And? So what? I'm here now."

What was I to do? He was being totally honest with me, which I respected. Although he cared for me, he didn't truly love me. I was a good time and an escape for him. And I had to surrender to that realization.

He gave me one last kiss before he left and that made it easier to accept his nonchalant, don't tie me down, free spirit ways. Besides loving and providing for his son, he could honestly live without a care in the world, and there was something beautiful about that.

LET IT GO

I DON'T REMEMBER the exact moment, but what had been blissful insanity finally turned into the resentful realization that I would never get the family I wanted by having sex with a man who already had one. Once an addict decides enough is enough, change will ultimately come.

To prevent myself from being tempted to contact Santiago, I started by deleting his contact information in my phone. Then I went back into my text message log and got rid of any text I had sent, saved or received from him. The last step was getting rid of the pictures in my phone, and it was probably the most agonizing part. I am such a visual person that the prospect of deleting pictures of his gorgeous body and face was tantamount to torture. I knew I would never be able to get those moments back: the picture Jeri had sent of him performing on stage, the ones of him downstairs in my kitchen wearing nothing but a towel, and the one of him I found on the bar's website. They were all gone now.

In order to move forward you have to stop living in the past, and that's something most addicts have a hard time doing. We allow events that happened five, ten, fifteen and even twenty years ago to affect us today because we haven't decided to let them go and live in the present. Now I understand why recovering addicts say, "I'm taking it day by day." That's what you have to do. If I start thinking about all the things in my past, I become consumed with trying to relive them. But I can't. It's the past.

Instead I need to look at my current circumstance and be thankful for what I have. The Lord has blessed me with so many things I take for granted: health, family, friends, education—and the list goes on and on. I've never been a person who compared myself or my situation to another person's. My mom instilled in me from childhood that God gives us all different gifts, so you never have to be jealous of what someone else has.

While I wanted to be in a passionate and loving relationship with someone I truly loved, that was in fact not the case. And the hardest thing for me to accept was that I couldn't control it. Yes, I could go back to an ex-lover or go find one of the many people who were currently infatuated with me and get into a relationship. But the real love I so desperately desired was something I couldn't fake or force. It had to happen in its own time, and my patience was still in an infantile state. So I was forced to let go of the fantasy that Santiago and I would be together.

SURRENDER

SO WHERE DID this leave me? I was open to falling in love with either a woman or man. If I fell in love with a woman, having the traditional family I dreamed of probably wouldn't be an issue. We could have the three kids I wanted and that would be it. Of course, if she couldn't get pregnant from the standard method we could do in vitro. Yet when I look back over my life, nothing has been easy or traditional.

Conversely, if I fell in love with a man I wouldn't be able to go the traditional route of having a child. There was always surrogacy. But then again, I was very adamant about my child having his or her biological mother in his life. Trying to manage that would definitely present a problem (for example, the problem of visitations) and would entail all sorts of unknowns.

Then I thought back to what Jeri had said when we met with Ammon. I had to stop trying to make everything perfect. She had given me a viable option of having a family and now maybe it was time to really consider taking it, especially since my 35th birthday was less than a month away and I had no real prospects of true love. Jeri would be a great mother, we would always be in each other's lives, and there was unconditional love between us. But we were both stubborn and controlling. Would the birth of a child create a strain on our friendship? I had to just take the chance.

I called Jeri and said, "Okay, I'm ready to try it!"

I didn't need to explain a word—she knew exactly what I meant and immediately went full throttle.

"Great. I'll call the doctor tomorrow and set up the consultation."

"Alright, see if you can set the appointment up for this Friday, since I'm off."

"Will do."

The next day she sent me a text informing me the appointment had been scheduled. I was all excited until I got her follow-up text asking if it was alright for her girlfriend to join us. While I didn't have anything against her girlfriend, this was about our baby, not their baby. Her including Stephanie from the first step was potentially a red flag and definitely something I felt I should keep in the back of my mind. Any child Jeri and I had would be exposed not only to our ways of life, but also to Stephanie's. I knew that I could easily begin overanalyzing the situation and that that might lead me to back out of the whole process, so I politely responded that I thought it should just be the two of us for now.

When I arrived at the doctor's office that Friday, Jeri was already waiting in the lobby. There was no doubt she wanted this baby as much or more than I did.

Dressed in her usual t-shirt, jogging pants and tennis shoes, the traditional high school coach's uniform, she began, "Can you believe we're actually going to do this? This means we'll forever be connected to each other."

Our worlds were so different. I was dressed in my typical corporate attire: dress shirt, slacks and oxfords. "I know. I can't believe it. We've known each other and have been in each other's lives for over thirty-three years."

"The fact that I'll be having a baby with my best friend is amazing." Her face was lit up and her eyes were shining.

The door opened and the nurse appeared. "Jeri Jones."

"Here."

"Alright, let's do it," I said, and she gave me that beaming smile I'd seen on her beautiful face countless times.

Dr. Patel, a middle-aged Indian man, came into the office; I greeted him and turned to the window. The scenic view could easily have calmed the fears of anyone contemplating going through the process.

With Jeri's file in his hands, Dr. Patel asked, "So you are ready to try this?"

"Yes!" she replied.

"And what about your husband?" he asked, looking over at me.

We looked at each other and laughed, knowing we were nowhere near getting married, but willing to play along for the time being.

"Yeah, I'm ready. We need to get this done quickly because I'm going to China at the end of this month."

"Is it for work?" Dr. Patel inquired.

"No, I'm going to celebrate my birthday."

"And you're not taking her?"

Jeri interjected, "No, he's the international traveler. I'm fine staying here."

"Okay, well, we'll need to do a semen analysis, and go from there. I'll have the nurse schedule you an appointment. To get an accurate sample you'll have to abstain from sexual intercourse and masturbation for three to five days."

That was not happy news, but if that was what it took, I would make the sacrifice. Besides, this was only the start of the sacrifices I would have to make for my child. I had to keep telling myself, it's no longer about you; it's about what's best for the child.

The office scheduled the semen analysis, and like a champ, everything came out perfect. Now it was time for Jeri's ovulation test. Luckily, everything was falling right into place and I would be able to give the actual sample before I went on my trip.

Was this a sign that God was giving his stamp of approval? In order for the timing to be optimal, I would have to come in at 8:30 a.m. when the lab opened and give my sample. The collected semen would then be washed and Jeri would be inseminated within an hour and a half of the initial collection. This was normally the time I would be at the gym, but I was more than willing to make an exception for such a grand occasion: I-Day (Insemination Day).

I arrived the morning of the insemination dressed for work—nervous yet excited. Would this finally be the day that I would actually start on the journey to getting the family I had wanted for so long? I walked up to the lab and signed in. The lady at the receiving counter said that both rooms were occupied, but that I was next.

As I waited for one of the rooms to open up, my mind was racing: Was I doing the right thing? Or was I about to make a mistake I'd never be able to come back from? Was I really ready to be a father and be responsible for another person's well-being? Would I make the same mistakes my father had? No, I told myself, I would never allow my child to feel that he wasn't loved. But what about the child having to transition between Jeri's house and mine?

"Burks!"

"Right here."

"Room one."

"Thank you."

As I locked the door and began the process of giving the semen sample that could change my entire life, excitement and fear kept dueling in my mind. Were Jeri and I being selfish by trying to force conception because we both wanted a baby? But then I realized that there was no turning back: I had to surrender to God's divine will.

I paused and took a seat on a chair. "God," I whispered, "if this is what you want for me, then allow Jeri to get pregnant. If not, I'm open to the family you'll provide."

With a smile on my face, I knew that I had finally reached the point at which I could put both my trust and future in God's hands and be content with the outcome. I thought back to how God had brought me through my addiction, and realized that this was a perfect moment, one I could never have envisioned. No matter what the outcome of the insemination process, I knew I was delivered now and moving toward the very best part of my life.

If one sex addict reads this book and says, I have a sexual addiction but I know God loves me and I'm going to establish a relationship with Christ so that I can be saved, my job has been done.

He who turns a sinner from the error of his way will save a soul from death. (James 5:20)

•

Acknowledgements

I CAN'T BEGIN without first thanking my Heavenly Father. Without your love and guidance I would still be bound by my addiction. Next I want to pay homage to the woman who has sacrificed more for me than anyone could ever imagine and more than I could ever thank her for, my mom. Thank you so much for instilling in me the vast amount of knowledge and insight God has given you. Dad, while we have had quite an interesting journey throughout my life, I realize that your love, although quite different from my mom's, is still love. Thank you. To my biological and extended family and friends, without your support I would not have been able to accomplish what I have. There aren't enough words I can say to express my sincere gratitude for all the love and support you've given me during this process. Last, but definitely not least, I have to give a special thank you to August Tarrier, Ph.D, Reshonda Tate Billingsley, Michael Biagas, and Moses Mason for all their support and work on the book. Much love and God's Favor until the next one.

About the Author

A.D. BURKS is a native Texan and true Renaissance man who sang at Carnegie Hall and wrote a song entitled .Renaissance Revolution. After earning a degree in Chemistry from Grinnell College, he pursued a music career while teaching in the Atlanta, Nashville and Houston public school systems. His strong sense of faith (and a little help from fate) provided him an opportunity to train and travel internationally under the same vocal coach as several Arista Records artists.

A.D. has a Master's in Business Administration from Rice University. Working in real estate development, he completed his own development projects and transitioned into corporate real estate for the world resource his state of Texas is known for: Oil.

With Sex & Surrender, A.D. returns to his first love, and what he considers his calling— creativity and spiritual growth. In this book, he hopes to share the experiences and life lessons he learned along the way.

37466899R00199

Printed in Great Britain
by Amazon